PALESTINIAN WOMEN OF GAZA
AND THE WEST BANK

PALESTINIAN

WOMEN OF

GAZA AND

THE WEST

BANK

Edited by Suha Sabbagh

INDIANA UNIVERSITY PRESS   BLOOMINGTON AND INDIANAPOLIS

"The Women's Movement during the Uprising" by Joost R. Hiltermann
first appeared in the *Journal of Palestine Studies* 20, no. 3 (spring 1991), pp. 48–57.
"The Role of Women in Intifada Legends" by Sharif Kanaana first appeared in
Contemporary Legend (1993), pp. 37–61. "Women in the Intifada" by Robin Morgan
is excerpted with permission from *The Demon Lover: On the Sexuality of Terrorism*
by Robin Morgan (New York, W. W. Norton, 1989) and *The Word of a Woman: Feminist
Dispatches* by Robin Morgan, *Social Text: Theory/Culture/Ideology* (spring 1989).
An earlier version of "The Declaration of Principles on Palestinian Women's
Rights: An Analysis" and part of the interview with Dr. Rita Giacaman are from
Arab Women: Between Defiance and Restraint, edited by Suha Sabbagh.
Olive Branch Press, an imprint of Interlink Publishing Group, Inc.
Copyright © Suha Sabbagh 1996. Reprinted by permission.

The paper used in this publication meets the minimum requirements of American
National Standard for Information Sciences—Permanence of Paper for Printed Library
Materials, ANSI Z39.48-1984.

Manufactured in the United States of America

Library of Congress Cataloging-in-Publication Data

Palestinian women of Gaza and the West Bank / edited by Suha Sabbagh.
p.   cm.
Includes index.
ISBN 0-253-33377-6 (cl : alk. paper). — ISBN 0-253-21174-3 (pbk)
1. Women, Palestinian Arab—Gaza Strip. 2. Women, Palestinian Arab—West Bank.
3. Women, Palestinian Arab—Gaza Strip—Social conditions. 4. Women, Palestinian
Arab—West Bank—Social conditions. 5. Women, Palestinian Arab—Gaza Strip—
Political activity. 6. Women, Palestinian Arab—West Bank—Political activity.
I. Sabbagh, Suha.
HQ1728.8.P35   1998
305.48'892740531—dc21   97-40148

1   2   3   4   5   03   02   01   00   99   98

CONTENTS

❀

Contents

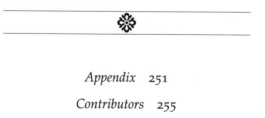

PALESTINIAN WOMEN OF GAZA
AND THE WEST BANK

SUHA SABBAGH

Introduction

Palestinians have been fighting Israeli occupation of the West Bank and Gaza since December 1987. The uprising that occurred between 1987 and 1991 is commonly known as the intifada and has penetrated Western consciousness through television images of youths throwing stones at soldiers. The term "intifada" is the only Arabic word to enter the English language in the last decade. In the Arab press the intifada was likened to the tremors of an earthquake, a metaphor that implies future political and social transformations in the region. Media analysts, reporters, Arab intellectuals, and commentators had much to say about the role of the "hidden forces," the Unified National Leadership of the Uprising (UNLU), and the outside leadership; yet most failed to assess accurately the contributions of women's institutions and the spontaneous support of middle-aged traditional women who sometimes formed human shields between the youths and the soldiers. What will be the effect of the politicization of these traditional women on the social change that some predict will transform the area and impact on the emerging Palestinian state? Will the women seek to alter their role in society, and what will be the response to that? This multidisciplinary work, written from an "insider's" point of view, seeks to answer these questions.

Television images of the intifada generally focused on youth. In part, the youthful image of the intifada reflects the age distribution of the

Suha Sabbagh

population on the West Bank, where 50 percent of the population is under fifteen years of age and 70 percent is under thirty years of age.[1] Yet it is not correct to assume that youths were the only participants. The intifada encompassed all sectors of society, and women's participation in particular is well recognized by the community. Laborers bused daily to Israel bore the brunt of the psychological stress, because the "shabab" (youths) of the intifada did not recognize their contribution; through their wages laborers sustained the youths and made it possible for them to participate in the resistance. Shopkeepers and businessmen sacrificed profits as they complied with the directives of the UNLU and upheld all commercial strikes. Camp dwellers responding to the tension and poverty in the camps mounted demonstrations and confronted the soldiers.[2] Urban and rural dwellers alike assisted their neighbors by providing the needy with food supplies during times of curfew. Others rushed the sick to hospitals, in spite of curfews, at the risk of their own safety. The assistance once extended to needy members of one's extended family was extended to one's neighbors. Some have argued that the general atmosphere in which men were required to express cooperation, caring, support and nurturing, compassion and empathy for one another—all traits generally attributed to women in a traditional culture—had a feminizing impact on society that augmented the appreciation for women's contribution and role. Some men learned to knit and made sweaters for male prison inmates, while others became sensitized to the need to help with household chores, especially if their wives were actively involved in the intifada. These ideas were new to a culture in which male and female roles were clearly demarcated.

Many uprisings against the Israeli occupation took place on the West Bank and in Gaza after 1967. But what distinguished the intifada was the mass mobilization of women from all walks of life: rural women, camp dwellers, and camp refugee women poured into the streets, marched in demonstrations, and organized sit-ins in front of blown-up homes. This was the first, spontaneous phase of the intifada, when mass demonstrations were formed as an expression of anger and frustration. Women initially went into the streets to tear their children from the grasp of the soldiers. They were acting in accordance with their traditional role as protectors. However, women soon came to realize that the position of the youths was a valid one and that occupation could end only through resistance; women then began to assist the youths by breaking up stones for them. Many women decided to try the liberating activity for themselves, as some photos show.

The initial impetus that drove women out of the private sphere of the home and into the public sphere of the street—to the extent that the terms private and public are applicable to life on the West Bank and Gaza at all—was simply the desire to protect their children. But women also expressed their willingness to question traditional values. Their very participation indicates a transformation of consciousness: through the spontaneous act of participating in the confrontation with Israeli soldiers, women have challenged their traditional role, which requires their exclusion from the public sphere. Their priorities have shifted from protecting their homes and traditional values to risking everything in order to loosen the grip of occupation. Given the influence that these women traditionally exert within the home, it is not difficult to imagine that the challenge to some patriarchal norms will have long-term repercussions for gender relations within the family, the exact nature of which remains to be seen.

Analysts have noted that women's participation dwindled in the same measure as the intifada began to lose its spontaneous nature and became institutionalized. The exact reason for this decline has been hotly debated in women's circles. Islah Jad, in a discussion in this volume, blames the UNLU for failing to give the women's issue the necessary attention and consequently for failing to attract women as the intifada became subject to the directives of the UNLU. Joost R. Hiltermann, on the other hand, argues that while not all the women who poured into the streets became mobilized, many did join the ranks of the women's work committees and other women's organizations as a result of their participation in the intifada. He further points out that these women had been courted by women's groups prior to the intifada with less positive results, because women were afraid to support what seemed to them to be a political program. The fact remains that the number of women who joined women's organizations during the intifada rose, although not enough to meet the goals and hopes of some intellectual and activist women.

The most significant effect of the intifada on women was the transformation that took place in women's consciousness of their roles. As they struggled with the soldiers to free their children, women overcame the internal barrier of fear that often prevented them from joining organized activities such as the women's work committees. Further, this development enabled them to challenge their position in the patriarchal structure. Women came to dominate the streets though their very presence there had previously been deemed improper. They were able to freely challenge certain traditions because the rest of society supported and recognized this challenge in the name of the "national cause"; that cause temporarily offered women an umbrella of protection against criticism that they were transgressing against age-old traditions. During the early phase of the intifada, women challenged nearly every symbol of male domination: they organized and joined street demonstrations; they worked side by side with men guarding each quarter; and they provided food to homes in times of curfew.

But the protection afforded women against social criticism in the name of working for *Al 'Amal Al Watani* (the national agenda) was a mixed blessing. Although women trespassed against the symbols of patriarchal domination with the blessings of society, they were simultaneously required not to question the central patriarchal paradigm, the power that men have over women's lives, until after the occupation ended. The argument against such a confrontation was that the direct questioning of this power could destroy the social fabric of the family, which was holding society together in the face of occupation. As in most Third World struggles, Palestinian women were being asked to put their agenda on the back burner[3] until national liberation had been achieved. But women's groups had studied the experience of Algerian women who fought side by side with men yet made very little progress after independence, and they were determined not to meet the same fate as their Algerian counterparts. When the intifada's spontaneous phase ended, most women's organizations and research centers decided to fight the battle on two fronts simultaneously:[4] national and women's rights were to be inseparable agendas. After the Oslo agreements, women's groups presented to the Palestinian Authority a women's bill of rights, which they wished to see become part of the national constitution. This bill, the Declaration of Principles on Palestinian Women's Rights (see appendix) calls on the political leadership to ratify all international conventions concerning the individual rights of women—including the International Convention for the Elimination of All Forms of Discrimination against Women—and to guarantee complete equality for women in the areas of political rights, civil rights, work opportunities, educational opportunities, personal rights, legal protection from violence, and the rights of women to participate in all levels of decision making. Years before the Palestinian-Israeli peace negotiations began in Washington, D.C., women's cadres prepared for the transfer of power by drafting secular personal status laws to replace the current *shariah*, or Islamic laws; conducted sessions designed to raise the consciousness of women to their rights and responsibilities; offered group sessions designed to prevent violence in the home against women and children; and conducted other sessions that focused on the rights of women in divorce. The gathering of information on women's issues in women's research centers loosely affiliated with the four factions of the Palestine Liberation Organization (PLO) sometimes took on the nature of a national obsession, and the information gathered covers nearly every aspect of women's lives. Further, this information was shared with the "outside world" by a virtual army of Palestinian women academics, organizers, and activists, who became globe-trotters, lecturing and attending conferences all over the world while their husbands were left behind to take care of the family.

The relation of Palestinian women to leadership roles is often a confused one. If "leadership" refers to individuals who transform reality, then the list of Palestinian women is an impressive one, indeed. However, in Western feminist terms, "leadership" is often employed as a synonym for political representatives, and the intifada, which is a mass uprising, has relied less on its leadership, the clandestine UNLU, than on mass organization and institution-building in which women organizers played a critical role. Still, the intifada led to the emergence of the Higher Women's Council, a unified body of women leaders representing women from the four main political factions. Their role is best evidenced by the influence they exercised on the UNLU's decision not to endorse the *hijab* (covering for the head, and sometimes the body, for women) because it was enforced by men. Finally, three women, Zahira Kamal, Hanan Mikhail Ashrawi, and Suad Ameri, participated as negotiators and as spokeswomen in the Middle East peace negotiations in Washington, D.C. Although the political representation of Palestinian women through them is in no way equal to the contribution of women, their presence does raise the issue of women's role in political decision making. During the first Palestinian elections on the West Bank in 1995, twenty women ran for office, and five won seats in the newly formed, eighty-eight-member parliament. Two women subsequently became ministers, Intisar Wazir, who was named minister of social affairs, and Hanan Ashrawi, who became minister of higher education.

Changed Lives

Analyses of the intifada note that it is not possible to speak of one social transformation that points in a positive direction without being reminded of numerous examples that point in the opposite direction. The intifada is in a continual state of flux since Palestinians must constantly devise new responses to changing methods of aggression. These seeming contradictions are also the result of the fact that social change has not been uniform. Palestinian society is characterized by a class system, urban and rural dwellers, educated elites and laborers, nationalists and fundamentalists—all of whom respond differently to social issues affecting women. The lives of some women who became involved in the work of the nation have been transformed, while the lives of others have become more oppressed.

Suha Sabbagh

The intifada brought about some positive transformations in traditional norms that symbolize women's dependency. The *mahr*, or dowry, which was bestowed by the bridegroom on the bride and included much gold jewelry, almost disappeared during the intifada. Some might debate whether men's or women's interests are served by reducing the mahr to a mere symbol; however, it is important to consider the kind of symbolism involved. In Muslim Arab culture, where the roles of men and women are clearly defined, the responsibility of providing for women rests squarely on men's shoulders.[5] Dropping the mahr means that women are economically responsible for themselves. If this norm is inculcated, it will mean that greater numbers of women will earn the right to work outside the home, assuming that job opportunities become available.[6]

The intifada spawned a number of marriages based on romantic involvement (as opposed to so-called arranged marriages). In a segregated culture, young men often resort to a third party to assist them in choosing the right marriage partner. The national agenda, by facilitating meetings between the sexes, made it possible for the current generation to choose their own marriage partners based on romantic involvement, although most young women insist that their choice is based on political and ideological compatibility.

For many women, however, the intifada had an adverse effect. In rural areas there was a substantial drop in marriage age for women, from an average age of eighteen to fourteen in some cases.[7] Unable to feed large families when construction work in Israel virtually came to a stop because of curfews and strikes, some fathers arranged for their daughters to marry at an early age. Others did not approve of political activism for women, and since schools were closed and parents were not always in a position to prevent their daughters' activism, fathers sought to arrange marriages for their daughters at an early age to protect their virtue. The ambivalence experienced by women who were caught at a moment in time when values were only beginning to shift is captured in the following excerpt from an interview with Siham Abdullah, a graduate of al-Najah University in Nablus (the full interview can be found in chapter three). Siham states that her mother, who is known for her courage in defying Israeli soldiers, has greater freedom than Siham herself because of her age and married status:

> *Are you afraid* [of participating in the struggle]?
> Of course I am, but not of the occupying power. With a mother like mine, how could I possibly be afraid of occupation. . . . I am afraid of remaining celibate, of not having children. Some men think that

women join demonstrations to meet men, and that could tarnish a girl's reputation and affect the rest of her life. Frankly, I am afraid of injury and of prison, because if I am maimed, there is very little chance of finding a man who will ask for my hand in marriage.

Political activist and organizer Amal Barghouthi is far more assertive. She succeeded in resisting her parents' decision to send her to teachers training school on the West Bank and attended instead the University of Jordan in Amman. Her experience with women's work committees and her knowledge placed her in a leadership position:

Changes in gender relations are at the moment [i.e., during the intifada] sustained by the high level of political energy among men and women.
Women are delighted with the recognition that they are getting, but . . . there will be a serious regression in gains made so far unless women organize by joining existing structures.

The dilemma now facing activists is how to convert into tangible results the gains women made during the spontaneous participation of women in street demonstrations. The idea of working simultaneously on both fronts, nationalist and feminist, was entirely new; it was introduced by the women's work committees when they began to emerge in the late 1970s. Here their views were reinforced in the course of time because women came to realize just how important their contribution to the struggle really is.[8]

Women's Organizations and Cooperatives

The first form of women's organization that emerged immediately after the 1967 war were welfare-type organizations. Raymonda Tawil's book *My Home, My Prison* is one of a few sources that offers information on the way women organized following the occupation in July 1967 as a reaction to the punitive measures imposed by the military government.[9] Tawil offers important details about specific events, such as women's active involvement in preventing changes imposed by the military government in the school curriculum and demonstrations carried out against the demolition of homes. She describes the conditions of the refugees evicted from their homes and settled temporarily around her house during the 1967 war.[10] The emphasis then on saving lives and providing sustenance carries through in women's welfare organizations to the present day. By and large, these early organizations were built around women's nurturing role. Any problems touching on the life of the family, school curriculum, food for needy families, or medical care became part of women's domain.

Welfare Organizations

The Society for the Rejuvenation of the Family (In'ash al-Usra), headed by Samiha Khalil, was founded in 1965, two years before the Israeli occupation of the West Bank and Gaza. In 1965 the budget of this small organization was five hundred dollars. Shortly before the organization was forced to shut down on the grounds that "it was teaching the slogans of the intifada," it was the largest organization of its kind in the West Bank and had a budget of $420,000. The organization was helping 15,000 women, including 4,800 women employed in traditional Palestinian embroidery projects in their homes, 152 full-time employees of the society, and 200 young women registered each year in its vocational programs. Fifteen hundred families were receiving sponsorship aid of $500 a year, including military prisoners and their families. In'ash al-Usra was not the only organization of its kind.[11] During the intifada, Palestinian society had a high percentage of women who were single heads of households, either because their husbands were in jail or employed in Gulf countries. Women have to rely on each other through a networking system to increase their income, and their welfare organizations play a very important role by providing financial, medical, and scholarship aid programs.[12]

Women's Work Committees

A new form of women's organization emerged in the late 1970s with the four women's work committees, affiliated with the four factions of the PLO.[13] While the welfare organizations were run from the top down, generally by urban, middle-class women who wanted to help women with lower incomes, the new organizations were more democratic and stressed self-help over welfare programs. The younger generation of women leaders felt that welfare organizations did not stress survival and self-help programs. The founders formed classes to provide health education; training in embroidery, office skills, and food processing; and to increase literacy. They also provided women with day care centers; women felt secure that their children were within reach while they were improving their survival skills. Most importantly, they engaged women in political discussions that soon turned into discussions about women's issues and women's rights.[14]

At the beginning of the intifada, when directives were issued by the UNLU calling for strikes or marches, women's work committees would translate them into a call for action by women and pass them on through their networks. They organized marches in which women called for the liberation of the land and for equality for women in a new Palestinian state headed by the PLO. At the beginning of the intifada, Israeli soldiers hesitated to use force against women, and women turned this constraint to their advantage. In more conservative villages women's participation was smaller, yet it signified a shift in what constitutes women's territorial domain. The women's work committees also benefited from the increased political awareness of women by drawing many new members into these institutions. They attracted women by offering classes in first aid and health education to compensate for poor access to medical centers in times of curfew. They also increased their day care hours to make it possible for women to participate in the intifada.

Popular Committees

The intifada saw the emergence of a mass base in an informal system of organizations called popular committees, which were designed to meet the needs of the community and enable them to resist; the committees consisted of both men and women working side by side. Members of the women's committees also joined the popular committees and transferred to them their institutional know-how. The two types of committees were able to supplement each other's programs. The popular committees were based on the principle of extending the care and support once reserved for members of one's extended family to all members of one's community. Under curfew and under restricted forms of mobility, one's neighbor is at least as important as a cousin who lives in the next village. Each neighborhood had a committee to deal with emergencies and ongoing services and supplies: serve food and baby milk, guard the neighborhood, maintain the clandestine education system, visit prisoners, and develop and staff the so-called "defense system." This last committee, the most visible one, consisted of the shabab, who engage the army by throwing stones.

With the exception of the defense committee, all committees had more than 50 percent female members. It is not difficult to see that women are more efficient in assessing the food and baby food requirements of households; first aid needs; and the need for urgent medical care, especially in cases of childbirth. The committees sought to meet these needs as best they could. Because schools were closed, women developed a clandestine education system in their basements and in community buildings; since it was illegal, teachers, if discovered, risked a prison sentence and a heavy fine. Pupils who attended had to hide their destination and their books from soldiers, and because of the surrounding anxiety and tension, many were not able to show the same concentration as they might have in a regular school.

Women's work committees matured in the process of lending their skills to the intifada. Before the intifada, competition was the norm between work committees affiliated with the different political factions; this sometimes led to duplication of the services offered in certain villages. During the intifada, all committees learned to work together and to coordinate their activities, a step that brought together activists from the various factions. Some analysts have argued that the agenda of the popular committees constituted a regression in women's rights because it represented an extension of women's traditional role of caring for the sick and the needy, something that was vital to the resistance but did not necessarily benefit women.[15] Others argue that while women's position was not significantly altered, their participation has earned them a stronger role in family decisions, including greater control over finances, their own mobility, and the education of their children.

Women's Food Cooperatives

In an attempt to meet the directives of the UNLU to boycott Israeli goods, the women's work committees established food cooperatives to produce jams, fruit juices, canned fruits, pickled vegetables, biscuits, and breads. Women did not have to learn new skills since canning is practiced in most Palestinian households. Methods of food preservation had to be improved, however, and the products were sold through shops or directly to customers. The effectiveness of the cooperatives in providing an alternative to goods imported from Israel was limited; but the experience afforded women a taste of economic independence and set an example of how women can contribute to the market while creating jobs.

In a published interview, Um Khalid, a forty-eight-year-old female worker in an agricultural cooperative in a village near the city of Ramallah, where she worked with twelve village women, had the following to say about her work and her new sense of self: "Now I feel that I'm able to fight for my full rights as a woman and as a human being. I am no longer just a housewife. No, I'm part of the work force that is creating direct change in my society. . . . By being productive, I can also be a full partner in establishing the structure of our society."[16]

Another successful cooperative called Our Production Is Our Pride Cooperative, had two branches on the West Bank and was formed shortly before the intifada. Its twenty-two women workers attended a course in marketing, production methods, and bookkeeping. Decision making was shared and so were the profits. Their jars of pickled cucumbers, olives, and stuffed eggplant were popular products in shops in the Jerusalem area. Many cooperatives gave women work that could be performed at home between household chores, for example, embroidering of articles of traditional dress and other items.

Assessment of the impact of cooperatives and other forms of home economies on women's lives indicates that increased income did not automatically alter the gender gap. Women still do their household chores in addition to their work outside the home. Yet participation in the cooperative decision-making process seems to have altered their perceptions of themselves. As one female worker put it: "As rural women, we have been working on the land all our lives; but we did not take a role in the decision making and we never dared to ask to be paid by our husbands or fathers. Now we can work as we did, but with more organization and taking part in the decision making."[17]

Women's Research Centers

In the assessment of most research institutions, women did not make substantial gains despite their hard work. And despite women's growing political activism, their status in society has not greatly changed. Similar conclusions were reached by the panelists at a women's conference held during the intifada at the National Palace Hotel in East Jerusalem on December 24, 1990.[18] The second point made during this conference, which was called Together toward Enlightenment and Equality, indicated that the early period of mass involvement by females in the intifada was followed by a retreat in women's rights. The most flagrant example cited is the imposition of Islamic dress codes where these rules had previously been relaxed. Two main reasons explain this regression: the emergence of a backlash against the progress made by women, and the failure of the intifada to achieve a political solution to occupation.

It is somewhat premature to dismiss or to diminish the positive impact of the intifada on women's lives. There have been some positive transformations in traditional norms that mark a shift in the direction of greater equality for women. But these changes have not permeated all levels of society equally. If we compare the situation in 1991 or 1992 with that at the beginning of the intifada, one must conclude that there had been no fundamental change in the position of women in Palestinian society. Yet all analysts concede that transformations in values did occur, some of which are mentioned below.

It is also important to remember that the personal situation of women writing about women's issues impacts on the nature of the research. One West Bank analyst confided that the negative conclusions regarding the lack of progress made by women are the result of the discrepancy between the aspirations of the women researchers and the gloomy conditions in which they live. Five years after the intifada, the failure to achieve any political solution to occupation, the economic devastation resulting from the Gulf War, and the emergence of a fundamentalist movement all combined to put the most optimistic advocate of women's rights in a state of despair that sometimes translated into self-reproach.

If documentation of women's participation can safeguard against the obliteration of women's rights after independence has been won, then Palestinian women's rights are well ensured. Several research centers belonging to different political factions publish regularly on women's issues. The Women's Affairs Center in Nablus published a quarterly journal in Arabic until 1995. The center trains researchers who have published studies on women in agricultural cooperatives; on the exploitation of nurses by local hospitals; on the choice of a career in journalism by women; and on the assessment of the women's movement in the occupied territories. In addition to interviews with local activists, the journal also published translations of articles by Robin Morgan and other Western feminists. Among its many activities the center sponsors lectures and house meetings to raise women's consciousness of women's issues.[19] Other research centers are doing similar work.

The Women's Resource and Research Center in Jerusalem publishes a monthly popular women's magazine, *Al Mara*, which deals with the social issues facing women. It has published an economic study entitled "The Socioeconomic Conditions of Female Wage Labor on the West Bank," which addresses such issues as holidays and health insurance for women; training available to women; and an assessment of women's awareness of their own labor conditions. Another study examined "Women Street Vendors," assessing women's income and status in society. The center continues to hold conferences and lectures in association with women's committees to inform women about their rights. The committees carried out a campaign and published information pamphlets on violence against women in the home; and they held consciousness-raising sessions in which women discussed their rights and their role in society.

The Palestinian Research and Development Group, known as Bisan and located in the Ramallah area, published the proceedings of the women's conference Together toward Enlightenment and Equality.[20] The conference was attended by nearly five hundred people. Its five academic papers and four workshops were highly critical of the gains made by women. A participant summed up the mood of the day when she said, "This is the first time we say out loud that there hasn't been a fundamental change in the role of women in Palestinian society." One of the papers dealt with the "Intifada and Social Issues,"[21] addressing the reasons behind the retreat from female participation during the second phase of the intifada. Another panelist argued that women's status had not been altered in proportion to their contributions to the national struggle. Women continued to be perceived exclusively as protectors of the home and were not fully represented at the political level, which could be seen from the fact that their representation in the Palestine National Congress did not exceed 10 percent. A third paper, "Intifada and Social Norms," states that the austere culture that developed during the intifada did not benefit women. Other centers not mentioned here have published studies on the roles of women, children, and the family. Should Palestinians have their own state, these studies may provide an analysis of social and development policy on which a new government might base its policies. It is to be hoped that through the documentation of their significant role, women will be able to achieve equal rights within the framework of a democratic Palestinian state.

Image and Reality

If indeed women's roles have changed, then this change must also be reflected in the language of the intifada—in novels, in legends, in poetry, and in the leaflets circulated by the UNLU. Literary critics, folklorists, linguists, and others have studied the language and imagery of this body of literature; the results indicate that folkloric anecdotes show the most positive transformation in the depiction of women while poetry shows the least change in this area. Although male poets include images of women's participation, they still focus on such biological attributes as long, flowing hair, a small waist, and other "feminine" characteristics when they could have portrayed women as equal partners in the struggle.

A number of legends about the confrontation with the occupier were spun during the intifada. In this volume, Sharif Kanaana analyzes the psychosocial conditions that are conducive to the emergence of such legends. He notes that stress and rising nationalism are two areas that constitute fertile ground for these stories, which portray local or national heros and heroines as accomplishing extraordinary feats against the enemy.[22] Some legends show a transformation in women's role, while others continue to cast women in the role of mythical mother and protector.

In the body of oral literature called legends, women's role is more positive than in the poetry written during the intifada. This is the conclusion of Ilham Abu Ghazaleh in her essay, and it is not surprising since the canons of Arabic poetry generally take a long time to change. Legends, on the other hand, do not have a structured form, and any changes in the perception of women can easily be incorporated in this form of anecdote.

Even prior to the intifada, Palestinian women have always perceived themselves as the stronger sex, according to the feminist novelist Sahar Khalifeh. Her main characters, a woman head of a household, a journalist, a prostitute, and a housewife, are trapped between poverty, occupation, traditional norms, and unchanging male perceptions. Yet, they grow and become stronger through their adversity and are able to make a contribution to society in many ways. In time society comes to value their contribution and to understand their position. Her women characters are politicized and display a hands on approach to life. At least one assumption carries through her work that gender conditions experience of occupation as she draws parallels between the oppression of women in a patriarchal society and their oppression under occupation. As they fight occupation they also fight against restrictive traditional values inculcated into their innermost self. She has an excellent understanding of subalternity, and her work brings a unique vision into the mechanism of power and subordination in occupation.[23]

The directives for mass mobilization during the intifada were issued in leaflets circulated by the UNLU; their language has been criticized for lumping together women, the older generation, and children as the segment of society that needs protection. The language used in these leaflets is part of a pattern of political discourse employed during times of national struggle. Here again canons of political discourse that impose on women a restrictive role that has no relation to women's role in the "outside world" are being questioned. Individually, each and every member of the UNLU had a sister or a mother who was politically active and must have been aware of the role of women. Needless to say, had there been more women among the ranks of the UNLU such a mistake might have been avoided.

Political Representation of Palestinian Women

The political representation of Palestinian women lags behind their contribution to the national struggle, and the offices they do hold reflect their traditional roles. In the Palestinian Red Crescent in Lebanon, women hold 40 percent of the higher positions. In the overall structure of the PLO, Palestinian women constitute roughly 6 percent of the higher authority of the organization. In the army in Lebanon, they held about 4 percent of the high-ranking posts. Of a total of 301 members in the Palestine National Council, the Palestinian parliament in exile, thirty-seven are women. In the structure of Fatah, the largest faction in the PLO, Um Jihad and Um Lutuf were the only two women members of the Revolutionary Council. In mass unions and syndicates, Isam 'Abdel Hadi is the only woman in a top position, heading—what else?—the General Union of Palestinian Women.[24] Several Palestinian fighters, such as Leila Khalid, became known for their militancy; however, the majority made their contribution in traditional ways. While the political representation of Palestinian women compares favorably with other Arab countries, this does not mean that Palestinian women are anywhere near close to achieving a measure of equality in political representation. Many believe that the women's movement will be in a position to negotiate like the other factions of the PLO once sovereignty is achieved; but this will depend on the level of democracy and political participation within the apparatus of the new Palestinian state.

A Phase of Regression

Comparing Women's Day in 1988 and in 1991, a prominent woman author has written:

> In the wake of the Gulf War and in the midst of continued curfew and restrictions on the Palestinian population, Women's Day 1991 passed almost without notice in the occupied territories. . . . The contrast to Women's Day 1988, during the first year of the uprising, was stark. On that day middle-class women in high heels, teenagers in jeans, and village women in traditional dress marched through the streets of Ramallah and other towns and villages throughout the West Bank and Gaza. Many women had tears in their eyes—not from the inevitable tear gas but from the exhilaration of a new spirit of women's solidarity and defiance.[25]

In the fourth and the fifth years of the intifada, the potential for a mass women's movement with the ability to address national and social issues was beginning to decline along with the declining figures in women's organizations. However, the number of hard-core women activists and women intellectuals was not affected, and many conferences were held in an attempt to analyze the three primary factors that were contributing to the decline in the women's movement: a) the failure of the intifada to bring about a political solution to occupation and the failure of the U.S. sponsored peace negotiations to produce any tangible results after one year; b) the emergence of a religious fundamentalist movement that succeeded in imposing the hijab on women and restricting their mobility, especially in the Gaza Strip; c) a sense of economic insecurity and personal vulnerability, generated, according to some, by the Gulf War, that brought women back into the fold of the extended family, reinforcing its patriarchal structures and values. The first phase of the intifada had been accompanied by a sense of euphoria because people felt that they were finally reclaiming their own destiny. Many social ills such as drug addiction, wife beating, and divorce nearly disappeared from the scene. These issues are addressed in this volume in an interview with Dr. Eyad el-Sarraj, a psychiatrist from Gaza. During this period, women's organizations flourished and more men came to support women's rights. The second, more pessimistic phase of the intifada set in roughly during the third year with the realization that tangible political gains were few. All other institutions were also affected. The financial situation was worsening because laborers either refused to work, or were refused work, on construction sites in Israel. Many institutions that commissioned women's embroidery in the past were now closed down by the occupation because of political activism. Many families had lost a child or a relative, others had relatives in prison, and in this general atmosphere a call for gender equality seemed less urgent than the question of daily survival. At that point, the failure of the Middle East peace negotiations to achieve any tangible progress toward ending occupation generated a pessimism that drew many women away from the political arena.

In Gaza women were being coerced to wear the hijab and to conform to an Islamic dress code that does not have its roots in the indigenous traditional culture. Rima Hammami has argued that imposing the hijab constitutes a backlash against women's changing roles. Supporting her views, Sarraj states that by turning to religion, fathers sought to reinstate their traditional authority within the family; this authority was challenged first by occupation and, during the intifada, by youths who no longer complied with parental regulations.[26] Since a feminist consciousness had not yet taken root in Gaza, women accepted this reimposition of male authority to avoid additional aggravation within the home. Some women wore the hijab out of conviction, others wore it as a form of divine protection against all forms of aggression.

Most analysts agree that the significance of the hijab arises from the struggle for control between the nationalists and the religious forces. If this is indeed the case, then the nationalists have not come to the assistance of women in the same measure as women have contributed to the struggle. At the prodding of the Women's Higher Commission but somewhat late in the game, the UNLU issued a leaflet chastising anyone who coerces women to wear the hijab. In the weeks that followed, women were not bothered, leading many to argue that had these leaflets been issued at the beginning of the campaign, women might have fared better.[27] During that period, by most estimates, the number of nationalists exceeded that of fundamentalists by two thirds. One must conclude, therefore, that many women nationalists wore the headdress against their wishes.

The Gulf War marks another downward turn in the rising expectations of women. The women's network and organizations had not been set up to deal with the fear of chemical warfare and the requirements for protecting one's family, for dealing with overcrowding due to twenty-four-hour curfews and family anxiety and stress. The inadequacy of the response is described as follows:

> The grassroots network of support developed during the intifada was, not surprisingly, inadequate to the emergency of regional and total curfew, with the partial exception of health committees and human rights work done by a number of organizations and activists to highlight the lack of protection afforded the Palestinian population. The role of the women's committees, however, was minimal at best. In towns, villages and camps, the sustaining network was the traditional one—family, kin, and neighborhood.[28]

As women returned to the fold of the patriarchal and extended family structure, their progress was halted and the economic survival of the family took precedence. A large percentage of families had hitherto survived on support from relatives, husbands, and sons working in Saudi Arabia and the Gulf states. Other families derived their income from local institutions that were financed by the Arab world. During the war, this income came to a near halt. As poverty spread, many young couples went back to live with the extended family, and this placed additional restrictions on women's behavior. A young man from Rajah refugee camp in Gaza viewed his wife's predicament as follows:

> After the intifada I lost all hopes of having a separate home. I simply could not afford to spend on two households [my parents' and my own], especially after my father and brothers had been laid off from their jobs. Being the youngest brother, I could not stop my family from interfering with my wife and my own affairs. They even went to the extent of forcing my wife to wear the veil inside the house.[29]

Finally, the fact that the women's movement was so inextricably linked to the nationalist movement meant that the women's movement suffered when the nationalist movement was in decline. And during the Gulf War the nationalist movement lost its centrality. Reflecting on this, Giacaman and Johnson write that just as the intifada in its initial stage offered remarkable opportunities for the development of the women's movement, the obverse is also true; the women's movement in the occupied territories, inextricably tied to the national movement, reflects each twist and turn of the national fortune.[30]

The shape that the fledgling women's movement will take in the future depends on the political future of the territories occupied by Israel.

In the Arab World the emergence of a feminist consciousness has always been linked to national liberation struggles, and this has both aided and hindered its development in a number of ways. What does the Palestinian example have in common with Algerian or Egyptian counterparts? To understand the Palestinian women's movement, it must be placed within the context of similar movements in the Arab world.

Feminism and Nationalism in the Arab World

A brief look at the modern history of the Arab world shows that some events have affected its population, including women, very deeply. Colonial occupation, the occupation of Palestinian land, and more recently the Gulf War, have shaped the views of both men and women in the area. The theorist and psychiatrist Frantz Fanon, who wrote for the Algerian revolution, has argued that all colonized people undergo three developmental phases as they move toward liberation. I would argue that the phases identified by Fanon are rather three political and intellectual currents that sometimes exist simultaneously. A glance at the modern history of the Arab world shows that these currents constitute three possible responses to a) Western policies in the Middle East, and b) economic and regional problems affecting the area. Here, we can take the current wave of Islamic revival as an example. But while this movement is more politicized than previous Islamic movements, it is certainly not the first time that the Arab world has turned to its Islamic roots for answers. Fanon has argued that a return to the religious roots of a culture belongs to the second phase.

Fanon traced his three political phases in the literature of native writers, arguing that the phases are chronological and culminate in national liberation. The attempt to understand the emergence of a feminist consciousness in the Arab world must take into account the three political currents. A feminist consciousness emerges during the struggle for national liberation. As women fight colonial occupation, they become conscious of their own oppression in a patriarchal culture. Fanon delineates these three phases through the literature of each phase. The first phase, under occupation, is an imitative phase. Fanon writes that during this period, the native is alienated from his culture and seeks to imitate literary genres and to absorb ideas that are Western. Since all educational institutions under colonization were built by the colonizers, education itself is informed by Western principles; contact with that educational system consequently alienates the native from his roots.

The second phase is understood by Fanon as an antithetical reaction to the first phase. In this phase we witness the re-emergence of forms of identity that are closely related to the roots of the culture, such as religious revivals or the concept of "negritude," also known as "black is beautiful." In literature, the native intellectual seeks a kind of cultural purity that is no longer possible. In other words, at this point, the unconditional affirmation of Western culture produces an unconditional affirmation of indigenous culture. The native intellectual seeks to return to a world that is uncontaminated by contact with the occupation, but this return to the past is not possible. Fanon places his trust in the third and nationalist phase, in the birth of a national consciousness that is part of the national struggle. At this point literature reflects a sense of solidarity with countries that are also undergoing decolonization. But the native intellectual is no longer self-conscious, he accepts the fact that some ideas are borrowed and some literary genres are Western in origin. New literary genres and new forms of writing emerge in this creative period, which generally sees the emergence of a large body of literature. It is during this third phase that women's roles begin to change; as they participate in the struggle, women break down traditional barriers, and their awareness of their own oppression under patriarchal structures becomes clearer.

In the Arab world today these three literary as well as political currents tend toward (a) importation of Western theoretical paradigms and ideas, (b) a return to the Arab-Islamic roots of the country in question, (c) or nationalistic trends that define themselves in anti-imperialist terms. The reliance on "knowledge" that is produced in the West, defined in (a) above, is not quite a political current or a question of intellectual choice as much as it is a necessity. All knowledge in the sciences and in the theoretical realm is produced from within or relies on Western thought. If the importation of knowledge is carried out in uncritical fashion, Arab intellectuals find themselves studying their own culture from a point outside that culture. The two remaining currents, nationalism (in all its variations, such as a greater inclination toward democratization or radical leftist theory), and religious Islamic currents sometimes occur simultaneously as competing ideologies. At times, though one trend may be dominant, the other current of thought is never totally supplanted.

In what follows we shall examine the leadership role that women played and continue to play at each juncture in the modern history of the Arab world. However, if by political leadership we mean women who hold political office, then our task is a limited one indeed, since few women have succeeded in breaking down this particular barrier of male domination. But if by leadership we refer to women who have had an impact on the community, women who have devoted their lives to building institutions, to bettering the lot of others, and to emancipating themselves and their sisters, then the list of Arab women might well exceed that of Arab men. Arab women have never been dormant; their roles and their struggles for emancipation, their perception of self, are grounded in the ideologies, the values, and the problems of the Arab world.

Male Reformers in Egypt and Women's Rights

In Egypt, the work of the early modernist writers from around the turn of the century shows a far greater degree of autonomy than that described by Fanon in his "imitative" first phase. The general consensus is that the period of early contact with European culture was also a period of cultural Renaissance in the Arab world, especially Egypt. Egyptian writers who traveled to Europe were exposed to Western literary schools from which they borrowed extensively upon their return to Egypt. Commenting on the impact of such borrowing, Edward Said noted that the adoption of Western genres, such as the novel, the play, the short story, and the biography, did not take place without a marked alteration in Arab writers' conception of reality. He argued that the novel in particular offers a view of reality that was foreign to Arab culture, because in Islamic thought, the act of imitating reality through the act of recreating the world constitutes a form of heresy. For example, reproducing the human form in art is considered inimical to Islam. Describing the intention of the novel, Edward Said has written: "The desire to create an alternative world, to modify or augment the real world through the act of writing (which is one motive underlying the novelistic tradition in the West) is inimical to the Islamic world view."[31] It is possible to assume that the idea of recreating the world opened up the possibility of recreating women's roles in this new worldview, which led to the debate on women's rights during this early phase. By borrowing literary genres and combining them with the indigenous intellectual tradition, writers demonstrated a creative fusion between the two traditions. But the extent to which this new creative fusion affected the possible new role of women is a question that still needs to be addressed.

Introduction

It is not surprising to see that during this early phase in the late nineteenth century, which marks a fusion of ideas between Arab and Western culture, new ideas about women's roles began to emerge in Egypt. What should be the role of Arab women? was a question that could only occur after an encounter with a different role for women, with that of Western women. Should women be educated and why? Until such time as a woman scholar proves that early reformers who called for the education of women were not all men, that women played a very active role, we will continue to hear that Egyptian male reformers led the way to the emancipation of Arab women, generally after their return from a trip to the European continent. The names of male reformers include Ahmed Fares El Shidyak, whose book *One Leg Crossed over the Other* (1855) supports women's emancipation. Another well-known name is that of Riffaa Rafi El-Tahtawi (1801–1871), who had studied in Paris and was concerned with modernizing the educational system in Egypt. A major concern for him was the education of young women. He put forward his views in *A Guide to the Education of Girls and Boys* (1872). In *Feminism and Nationalism in the Third World*, Kumari Jayawardena affirms that during this period nearly every aspect of women's emancipation was being discussed, with very little agreement among authors.[32] She argues that the debate sparked a sizable amount of literature on women's rights, which appeared in the form of books, magazine articles, and poetry.

Egyptian male reformers of this period made a clear distinction between religion and practice or tradition, arguing that it is the latter that often led to the subjugation of women. Many argued that a return to "true" Muslim principles would enable women to gain greater rights. The most outspoken male reformer of this period was Qasim Amin who, after a visit to France, argued that what had become the norm for female behavior was not ordained by the shariah or the Quran. In his book *Tahrir al-Mar'a* (Women's emancipation [1899]), he stressed the need for women to work outside the home—a new concept for a culture that was steeped in the notion that men are the providers for women. He also argued against the prevalent customs of covering the female body and secluding women within the home. He was for the improvement of women's rights in divorce and for a woman's right to have a greater say in choosing her husband. Amin was the author of the statement, "there can be no way of improving the state of the nation without improving the position of women,"[33] which was to become the slogan for male and female reformers in later years. It is not surprising that his views were controversial; for although he argued from within Islamic principles, his ideas about the role of women were clearly influenced by the role of women in European countries. Amin answered his critics in a second book entitled *al-Mar'a al- Jadida* (The new woman [1900]), in which he developed his concept of equal rights for men and women. Within the span of a few years women would become quite capable of using the pen to champion their own cause very effectively.

National Liberation and the Emergence of a Feminist Consciousness

Fanon places his trust in the third phase, the process of decolonization that brings about the birth of a national consciousness. National consciousness is, according to Fanon, reflected in "national culture," which includes both literature and folklore. He attributes the emergence of new literary genres to this period, when the native writer is no longer self-conscious about the origins of literary genres that blend what was acquired from the West with indigenous genres to produce the literature of liberation.

Implicit in Fanon's concept of "national culture" is the emergence of a feminist consciousness that seeks a greater degree of equality with men. The feminist consciousness is born in the context of resistance to outside domination, on the one hand, and to feudal monarchies and traditional patriarchal and religious structures on the other. The initial impetus that drove women to participate in the national liberation struggle is often a traditional motive: the spontaneous outpouring of anti-imperialist feeling, as was the case with Egyptian women who demonstrated in the streets of Cairo against British occupation or, more recently, Palestinian women's desire to protect their children in the early days of the intifada. However, in the process, as women move from the private sphere of the home and into the public sphere of the street, women express their willingness to question traditional values that require their exclusion from the political sphere. Their participation in the national liberation struggle indicates that their consciousness has been transformed: women have started to question age-old values that require their seclusion in the home. Their priorities have shifted from being the guardians of tradition to risking everything in order to loosen the grip of colonization. It is at this moment that a feminist consciousness seeking greater equality with men begins to form. The struggle therefore often takes place on two fronts simultaneously: feminist and nationalist.

In the modern history of the Arab world, three countries come to mind with regard to the issue of women's participation in a national liberation struggle: Egypt, Algeria, and Palestine. Many people remember the images of the intifada on the evening news, images that showed middle-aged women in traditional dress forming human shields between their children and the army in the streets of their towns on the West Bank and in Gaza. As early as 1919 Egyptian women demonstrated in the streets of Cairo, chanting nationalist slogans through veils covering their faces. Algerian women passed messages and transported arms at greater risk to their personal safety during the struggle for decolonization.[34]

Nationalism and the Women's Movement in Egypt

Women's participation, at the turn of the century, in growing political resistance to colonial rule in Egypt has had an influence on the emergence of a women's movement that has called for the education of women, for bettering women's position within marriage, and for the right of women to work outside the home. The turn of the century saw the emergence of an educated elite, including lawyers and teachers, who, along with landowners and peasants called for the expulsion of the British from national soil. This group, headed by Saad Zaghlul, in time became the Wafd Party and had the backing of many intellectuals who supported greater rights for women. Saad Zaghlul had been a staunch supporter of women's rights to education, and his perspective was secularist. By 1922, when Egypt gained its independence from the British, political activism and street demonstrations in which many women participated had led to the emergence of a political movement that also recognized the rights of women. A number of women, now considered to be early Egyptian feminists, rose to prominence through their writings at this time.[35]

One of the most influential women writers of this period was Malak Hifni Nassif (1886–1918). She used the pen name Bahissat al-Badiaa, meaning Researcher from the Desert, at the edge of which she lived during her married years. She was vocal in her criticism of all the institutions that form a woman's life: veiling and seclusion, denial of education, polygamy and divorce, and denial of the right to work outside the home. It is assumed that her unhappy marriage had some influence on her writings. However, she had the opportunity, unlike many other women of her time, to receive an education. And she was among the first women in Egypt to qualify as a school teacher, though her marriage prevented her from practicing her profession. In 1911 she was asked to present her views on the emancipation of women to the Egyptian Legislative Assembly; she set forth an impressive program that included compulsory elementary education for women. Some of her program was implemented.

SUHA SABBAGH

Equally important is May Ziyada, who had a literary salon in her home. Her writings were well received in the circles of male literary critics. At a time when most women were still veiled, she mixed freely with male intellectuals. In Egypt this period saw the emergence of fifteen journals that published on women's issues; May Ziyada was a regular contributor.

In the West, Huda Shaarawi (1882–1947) is known for her theatrical gesture of throwing her long veil into the Nile after returning from a trip to Italy. In the Arab world she is best remembered for opening a school for girls and for her participation in anticolonialist activities. On several occasions she petitioned the British High Commissioner to stop the use of violence against street demonstrations. Huda Shaarawi is remembered for forming, together with other middle-class women, the Egyptian Feminist Union. This organization fought hard to achieve education and other social benefits for women, including changes in personal status laws. Shaarawi was also the founder of a journal for women published in French, *l'Egyptienne*, which dealt with the issue of polygamy and other infringements of women's rights from a perspective that remained Islamic.

The nationalist struggle in Egypt offered women the opportunity to voice their demands for greater equality and to be heard. This early period also saw the emergence of many publications in which women's issues were hotly debated. However, interest in women's rights began to decline in the 1930s, and in time the feminist movement lost its early appeal.

Women and the Algerian Struggle for Independence

Frantz Fanon, who was sensitive both to the use of language and to all forms of oppression, lapsed when he named his concept, born out of the struggle, the "New Man," thus excluding from the concept Algerian women whom he admired precisely because of their contribution to the liberation of their people. In his essay "Algeria Unveiled," Fanon places a great deal of emphasis on the inner struggle of women who, in order to pass messages, found themselves walking for the first time without the protection of a veil;[36] he also writes about the dilemma of a woman who had emancipated herself from the veil but found it necessary to don it again in order to smuggle arms. However, Marnia Lazreg argues that Fanon's emphasis on veiling or unveiling is a vestige of Fanon's Western perceptions, an expression of a culture that is obsessed with the veiling of Arab women.[37] Yet Fanon understood the essential role of women. The tasks that Fanon describes as entrusted to Algerian women included the bearing of messages and complicated verbal orders learned by heart, sometimes despite the complete absence of schooling. Women were also called upon to stand watch, often for more than an hour, outside a house where district leaders were in conference.[38]

Whereas Fanon takes the position that Algerian women had always been extremely powerful within the home and that the revolution forced them to show equal tenacity in the political sphere, David Gordon maintains in an essay on "Women of Algeria" (1968) that women followed the orders of male leaders of the struggle.[39] He writes: "Women did not become part of the struggle early on but were included in 1955 when men realized that women could be useful because French soldiers, who perceived all Arab women to be docile, never suspected these women of being capable of acting as messengers, arms smugglers etc." Gordon's essay gives useful details on the experience of women who were imprisoned for their refusal to divulge information, but he argues that the emancipation of women occurred because the patriarchal structure was crumbling. During the struggle, patriarchy collapsed—a father could no longer give orders to a daughter he knew would be working for the national cause. Finally, women fighting side by side with men could not be considered passive. While Gordon maintains that the struggle did not raise the issue of liberation for women since Arab women followed orders given by the male leadership, Fanon argued that Algerian society was outwardly patriarchal while underneath a matriarchal structure had always ruled and the anticolonial movement simply released the power of women.

How did Algerian women perceive their own role? This question has been asked by Bouthaina Shaaban, a feminist from Syria.[40] She writes, "In answer to my question whether women organized operations or obeyed male orders, an Algerian woman said that the men carried out our (women's) orders. We were the only ones who planned operations. . . . We used to take someone to a hospital, pretending that he or she was ill. Once they were in there we changed their clothes, dyed their hair and they went out the opposite door completely new persons carrying arms and ready for the next new operation. The town was divided into six parts. Mme. Bouzienne, for example, would come here from one direction wearing the veil and black shoes. She would come in, hold a meeting, plan an operation, then give her clothes and shoes to a man in the meeting and go out in another direction in a blouse and skirt with matching shoes and bag and uncovered hair. If she came in with black hair she would leave with red hair. We were constantly changing men's clothes, dyeing their hair and ours too, and doing our best to reduce the risk of being found out by the enemy. All this was thought of and carried out by women. The men had no idea of all these possible ways of hiding our identity and outwitting the French authorities."[41]

Contrary to Gordons' views, Shaaban shows that Algerian women believe that their struggle against colonization emerged in 1930 rather than during the struggle for independence in 1954. In the 1930s they launched their first serious campaign for educational reform and sought to reintroduce the generation educated in French schools to their Arab-Islamic cultural roots. They also believe that they were the ones who thought up the operations and that men followed their orders.

It is difficult to establish the exact number of Algerian women who participated in the struggle; according to the records of the Ministry of the Mujahidin, since Algeria's independence, only 10,949 women have claimed status as former militants.[42] This figure is considered to be far below the number of women who actually participated in the struggle since the many thousands of women who provided shelter and food for the militants did not always report their contribution. While the world remembers the name of a militant woman such as Jamila Bouhired, who took up arms and conducted several operations against the French before she was jailed and severely tortured, a vast number made their contribution in more traditional ways. For example, nearly half of the 205 women militants on whom accurate information has been obtained were nurses.

What was the male attitude of the FLN to women's participation? According to Marnia Lazreg's study, which is by far the most detailed work on Algerian women and which appeared in 1994, thirty-two years after independence had been won, the participation of women brought out men's ambivalence toward women's roles in society as well as in the struggle against colonial rule. She refers to a woman who participated in the revolution and who noted that a notable guerrilla leader lectured women on the need to devote themselves to the care of the civilian population and to spare themselves the risk of battle.[43] The attitudes of the PLO leadership in Lebanon was similarly ambivalent toward women's participation.

The failure of Algerian women to make serious strides toward equality after the new state was established is addressed in both Lazreg's work and by Bouthaina Cheriet, who has argued that "there is no more telling indicator of the vast dialectic between tradition and modernity than the position of women."[44] Based on the Algerian experience, Cheriet advances an interesting thesis that in the postindependence state, feminism and fundamentalism emerge as two conflicting forces directed against the corruption and the failures of the secularist nationalist state. She views these two conflicting movements as pioneering forces in Algeria's political democratization and notes that in the 1980s, the state clamped down on fundamentalist Islamists and on feminists because both had demonstrated their disapproval of the power elite's ambivalence toward their status. Feminists were detained for demonstrating against a reactionary personal status bill.

According to Cheriet, "the inability of Algerian women to make serious strides toward equality in a postindependence state does not reflect on the women's movement but can be traced back to the national elites, which barely reformed the apparatus of the colonial state they inherited. Civil society, and with it the women's movement, was dealt a heavy blow in the process, and this has worked to the advantage of the state." Hisham Sharabi has advanced the same idea, arguing that over the last one hundred years the patriarchal structures of Arab society, far from being displaced or truly modernized, have merely been strengthened and maintained in deformed "modernized" forms.[45]

Writing on Palestinian Women

After a long period of near total absence, writing on Palestinian women showed a marked increase in the 1990s. Four books appeared in 1992 alone,[46] and nearly every major book published on the intifada contains what has become an obligatory chapter on Palestinian women. Within the last seven years, articles on Palestinian women's involvement in the intifada have appeared in *Middle East Report, Khamsin*, and *Race and Class*. The discussions deal with the role of Palestinian women in the territories occupied by Israel since 1967, emphasizing primarily the years of the intifada. As such, they do not fully cover the long-term involvement of Palestinian women in the national struggle. The literature on Palestinian women is still far from complete.

The studies discussed below complement each other both in their theoretical perspective and in the material they present. Written in the form of a journal, Philippa Strum's *The Women Are Marching* offers a comprehensive view of women's emergence into leadership roles and the ensuing transformations in gender relations. It offers the reader a glimpse of daily life during the intifada from the perspective of an empathetic American-Jewish visitor. Orayb Aref Najjar's *Portraits of Palestinian Women*, offers intimate interviews with women activists, intellectuals, homemakers, and professionals. While Strum's book describes the roles performed by women community leaders and intellectuals, Najjar's interviews offer access to the personal journey of the same women, who explain why they made the choices they made. Theresa Thornhill's *Making Women Talk* is about the interrogation of women in Israeli jails. The book is based on nineteen statements by women, including two Jewish-Israeli women and an Arab citizen of Israel. Written in an impartial tone, the text describes the methods of abuse designed specifically to extract confessions from women. Elise G. Young's book, *Keepers of the History*, is an ambitious work that proposes an alternative feminist theoretical construct through which to interpret the Israeli-Jewish conflict. Najjar and Strum propose that a feminist consciousness emerges in the Third World during national liberation struggles; they see the solution for women in a fight for greater rights in the new state and in patriarchal structures. Young, on the other hand, argues that the concepts of the nation-state, national liberation struggles, and the extended family are all based on the principle of "phallocracy" and are, therefore, inherently opposed to full equality for women.

Philippa Strum's diary entries are written in a "hurried" style and give the impression that writing must play catch-up with the fast-moving events of the outside world. Her style also projects a feeling that the author is trying to keep up with the rapid rate of change in gender relations as they affect the lives of women and that she has to sum up a long and successful story of women's institution-building within the limited space of a few pages. Strum's work is interspersed with interesting anecdotes that bring the narrative to life. There is one, for example, about a demonstration at which women wielding pots and pans attack an Israeli military patrol and force the soldiers to release a youth they have arrested. Strum also narrates how some women died, killed by chance, as was the forty-five-year-old Bethlehem housewife who was shot in the eye at a market during a demonstration.

Strum avoids the pitfalls of an analysis that imposes a Western vision of feminism on the role of Palestinian women. She points out similarities with the experience of women in the United States when possible, yet the cultural and political differences are never glossed over since women's actions are understood within the political context of occupation.

Orayb Najjar is a social historian par excellence. Her interviews are divided into five sections, each showing the impact of a historical event on women's lives: loss of Palestine; loss of farmland; encounters with the occupiers; women and institution-building; and women and education, art, and journalism. The interviews are contextualized in an introduction to each section that addresses the general reaction to a given problem before the author turns to the personal reactions of individual women. Among the questions the author deals with in the chapter "Coping with the Loss of Palestine," which precedes the interviews, are those of how loss of the land impacted gender relations within the Palestinian family and how the roles of women changed when their husbands were away. Many interviews are followed by an update that describes the birth of a child or the solution to a problem that had earlier seemed insurmountable. The book is a monument to the resilience of Palestinian women, many of whom were able to overcome incredibly difficult personal lives and a great deal of adversity.

Whereas interviews with women prisoners in Najjar's book reveal the psychological impact of their ordeals, the purpose of the interviews in Theresa Thornhill's book is to show the methods of interrogation employed by the Israeli security apparatus. The interviews reveal that all forms of torture are acceptable as long as they do not leave detectable marks and can, therefore, be labeled "moderate." The courts, which are also part of the military system, consider "moderate" torture to be acceptable. And as attorneys Felicia Langer and Leia Tsemel argue here, it is only a short step from there to accepting statements made under "moderate" torture as admissible.

Elise G. Young's book proposes an alternative feminist theoretical construct for interpreting the Arab-Isreali problem but also has far-reaching ramifications for our understanding of all forms of violence against women everywhere. While the works of Strum and Najjar in particular argue that national liberation struggles bear within them the potential for the emergence of a feminist consciousness and that this promise was partially fulfilled in the occupied territories through the new roles assumed by women, both of these authors are aware that the control men exert over women's lives—whether in the patriarchal structure of the extended family or the equally patriarchal structures of the Palestine Liberation Organization (PLO)—will not disappear overnight. Young, on the other hand, argues that all forms of nationalism, including national liberation struggles and the modern Western nation-state, are based on the principle of phallocracy and are inherently opposed to full equality for women. Women's relationship to the land, she argues, is different than that of men, which is generally one of domination, similar to their relationship with women. Young concludes that whether from the perspective of the invader or the invaded, the ruler or the ruled, the nationalist struggle for control of land is not the same struggle for women as it is for men.

It is possible to see here how Young arrives at her premise, which states that violence against women is linked to violence against nature and violence against race. Within this construct she draws interesting correlations between a woman raped in Central Park in New York, a woman shot on her balcony in the intifada, and the Holocaust. She traces the roots of the control over women to the early days of the three patriarchal religions, showing how in the Bible the story of Sarah and Hagar is also the story of the triumph of patriarchy over matriarchy. At this point, however, it is possible to see only that the three forms of violence—against race, against class, and against gender—share the same paradigm. I do not think Young has shown, or that anyone else can prove conclusively, that colonization, violence against race, and violence against nature have their roots in violence against women, although similarities do exist between the three forms of violence.

Palestinian Women: Identity and Experience, edited by Abba Augustin, is a book that bridges the gap between academia and a general readership, offering a unique gender perspective on the social history of the Palestinians in the occupied territories.[47] In contrast to the dominant historical discourse, social history considers the way in which individuals react to major historical change. The contributors to Augustin's volume, all women, view their social history from a feminist perspective. At least one underlying assumption carries through all the contributions: gender conditions the experience of occupation. All the authors write from a position in which the questioning of patriarchal norms is mediated through a national agenda.

The contributors were chosen from all walks of life and include an activist, Yusra Berberi, from Gaza; an artist, Vera Tamari, a housewife and the product of an upbringing between Palestinian and German culture; a clinical psychologist, Najah Manasra; and many others. All narrate their experience in an eloquent, personal style without ever losing sight of the experience of the group. This is achieved by weaving back and forth between a third and first person narrative that emphasizes the solidarity between the speaker and the group, a technique that does, at times, give the narrative a rather self-conscious quality, as if the women interviewed were conscious of being spokeswomen for Palestinians. Yet the narrative is never apologetic, and it maintains a critical feminist standpoint throughout as the various authors narrate their experience of occupation and of the constraints and challenges forced on them by tradition, as well as the victories and fulfillment they have experienced. The role of Augustin goes well beyond that of the average editor since some of the contributors no doubt experienced, to varying degrees, the barrier of language. Yet the text as it appears, while faithful to the privileged insider's viewpoint, reads smoothly and maintains the personal and eloquent quality of the narrative.

Amal Kawar's *Daughters of Palestine* is based on interviews with women leaders in the PLO.[48] Her investigation focuses on the women's leadership and how it evolved in conjunction with developments in the history of the Palestinian struggle after the establishment of Israel in 1948. This is the only examination of the full history of women's involvement in the Palestinian National Movement from the revolution in the mid-1960s to the Palestinian-Israeli peace process in the early 1990s. The importance of this book lies in the author's ability to explain how these women were able to overcome some of the social barriers that traditionally prevent women from entering the political arena.

Three excellent essays on Palestinian women appear in *Arab Women*, edited by Judith Tucker.[49] The perspective they adopt challenges a monolithic view of the Arab world while avoiding the pitfalls of a defensive position. This collection of essays assumes that, in spite of diversity, the Arab world constitutes a cultural and historical unit that provides a shared context for women. The role of Palestinian women is understood here through the relationship between feminism and nationalism in the articles by Julie M. Peteet, Souad Dajani, and Rosemary Sayigh. Taken together, these three articles raise the question of how diasporan women's experience compares with women's lives inside the occupied territories.

Souad Dajani's essay, "Palestinian Women under Israeli Occupation," addresses the conditions for Palestinian women under occupation and the implications for future developments.[50] Dajani writes that the West Bank has been transformed into a colony for Israel's economy and that the situation of women reflects the economic exploitation that has led to the destruction or transformation of indigenous structures such as the family, to land expropriation, and to the proletarianization of the population.

Dajani's article draws on statistical data available since 1967 and shows how the subjugation of Palestinian women to Israel's economy has operated on two levels—indirectly through unpaid housework, with Palestinian women assuming the role of reproducing the labor force for the Israeli market; and directly through wage labor. A number of important issues are tackled in this informative essay; they could easily serve as an outline for a book on Palestinian women in which issues of development are addressed at greater length.

The work of three Palestinian women writers—Sahar Khalifeh, Raymonda Tawil, and Soraya Antonius—is the subject of my article "Palestinian Women Writers and the Intifada."[51] I consider their work to be a national allegory of the Palestinian situation; it differs, however, from that of male writers since the allegory takes place between two poles and the questioning of patriarchal norms is therefore mediated through the national agenda.

SUHA SABBAGH

About This Work

The intention of this collection of essays is to add to the discourse on Palestinian women within the tradition of writing on women in the Third World. The aim is to accommodate both women's nationalist and feminist concerns, without selectively stressing one form of victimization over another. Academic research in the United States has not yet shown a genuine interest in the theoretical implications of the emergence of a feminist consciousness from within the folds of a national liberation movement. Women's struggle is correctly defined as one against a patriarchal paradigm, against the principle of "phallocracy," as Elise Young has called it. What are the implications of this dialectical relationship between feminism and nationalist concerns for the emergence of the Palestinian women's movement and, by extension, for all Third World women's movements born of the process of decolonization? The problem is most urgent at present for Palestinian women as they fight to include their demands in the constitution and in the structures of an emerging Palestinian state. Therefore, it is important to pose the following question at the scholarly level: How can we develop new feminist paradigms capable of accommodating the feminist and the nationalist components without giving priority to one over the other?

Study of Palestinian women's roles during the intifada provides an opportunity for addressing these theoretical issues. Failure to address them would mean that the study of Third World women's movements would continue to suffer from a one-sided view that focuses exclusively on either feminist or nationalist content.

The essays presented here examine women's participation and its relationship with the regional conflict, including recent political factors and the internal psychosocial dynamics of the culture. The goal is to define the conditions that affect the changing role of Palestinian women and the dynamics that affect their participation in the struggle, while avoiding the pitfalls of an analysis that views women in resistance as mythic heroines outside of time, a metaphor that has in the past earned women very few rights after liberation. The second goal is to examine the way in which the culture has recorded the role of Palestinian women in the literature and language of the intifada. The majority of the essays are by academic women and men living in the occupied territories. Two American women, known for their deep concern about conditions for Palestinian women, write about their encounters with women they knew before and during the uprising. Most Palestinian women authors are engaged in the production of knowledge about themselves. While the constraints imposed by the use of a foreign language and Western paradigms must be acknowledged, the work as a whole seeks to define the experience of women from a perspective that is internal to the culture and that reflects both the feminist and the nationalist aspirations of women in the territories occupied by Israel in 1967.

Part one deals with women's active participation in the intifada, which often took the form of institution-building, and the ensuing transformations in gender relations. Joost R. Hiltermann's essay deals with the development of women's organizations and the women's movement and focuses on their role during the intifada. The essay by Islah Jad deals with the changes in the roles of family members as a result of the involvement of women in the intifada. Philippa Strum's essay, written after her book, *The Women Are Marching*, offers a less optimistic assessment than the one she had previously expressed. Here she focuses mainly on the changes in women's traditional roles as a direct result of political involvement. Zahira Kamal's essay examines the objectives of the women's movement as defined during the intifada years.

Part two deals with the way in which transformations in women's roles have been recorded in the culture through poetry, novels, and the folklore of the intifada. It poses the question: Has the image of women changed in the male and female subconscious to the same degree that the role of women has changed in the outside world? Ilham Abu Ghazaleh has surveyed all the poetry written during the years of the intifada. She concludes in her essay that the image of women has changed very little. Although male poets recognize the participation of women in street demonstrations, for example, they still emphasize the biological role of women or their physical attributes. Sharif Kanaana has collected and analyzed two hundred and fifty anecdotes or "legends" about the intifada. He concludes that in folklore the image of women shows the most noticeable positive transformation; women are viewed as active, strong, and creative. An interview with a well-known Palestinian feminist author, Sahar Khalifeh, describes the interrelations between her writing and her life. And finally, two short stories by Hanan Mikhail Ashrawi show the thinking of a Palestinian feminist intellectual and spokeswoman for her people.

Part three deals with the impact of tradition and occupation on the rights of women and their emotional well-being. Robin Morgan's essay presents her impressions upon her return to the occupied territories after the intifada had taken a serious toll on women's lives and on their human rights. Dr. Eyad el-Sarraj proposes in an interview that during the intifada women became the role models for their male and female offspring because of their resistance, while respect for fathers diminished because they continued to work for the occupiers. Within this context the reinstitution of the hijab (head cover for women) is seen as a means for reestablishing the father's authority within the home. In an interview, Hanan Mikhail Ashrawi addresses the violation of women's rights under occupation and in a patriarchy. Five women discuss, in the form of interviews, the moment at which they became aware of their oppression as women and as an occupied people and the relation they see between the two. And finally, in the essay by Rita Giacaman and Penny Johnson, the authors assess the women's movement four years after the beginning of the intifada.

The fourth section was written after the Oslo Accords were signed in 1993 and addresses the Declaration of Principles on Palestinian Women's Rights, a document designed to integrate the rights of women into the constitution of a future Palestinian state. Amal Kawar's essay deals with women's activism after Oslo and other developments during the years that followed the establishment of the Palestinian National Authority. The volume ends with my analysis of the Declaration of Principles on Palestinian Women's Rights and with the third and final draft of the document itself, presented as an appendix.

It is hoped that this book will serve as a record of both Palestinian women's struggles and their moments of victory. Elias Sanbar comments on the lack of research on Palestinian women in Arab and Palestinian institutions and sees it as a result of the "psychocultural effects of Palestine's 'deconstruction' on the generation of intellectuals that began to work after 1948." He notes that in their efforts to understand the "power of the Zionist movement and its international backing . . . research into Palestinian history, society and culture appeared of secondary importance. . . ."[52]

Taking Sanbar's point one step further, it is possible to argue that research focusing primarily on the victimization of the Palestinians does not allow for a simultaneous examination of the empowerment of women. Palestinian women's "herstory" is a story of empowerment, of gaining greater rights from patriarchal structures, of a double resistance; it is difficult if not theoretically impossible to accommodate this story in a work aimed primarily at exposing Zionism from the point of view of its victims. Women have been victimized like the rest of Palestinian society, but there is simultaneously a story of liberation from male domination. While conceding that it is difficult to include both moments, these theoretical constraints should in no way prevent us from telling the story of women's struggles and their moments of victory.

Introduction

NOTES

1. Rita Giacaman, "Palestinian Women in the Uprising: From Followers to Leaders," *Journal of Refugee Studies* 2, no. 12 (1989): 139–46.

2. See ibid. for a detailed description of the factions that participated in the intifada.

3. See the magazine interview with Hanan Mikhail Ashrawi, "*Ms* Exclusive: The Feminist behind the Spokeswoman—A Candid Talk with Hanan Ashrawi," *Ms* (March–April 1992).

4. Ibid. Ashrawi states that Palestinian women studied and learned from the Algerian women's experience. She maintains that in Algeria women implemented male-dominated political theory while Palestinian women are focusing on their own agenda.

5. Palestinian men have always shouldered the responsibility of providing for the family, irrespective of the difficulties of finding employment and the harsh conditions of labor on construction sites in Israel.

6. For an account of social transformations that have affected the lives of women during the intifada, see Philippa Strum, *The Women Are Marching: The Second Sex and the Palestinian Revolution* (New York: Lawrence Hill, 1992), pp. 137–53.

7. See the results of a study conducted by Najah Manasra and published (in Arabic) in *Al-Katib* (April 1990).

8. See Joost R. Hiltermann, "Trade Unions and Women's Committees: Sustaining the Movement, Creating Space," *Middle East Report* (May-August 1990).

9. See Raymonda Hawa Tawil, *My Home, My Prison* (New York: Holt, Rinehart, and Winston, 1979).

10. Even as early as 1967, involvement in the national agenda afforded women some protection against charges that they were transgressing against traditional norms and behavior.

11. For information on the In'ash al-Usra organization, see Orayb Aref Najjar, "Palestinian Self-Reliance on Trial," *Christian Century*, November 23, 1988, pp. 1070–72.

12. Ibid. The head of In'ash al-Usra, Samiha Khalil, ran for president against Yasser Arafat during the first presidential elections in 1995. When In'ash al-Usra faced a severe financial crisis in 1984, Khalil refused offers of aid from organizations that did not support the principle of self-determination for Palestinians.

13. The four women's committees are affiliated with political parties as follows: the Federation of Palestinian Women's Action Committees (FPWAC) with the Democratic Front for the Liberation of Palestine; the Union of Palestinian Working Women's Committees (UPWWC) with the Communist Party; the Union of Palestinian Women's Committees (UPWC) with the Popular Front for the Liberation of Palestine; and the Women's Committee for Social Work (WCSW) with Fateh, by far the largest mainstream political group.

14. Joost R. Hiltermann, "The Women's Movement during the Uprising," in this volume.

15. See Islah Jad, "Patterns of Relations" (in part 1 of this volume) on the impact of the intifada on the Palestinian family.

16. See Saida Hamad, "Intifada Transforms Palestinian Society, Especially the Role of Women," *Al-Fajr Jerusalem Palestine Weekly*, March 13, 1989.

17. See ibid.

18. The conference was covered on the West Bank in an article titled "Openness and Frankness Dominate Discussion of Women's Role," *Al-Fajr Jerusalem Palestine Weekly*, December 24, 1990, p. 8.

19. The Women's Affairs Center is headed by Sahar Khalifeh, a prominent feminist novelist who has published six novels that have been translated into nine languages. For an analysis of her work, see Suha Sabbagh, "Palestinian Women Writers and the Intifada," *Social Text: Theory/Culture/Ideology* (spring 1989).

20. The Bisan Center for Research and Development is headed by Izzat Abdel-Hadi; Eileen Kuttab is director of the Women's Research Committee.

21. Eileen Kuttab argues that the intifada had two phases. In the first phase women were more active, while the second period saw women retreat from their demands for equal rights. She cites the following reasons for the decline in women's participation in the struggle: 1) lack of a policy on the part of the national forces to liberate women from the constraints of traditional norms; 2) both the women's movement and the national forces lacked a clear and pragmatic agenda for dealing with women's issues and a clear women's program; 3) women formed an important part of the popular committees and local committees, and when these committees began to decline, so did women's participation; 4) the rise of fundamentalism brought about the segregation of the sexes.

22. See Sharif Kanaana, in part 2 of this volume, on the role of women in intifada legends.

23. See Sabbagh, *Palestinian Women Writers*, for a discussion of her work.

24. See "The Rights of Women in the Future State of Palestine: An Interview with Yasser Arafat," conducted by Suha Sabbagh, *Arab Studies Quarterly* 15, no. 2 (spring 1993).

25. See, in part 3 of this volume, "Intifada Year Four: Notes on the Women's Movement," by Rita Giacaman and Penny Johnson.

26. See the interview with Dr. Eyad el-Sarraj (in part 3 of this volume) for an analysis of the psychological impact of the intifada.

27. Rima Hammami has argued that the "modest dress code" sought by Hamas suggests that the movement has its roots in the fundamentalist religious movement that is sweeping the Arab world. At no previous time in their history have Palestinian women worn the headdress or the long overcoat. Rather, this attire is worn by women belonging to the recent Islamist movement in the Arab world ("Women, the Hijab, and the Intifada," unpub. paper, Birzeit University).

28. See Giacaman and Johnson, "Intifada Year Four."

29. Quoted in Jad, "Patterns of Relations."

30. Giacaman and Johnson, "Intifada Year Four."

31. Edward W. Said, *Beginnings: Intention and Method* (New York: Basic Books, 1975), p. 81.

32. Kumari Jayawardena, *Feminism and Nationalism in the Third World* (London: Zed Books, 1986), p. 46.

33. See Thomas Philip, "Feminism and Nationalism in Egypt," in *Women in the Muslim World,* ed. Lois Beck and Nikki Keddie (Cambridge: Harvard University Press, 1980 [1st ed. 1978]), p. 279.

34. See Marnia Lazreg, *The Eloquence of Silence: Algerian Women in Question* (New York: Routledge, 1994).

35. See Jayawardena, *Feminism and Nationalism,* p. 51.

36. See Frantz Fanon, *A Dying Colonialism* (New York: Grove Press, 1965), pp. 35–64.

37. See Lazreg, *Eloquence of Silence.*

38. Ibid., p. 53.

39. David C. Gordon, *Women of Algeria: An Essay on Change* (Cambridge: Harvard University Press, 1968).

40. See Bouthaina Shaaban, *Both Right and Left Handed: Arab Women Talk about Their Lives* (London: Women's Press, 1988 [Bloomington: Indiana University Press, 1991]).

41. Ibid., pp. 196–97.

42. Djamila Amrante, "La femme Algérienne et la guerre de libération nationale," pp. 3–4 in *Combattantes de la lute armée, les femmes aussi écriront l'histoire* (Algiers, 1982), a monograph issued by the magazine *El Djazairiya* on the twentieth anniversary of independence and cited in Lazreg, *Eloquence of Silence,* p. 119.

43. *El Moudjahid,* no. 47, August 3, 1959, p. 381, as cited in Lazreg, *Eloquence of Silence.*

44. Bouthaina Cheriet, "Islam and Feminism: Algeria's Rite of Passage to Democracy," in *State and Society in Algeria,* ed. John P. Entelis and Phillip C. Naylor (Boulder, CO: Westview Press, 1992).

45. Hisham Sharabi, *Neopatriarchy* (New York: Oxford University Press, 1988).

46. Orayb Aref Najjar with Kitty Warnock, *Portraits of Palestinian Women* (Salt Lake City: University of Utah Press, 1992), introduction by Rosemary Sayigh; Philippa Strum, *The Women Are Marching: The Second Sex and the Palestinian Revolution* (New York: Lawrence Hill Books, 1992); Theresa Thornhill, *Making Women Talk: The Interrogation of Palestinian Women Detainees by the Israeli General Security Services* (London: Lawyers for Palestinian Human Rights, 1992); and Elise G. Young, *Keepers of the History: Women and the Israeli-Palestinian Conflict* (New York: Teachers College Press, 1992). The four volumes were reviewed by Suha Sabbagh in *Journal of Palestine Studies* (summer 1993): 94.

47. Abba Augustin, ed., *Palestinian Women: Identity and Experience* (London: Zed Books, 1993). This volume was reviewed by Suha Sabbagh in *Journal of Palestine Studies* (autumn 1994): 101.

48. Amal Kawar, *Daughters of Palestine: Leading Women of the Palestinian National Movement* (Albany: State University of New York Press, 1996).

49. Judith Tucker, ed., *Arab Women: Old Boundaries, New Frontiers* (Bloomington: Indiana University Press, in association with the Center for Contemporary Arab Studies, Georgetown University, 1993). For a review of this volume, see *Journal of Palestine Studies* (spring 1995): 102.

50. Souad Dajani, "Palestinian Women under Israeli Occupation," in *Arab Women*, ed. Tucker.

51. Suha Sabbagh, "Palestinian Women Writers and the Intifada," *Social Text: Theory/Culture/Ideology* (spring 1989). For a description of novels by Palestinian women, see Miriam Cooke, *Women and the War Story* (Berkeley: University of California Press), pp. 195–219.

52. Elias Sanbar, "Le vécu et l'écrit: historiens-réfugiés de Palestine," *Revue d'études palestiniennes* 1, no. 1 (autumn 1981): 62–75.

PART ONE

Defining the Role of Women

.1.

JOOST R. HILTERMANN

The Women's Movement
during the Uprising

The early days of the uprising in the occupied territories yielded striking images of Palestinian women marching in the streets, schoolgirls
throwing stones at soldiers, older women carrying baskets of stones on
their heads to supply younger demonstrators, women arguing and
tussling with the authorities to win the release of an arrested boy. Given
this unaccustomed public profile, some commentators began referring
to the intifada not only as "shaking off" military rule but as a social
revolution in its own right in which the younger generation rebelled
against its elders, street activists rebelled against the authority of the
PLO, and women rebelled against their traditional place in a patriarchal
society.

By the third year of the uprising, this assessment of the intifada's
effect on women had already revealed itself as premature: despite
women's activism, their social and political position in society had
remained essentially the same. Still, it would be wrong to dismiss totally
the intifada's implications for women; women's awareness of their
rights has been significantly enhanced, and more women than ever
before have been mobilized—beyond their participation in demonstrations—in organizational structures channeling their energies toward
satisfying the needs of a society under siege. Perhaps more important,
women have begun seriously to address the issue of their rights and

roles in the struggle for national liberation, a subject barely alluded to before the uprising except by a handful of committed activists.

Mobilization during the Intifada

What sets the uprising apart form previous years in terms of women's activism is the fact that it is not just students and one-time activists who participate in direct confrontations with soldiers but women of all ages and from all sectors of society, especially women from villages and refugee camps. These are women who, during the years prior to the uprising, had been courted by organized women's groups but who had not, despite their sympathies, become part of any formal framework. The uprising spurred these women to work for the national cause in a situation of real emergency: "Because our program [before the uprising] was explicitly political, economic, and cultural, women were afraid to join," one Nablus activist explained; "but during the uprising, our program began to address reality. Now women are more eager to join because they want to address problems in their lives."[1]

From the early days of the uprising, women's activism was partly spontaneous and partly organized by the four women's committees that together constitute the modern women's movement in the occupied territories. These committees had all grown out of the Women's Work Committee, founded in the late 1970s on the spur of the national movement then gathering force as high school and college students turned their activism to mobilizing other sectors of the population. A number of the founders were graduates of Birzeit University. Many had clashed with the Israeli army in demonstrations in the early and mid-1970s, and their activism was fueled by a growing realization that Israel was not going to relinquish the occupied territories voluntarily and that the existing local institutions were ill equipped to cope with a prolonged military occupation. Moreover, the kind of broad-based movement the founders envisaged was seen as an effective protection against the loss of cadres, an important consideration given the frequency with which heads of universities, charitable associations, and other institutions were deported or imprisoned by Israeli authorities.

The founders of the Women's Work Committee had been particularly impatient with the charitable societies that had hitherto dominated women's activities in the occupied territories. The charitable societies provided services to women without teaching them the elementary skills that would enable them to help themselves. In contrast, the new Women's Work Committee started a program of education not only in the towns but also for the first time in the villages and refugee camps throughout the West Bank and Gaza Strip. The program involved classes in literacy, health, education (including first aid), and skills-training classes (for example, in embroidery, food processing, and so on), usually at member's homes or at makeshift committee offices. The committees also set up day care centers, which made it possible for women with small children to work outside the home. Through the various programs, the women began engaging in political discussions, thus raising their awareness not only concerning the national question but also concerning the issue of women's rights in Palestinian society.

In the early 1980s, the original Women's Work Committee split into four committees, reflecting the factionalism in the Palestinian national movement in general. The largest of the successor organizations are the Federation of Palestinian Women's Action Committees (FPWAC), which identifies with the political program of the Democratic Front for the Liberation of Palestine (DFLP), and the Union of Palestinian Women's Committees (UPWC), which adheres to the political program of the Popular Front for the Liberation of Palestine (PFLP), and the Women's Committee for Social Work (WCSW), which supports Fateh. Finally, there is the Union of Palestinian Working Women's Committees (UPWWC), which is affiliated with the Communist Party. The larger committees all have memberships in the thousands; the FPWAC alone claims to have some ten thousand active members.

The WCSW is the closest ideologically to the earlier charitable societies in that it provides social services to women rather than mobilizing them. The other three committees are quite similar in their work, although they tend to focus on different categories of women in their recruitment strategies: thus, the UPWWC has organized primarily working women, the FPWAC concentrates on housewives, while the UPWC tends to have an educated, urban middle-class membership, often young women who have come out of the student movement. The real difference between the committees lies in their political identification and therefore the positions they take on national issues.

After the intifada broke out, the four committees stepped up their efforts to mobilize their own members and sympathizers and to absorb new recruits. Concentrating on the areas of their greatest strength, they extended the schedules of child care centers to accommodate women active in the uprising and geared health education classes to first aid as casualties mounted in the neighborhoods, especially as a result of beatings and tear gas.[2]

In the early stages of the uprising, the women's committees lent their organizing and leadership experience to the emerging popular committees in villages, refugee camps, and urban neighborhoods throughout the territories. Indeed, during the early period, the work of the women's committees and of the popular committees was virtually indistinguishable. Women's committee activists would join local popular committee members to organize relief or emergency services following Israeli army raids, to pay solidarity visits to the families of martyrs and detainees, to provide material assistance whenever necessary, to work on behalf of prisoners, and to arrange prison visits via the Red Cross. Women also distributed leaflets, discussed politics openly for the first time, and urged people who remained unconvinced to participate in the uprising.

Overall directives issued by the Unified National Leadership of the Uprising (UNLU) were translated into specific calls to action for women by the women's committees. In a landmark joint program of the four committees on March 8, 1988, celebrating International Women's Day, women were called upon to participate in popular committees and trade unions, to boycott work on strike days, to confront soldiers and settlers, and to promote a "home economy" of locally produced food and clothing.[3] In keeping with the UNLU's calls, women were prominent in efforts to monitor prices charged by merchants and to ensure compliance during commercial strikes and boycotts of Israeli goods, and especially in providing alternative education to children in homes, churches, and mosques after the closure of schools. Women were particularly active with the popular committees in urban neighborhoods, playing a lesser role in the villages and camps.[4]

Throughout the uprising, the women's committees organized marches, and activist women and schoolgirls participated in demonstrations and confrontations with the army; it is remarkable that despite their prominence in such actions, women suffered relatively few casualties.[5] The level of women's participation has varied from locality of locality, being lower in more religious or conservative areas such as al-Khalil (Hebron), where a turnout of one hundred women in a demonstration is considered good,[6] and far higher in towns such a Ramallah, where despite a smaller population a demonstration may draw as many as five hundred to one thousand women.[7] Slogans have included not only demands for an independent state but for women's liberation as well. During a march in Ramallah commemorating International Women's Day on March 8, 1988, for example, "women unfurled banners, posters, and flags and began their silent procession to the center of town. The banners and slogans called for women's liberation, for an independent state with the PLO as its leadership, for an end to the occupation, and for an end to Israeli brutality."[8]

Although women were active in the popular committees, it is not clear if they made any gains in their rights as women through such involvement. On the one hand, women engaged for the first time in collective political actions in the streets, occupying a space traditionally reserved, with few exceptions, for men. Their politicization is bound to have a long-term impact on their role in society. But on the other hand, as Islah Jad, a Birzeit University lecturer, has argued, the "essential goal" of the popular committees was merely "to find new members for the mass organizations of each faction. . . . Women's role in the popular committees became an extension of what it traditionally had been in the society: teaching and rendering services," without ever going beyond that.[9]

Women's Production Cooperatives

In the only clear effort at totally independent action during the uprising, the women's committees began to establish women's productive cooperatives in response to the food shortages caused by army curfews and the boycott of Israeli products. These cooperatives produced relatively simple foodstuffs, such as fruit juices, pickled vegetables, canned goods, and jams, as well as clothing, embroidery, and picture frames for the local market. Women were in charge of all stages of the production process and shared the profits. They sold their wares through offices of the women's committees or through merchants who identified with the committee's work. The number of cooperatives has remained fairly limited, however. More commonly, women affiliated with the women's committees produce goods directly in their own homes to be sold by the committees through the outlets already mentioned.

The goals set for cooperatives were ambitious, though not always very clear. Pamphlets distributed by the Union of Palestinian Women's Committees (UPWC) asserted that the objective of the committee's production project (entitled "Our Production Is Our Pride") was "to build the basis for women's emancipation by constructing economic projects."[10] But of the project's five main aims and principles, only two pertain to women: "The transformation of women's traditional role in the domestic economy into a positive role in the national economy," and "The provision of opportunities for the participation of women in economic enterprises as a basis for economic independence and social emancipation."[11] Moreover, the UPWC did not explain how a "positive role in the national economy" will enhance women's social and political status and lead to social emancipation, nor how the cooperatives can contribute to this transformation.

Assessments of the results of women's cooperatives and production efforts have been mixed. While the cooperatives clearly afford a measure of economic independence for women, they do not necessarily provide the stimulus for women to become more active in community life. As Islah Jad has argued about the cooperative effort, "setting up a women's production cooperative in the countryside does not automatically lead to changes in the gender-based division of labor, nor to an upward reevaluation by men of women's work."[12] Expressing a widely held view, a UPWWC activist noted: "Our position in the political struggle has changed, but our position in social life has not."[13] A Nablus activist complained that "men are still making the decisions. If a woman is active, the neighbors start talking. So it will take a long time of struggle, and we won't automatically get our rights as women when we get our state."[14]

Nevertheless, cooperatives have had positive results and probably constitute one of the more significant achievements of the uprising. According to a UPWWC activist, the establishment of the UPWWC's cooperative in the village of Idhna near Hebron "helped to bring the issue of women onto the agenda"; participation in the cooperative "increased women's social consciousness. Women realized that they had the same abilities as men. It helped them get out of the family circle and help out in the bad economic situation, since men were either jailed or unemployed."[15] Even if resistance to change is stiff, women's issues have been put on the agenda, and for the first time, women have begun to discuss their status in society. While women during the uprising may have "enlarged or extended their traditional role rather than adopting a completely new role," as Rita Giacaman and Penny Johnson have pointed out, aspects of this role "have become a source of resistance because women have transformed their family responsibilities to encompass the entire community."[16] According to an activist in the village of Kufr Na'meh (Ramallah), the fact that women participate in marches, demonstrations, and confrontations with the army, get injured or killed, go to town to sell produce in the market, visit relatives in prison, and join political events in Ramallah or Jerusalem has changed their overall position. Because of the uprising, women have strengthened their role in the family, often have control over money, can refuse to obey certain orders, or can decide which school their children attend. She called the position of women "outstanding" compared with the years before the uprising.[17]

There is no doubt that the active participation of the women's committees in the uprising and the economic contribution of the cooperatives have not translated into the significant concrete changes sought by women. But the daily struggle in the streets has brought activists from the various factions in the national movement closer together. In the words of one activist, "because of neighborhood work, women from the different blocs are now blending, developing strong personal relationships, and struggling side by side."[18]

In the women's movement this has led to greater formal cooperation, which eventually crystallized in the establishment of the Higher Women's Council (HWC) in December 1988. The Council united the four committees in one forum; women leaders felt that only through the joint action made possible by such a body could the crucial issues of education and the legal situation created by the religiously based family law be addressed effectively.[19] The council's aim was to unify the women's movement around the twin themes of women's social struggle and the struggle for national liberation. It also strove to find a proper balance between the two so as to prevent the return of women to their traditional social roles following the national victory. In this regard, activists repeatedly reminded their peers of how Algerian women, who had played so important a role during the revolution, had fared following Algerian independence in 1962.

In terms of national struggle, women activists have been unable to take a more prominent role in the leadership of the uprising. Although it is likely that the UNLU has at one point or another included women, its members have generally been men, as the language of its communiques and the pattern of arrests and deportations suggests.[20] An examination of UNLU communiques reveals not only a striking disregard for women's issues and the role of women in the uprising—as compared to the attention paid to other sectors of Palestinian society—but also an attitude toward women that is profoundly traditional, patriarchal, and condescending. For example, when the UNLU addresses the participants in the intifada, it invariably refers to "our sons," "brother doctors," "brother workers," "brother businessmen and grocers," and so on.[21] When women are mentioned, it is usually as "mothers," that is, women are mentioned only in relation to others, their sons, rather than in their own right. Alternatively, they are grouped with children and old men and all people "who are suffering."[22] Women are commended for their "steadfastness," for "standing firm," and for "protecting the uprising," not for participating in it.[23] In communique number 21, the UNLU invites "students, workers, merchants, peasants, and strike forces" to carry out acts of civil disobedience. Women are notably excluded, despite the obvious activism of the women's committees.

Thus, the role of women is marginalized; women are cast as protectors of the uprising and of those who supposedly make the uprising: their male relatives. There are, however, slight departures from this pattern. In communique number 5, the UNLU called on "mothers, sisters, and daughters to work side by side with their husbands, sons, and brothers." But even here, despite the call to action, it is not a given that women would work "side by side" with men, nor is it recognized that in fact they had been doing so from the beginning of the uprising, or even before.[24] In August 1988, when the UNLU tried to fill the institutional vacuum created by King Hussein's formal withdrawal of his claim to the West Bank by reinforcing the popular committees and other grassroots organizations, it for the first time made a strong appeal to the women's committees, among others. The UNLU reminded the women's committees that they had to "shoulder a special responsibility in organizing sit-ins and other appropriate activities" in solidarity with men and women prisoners. After all the committees had been doing during the preceding eight months, this must have been a puny, if not offensive, reminder of the status quo to women organizers.[25]

International Women's Day has proven to be the only occasion when the UNLU devotes substantial attention to women's participation in the uprising, but again the record is mixed. In 1988, the UNLU did not go further than including a call for demonstrations on March 8 as part of its weekly schedule of events.[26] In 1989, the UNLU went further, to "salute the Palestinian woman" and to declare its "admiration for her heroism in the national struggle." The UNLU referred to women's organizations, urging a "strengthening [of] the unity of the women's movement in the State of Palestine within the framework of the Unified Women's Council." But again, all references were made in the context of the UNLU's weekly schedule.[27] In 1990, the UNLU went so far as to name its communique "The Woman's Call," and reserved a special section for women; but it made sure that they were referred to in the "proper" context, that is, in relation to men:

> Progressive nations celebrate International Women's Day on March 8 as a day of struggle for the world's women's masses. While celebrating this great day, in the name of all the sons of our people, we congratulate the world's women's masses and the masses of the Palestinian women's movement and its vanguard organizations, hailing every working woman, woman struggler and housewife, and especially our imprisoned strugglers. We also pay tribute to the struggling role of the Palestinian uprising's women's movement, to every mother who has lost a son, daughter, husband, or brother, and to every woman who meets with a struggling daughter or a heroic son from behind the Bastille of the Zionist enemy.[28]

In the same leaflet, the UNLU congratulated mothers on Mother's Day, calling their "sufferings and pain the source of our strength and determination." Almost in the same breath, the UNLU exhorted "our sons at school to adhere to school times," and praised Palestinians for making history "through the blood of our sons."[29]

Palestinian women activists do not appear to have publicly challenged the leadership's approach to the women's question. To the contrary, they occasionally provide interesting rationalizations for the approach. An activist in Arrabeh (Jenin) contended that the UNLU preferred not to focus on women in its communiques because it did not want to draw attention to them, with a view to protecting them, because it understood women's important role in the uprising.[30] On the other hand, the women's movement has sought to capitalize on the declaration of independence by reminding women that they are "entitled to preserve all the gains already achieved on the national level" but that they "must also continue fighting for their liberation and for a radical and comprehensive solution to their economic, social, and gender problems." Most importantly perhaps, women were told that they "must participate in developing legislation and a constitution, which will give women equal rights with men. . . ."[31] The word "entitled" suggests a certain defensiveness, but the overall tone is assertive, as the committees seek to translate political gains into concrete steps toward furthering women's rights.

Conclusion

In September 1989, the UPWWC put the following questions to its membership:

> Has the intifada changed the perception of women's role in Palestinian society? Has it changed the way women themselves perceive their roles? These questions have to be reckoned with by the Palestinian women's movement to enable it to keep pace with the fast-moving events of the intifada. . . . What assurances do women have that they will not be asked to return to their traditional, domestic roles if and when national independence is achieved?[32]

The UPWWC reports that members in branch meetings frequently raise the question, "When can we have birth control?"[33] The UPWWC concludes that "if the Palestinian women's movement is to grow and develop, it must address itself to women's issues."[34]

The two other progressive committees, the PFLP-related UPWC and the FPWAC, the ideology of which is close to the DFLP, have echoed such sentiments. In lectures, meetings, and publications, women activists set off a lively debate on the relationship between the women's struggle and the national struggle. One UPWWC representative said:

> We haven't had a feminist agenda. We have been preoccupied with political concerns, and as a result we often became traditional in our approach, because we didn't want to become alienated in our society. We weren't necessarily aware that we were not on the right track. Recently, we have come to realize that this approach doesn't work. We realize that if we don't raise issues now, we won't be able to push them later on, and we'll be abused by the national movement.[35]

The UPWWC therefore started holding lectures about early marriages, divorce, personal status law, the division of labor at home, and other social problems relevant to the lives of women.

In 1988 and 1989, women in the occupied territories came under growing pressure form the insurgent Islamic movement to wear a head scarf (hijab) in public. Many secular women, especially community activists, resisted such pressures. By the end of 1989, however, the campaign had succeeded in the Gaza Strip, where women could no longer appear in public without a head scarf, and it had made major inroads in the West Bank as well. Neither the UNLU nor even the women's committees were effective in countering the practices of the Islamic Resistance Movement (Hamas), and this may have contributed to the success of the hijab campaign in Gaza.[36] Some women activists later tried to explain the national leadership's and their own action by claiming that

> we couldn't act earlier in Gaza, because the time was not right. The intifada was at its height, and we didn't want to create internal differences while fighting the occupation. Because Hamas will throw stones at us, we will throw stones at them, and the army meanwhile can take a break. Only now that the intifada has a solid grounding is it possible to address these issues. It is late now to act against this religious coercion, but not yet too late.[37]

Such setbacks, however, do not augur well for the prospects of achieving further gains for women, and they have undermined the credibility of the women's movement. The status of women in the intifada and in Palestinian society in general will therefore increasingly depend on whether the women's committees, as the vanguard of the women's movement, will be able to match their important objectives—which they have articulated with growing vigor since the declaration of independence in November 1988—with concrete action.

NOTES

1. Interview, Nablus, December 17, 1989.

2. Federation of Palestinian Women's Action Committees (FPWAS), Newsletter, March 8, 1988, p. 11.

3. Quoted by Islah Jad (who interviewed women in villages and refugee camps), "From Salons to the Popular Committees: Palestinian Women, 1919–1989," in *Intifada: Palestine at the Crossroads,* ed. Jamal R. Nassar and Roger Heacock (New York: Praeger, 1990), p. 134.

4. Ibid., p. 135.

5. Al-Haq reported at the end of the first year of the uprising that fifteen women had been killed by the army, as compared with 189 men. See Al-Haq, *Punishing a Nation: Human Rights Violations during the Palestinian Uprising, December 1987–1988* (Boston: South End Press, 1990), p. 12.

6. According to an interview, Hebron, June 13, 1990.

7. From personal observations and interviews, March 1988. The FPWAC reports that six hundred women participated (Newsletter, March 8, 1988, p. 9). Other estimates exceed one thousand.

8. FPWAC, Newsletter, March 8, 1988, p. 9.

9. Quoted by Jad, "From Salons to the Popular Committees," p. 135.

10. Union of Palestinian Women's Committee (UPWC), "Our Production Is Our Pride" (undated, available from UPWC).

11. Pamphlet written by Kathy Glavanis and Eileen Kuttab, Department of Sociology, Birzeit University (undated, available from UPWC).

12. Jad, "From Salons to the Popular Committees," p. 136.

13. Interview, Ramallah, December 20, 1989.

14. Interview, Nablus, December 17, 1989.

15. Interview, Ramallah, December 20, 1989.

16. Rita Giacaman and Penny Johnson, "Palestinian Women: Building Barricades and Breaking Barriers," in *Intifada: The Palestinian Uprising against Israeli Occupation,* ed. Zachary Lockman and Joel Beinin (Boston: South End Press, 1989), p. 161.

17. Interview, Kufr Na'meh, June 12, 1990.

18. Interview, Ramallah, December 20, 1989.

19. See, for example, "The Unified Women's Councils: The Women's and Nationalist Function of the Covenant," FPWAC, Newsletter, March 1989, p. 6.

20. This assessment is shared by Giacaman and Johnson, "Palestinian Women," p. 165. The Israeli authorities arrested people they referred to as members of the UNLU on several occasions in 1988 and 1989. All were men.

21. For references to "sons," for example, see UNLU communiques nos. 3 ("O brave sons of our people"), 9 ("We address a militant greeting to the sons of Qabayta"), and 23 ("We have no choice but to depend on ourselves to educate ourselves and our sons"). For references to "brother," see communiques nos. 1 and 14.

22. For examples of references to women as "mothers," see UNLU communiques nos. 8 ("our love for all mothers of this homeland"), 29 ("mother of the martyr"), and 53 (celebrating Mother's Day). For references to women in the context of victims of the occupation, see communique no. 24, which intones:

"In the name of our people under curfews and in prisons, the bereaved, children, women, and the elderly who are suffering from the repressive measures of occupation. . . ."

23. See UNLU communiques nos. 12 ("Our children, women, men, and youths stand firm against the ruthless Zionist military machine"), and 32 ("The UNLU also values the role of the Palestinian woman in furthering steadfastness, uplifting the morale of our people, and in protecting the uprising").

24. Similarly, in communique no. 7 or 8 (unclear from Lockman and Beinin, *Intifada*, which reproduces it), schoolgirls are encouraged to go to school every day and organize demonstrations, despite the fact that they had been doing so for at least a year prior to the uprising, often taking the initiative, at least from my own personal observations in Ramallah.

25. UNLU communique no. 23, August 5, 1988.

26. Interview, Kufr Na'meh, June 12, 1990.

27. Interview, Ramallah, December 20, 1989.

28. UNLU communique no. 53, March 6, 1990.

29. UNLU communique no. 53, March 6, 1990.

30. Interview, Arrabeh, December 16, 1989.

31. These are citations from an editorial published in the FPWAC Newsletter of March 1989; however, they reflect the position of all three of the progressive women's committees.

32. "The Intifada and the Role of Palestinian Women," *Voice of Women* (Newsletter of the Union of Palestinian Working Women's Committees), vol. 1, no. 2 (September 1989), p. 1.

33. Ibid., p. 4.

34. Ibid., p. 10.

35. Interview, Jerusalem, October 21, 1989.

36. See the excellent article by Rima Hammami, "Women, the Hijab, and the Intifada," *Middle East Report*, no. 164–65 (May-August 1990), pp. 24–28, 71.

37. Interview, Ramallah, June 5, 1990.

.2.

TRANSLATION BY MAGIDA ABU HASSABO

Patterns of Relations within the Palestinian Family during the Intifada

As a basic unit of society, the Palestinian family is influenced by the political, social, and economic changes that affect the society as a whole. In turn, these transformations reflect on the ability of the Palestinian family to fulfill its traditional role of providing economic, political, and social support to its members. The changes that affect the family influence its members in different ways. This chapter will look at the changes in the role of women, traditionally revered as wives and mothers. It will examine the ways in which the position of women within the family structure have been affected by the intifada and by the rise of national consciousness in the occupied territories since 1967.[1] The underlying question that will be asked is, Has the intifada fostered the development of new roles for Palestinian women?

During the first six months of the intifada women played a dynamic and active role in determining the course of the uprising against occupation. In its fourth year, the intifada changed in character, and the transformation brought about a decline in women's participation. The spontaneous popular uprisings that characterized the first six months of the intifada and that often involved the participation of an entire camp, village, town, or a whole area of a city, were no longer the major forms of public expression. In the later phase of the intifada, the masses became organized around the United Leadership and were guided by its policies and directives. The intifada lost its early spontaneous nature as it became guided by the directives of the clandestine United Leadership issued through *bayanat* or written releases distributed to the population. This does not totally eliminate the spontaneous reactions to the frequent provocations by the Israeli army, such as the events of Beit Sahour, Beta,[2] and other similar offensives on camps and villages in which women, and all other members of society, continue to participate.

It has generally been noted that after the first six months of the intifada women's participation began to decline. It is, therefore, possible to propose that there is a connection between women's early participation and the spontaneous nature of the first six months when women poured into the streets, breaking away from their traditional role. It is also possible to see a similar connection between women's waning participation and the emergence of a more organized and less spontaneous form of resistance during the later phase. In other words, women showed less willingness to participate as the intifada responded to the directives of the United Leadership. It is not entirely clear at this point whether women's waning participation is a reflection of their objection to the policies of the United Leadership or whether it reflects their objection to organized, as opposed to spontaneous, forms of resistance. Are women reluctant to accept directives from an all-male leadership? Or is it possible to surmise that their participation is a reflection of the fluctuating nature of women's role, which gains or loses importance with the intensification or retreat of the nationalist struggle? Palestinian women are still burdened with domestic responsibilities, and it is possible that these duties, coupled with the pressure placed on women by family members who opposed their participation, forced women back into the domestic sphere.[3]

Women are not the only segment of society whose participation in the intifada fluctuated. And throughout the early period, the response rate of females (mostly students) below the age of eighteen exceeded that of males over the age of forty. There are certain limitations imposed on this study that must also be considered here. For example, the study does not claim to have examined all areas of women's participation. The directives of the United Leadership called on the population to participate in demonstrations, regular strikes, and sit-in strikes, in the writing of slogans, the raising of the Palestinian flag, support of political prisoners and detainees, commemoration of martyrs, and the reviving of the home-based economy, including cultivation of small-land holdings.[4] This study does not claim to have examined women's participation in all these activities, since the necessary field work for such research has not been undertaken. However, it outlines changes in social relations on the basis of some preliminary observations. And it has been observed that as the early fury of the intifada started to decline, new types of social, economic, and political problems began to emerge. These problems, in turn, began to affect the patterns of relations within the family, especially with regard to women. We will examine these patterns below.

Impact of the 1948 War on the Palestinian Family

While the political, military, and economic foundations of Palestinian society were almost completely destroyed following the 1948 war, the structure of the Palestinian family remained intact everywhere. Nuclear and extended families survived as strong institutions capable of securing political, economic, and social protection to their members, whether at times of rejoicing, such as weddings, births, building a new house, or celebrating the return of relatives from abroad—or at times of mourning or illness. The role of the family was to provide amenities for the individual generally provided by the state in Western countries. The family was the vehicle for financial security and protection against rampant unemployment. Threats faced by one member of the extended family, or mistakes committed by another, were confronted and felt by the extended family as a whole.

In fact, the political uprooting of Palestinians served to strengthen the structure of the extended family, for unemployment increases dependence on other family members and in this way strengthens the ties within the extended family structure. In return for the financial security offered by the family, individuals devoted considerable time and effort to maintaining good family ties with one another and with the family as a unit. There is very little research on the sociomarital changes that affected the role of women during the period under consideration. However, it is possible to assume that the structure of the family remained hierarchical, with variables such as age and gender shaping the pattern of relations among its members.[5] The father represented the top of the hierarchy, with central decision-making authority, especially in cases of marriage, divorce, and inheritance. Following the father were the other male family members, who bore a conventional obligation to support the family economically. Females ranked at the bottom of the hierarchy, with little or no share in decision making.

Effects of the 1967 War on the Palestinian Family

Following the defeat of the Arab regimes in 1967 and the resulting Israeli occupation of the rest of Palestinian land, the West Bank and the Gaza Strip, major changes started taking place in the patterns of social relations inside the Palestinian family. The factors that contributed to these changes can be summarized as follows:

The economic factor. Under the Israeli occupation, the Palestinian economy was systematically destroyed and subjected to the needs of the Israeli market. Vast lands in the West Bank and Gaza Strip were appropriated either for military purposes or for expanding Israeli settlements, a process that subsequently led to the marginalization of the agricultural sector. This in turn led to a mass migration of Palestinians, especially the younger generation, and to an increased dependency on Israeli-controlled labor. In other words, young Palestinians were forced to shift from agriculture as an independent means of existence to wage labor under an alien economy.[6] This significant development had serious implications for the patterns of social relations within the Palestinian family. The new setting was characterized by the following: 1) a tendency on the part of young Palestinians to show greater independence from their families by moving to separate housing after marriage; 2) a marked decline in the number of arranged marriages and, to a lesser degree, in the number of marriages between relatives. More room was allowed for girls to have a say in choosing a husband, even though customs attached to the marriage ceremony remained unchanged;[7] and 3) new modes of living and consumption attitudes. This process accompanied the introduction of electricity and water supplies to traditional households, thus cutting down the amount of domestic work done by women but at the same time placing new demands on them to attend to their households and families.

Despite these changes, the emerging nuclear family was only nominally independent.[8] In practice it still retained strong economic and social ties with the extended family because the economic changes mentioned earlier were not fundamental enough. The commitment of wage laborers to their land, their unstable working conditions, and the continuation of the private ownership system, were all factors that hindered the development of a new social structure. Nevertheless, there was an evident decline in the role and influence exerted by the extended family, especially in serious decisions such as the choice of a marriage partner.[9]

Education. Education became another major factor in changing the patterns of social relations within the Palestinian family. As the advantages of education started to be reflected in better economic and employment opportunities, Palestinians began to encourage their sons, and often their daughters, to pursue higher education. Schools and universities became important means of communication with the world, outside the family, the village, or the camp. In time the emphasis on education was to contribute to the emergence of a national consciousness among students. It is a development that has contributed to liberating women from certain traditional constraints on mobility and the segregation of the sexes, as we shall see below. Subsequently, women gained new freedoms that allowed them to choose their future husbands from outside the family circle, though the final word still rested with the family.

Impact of the Palestinian national movement. The demands of the post-1967 war period channeled the society's sense of commitment from the smaller needs of the family to the greater cause of national struggle. Moreover, by offering equal opportunities for struggle and by enhancing people's sociopolitical consciousness, the national movement allowed a new and a more democratic environment to replace the traditional family setting. This was especially evident in the case of women. Palestinian women who participated in the movement developed a new social awareness that was best exemplified in their attitude toward marriage; they assumed a more positive role in limiting and generally defining the expenses traditionally associated with the marriage ceremony, for example, the large bridal dowry, or the purchase of excessive amounts of gold jewelry for the bride.

The nationalist movement enforced a new role for women by encouraging them to challenge the traditional family authority, the outcome of which was a new image of an independent, outgoing Palestinian woman that contrasted with the historically bound definition of a helpless, politically immature woman. This radical social transformation was strongly reflected in the culture and literature of Palestinian society. Folk songs, poetry, and even new wedding practices that flourished in the mid-seventies inspired women to break away from the old traditions and assume new roles in the nationalist movement.

With such dramatic developments sweeping over Palestinian society, the old family structure could not remain unchanged. A less centralized and more democratic set of relations started to materialize. This was exemplified in the diminishing role of the father as the head figure and sole decision maker, and the incorporation of the opinions and political ideologies of different family members, sometimes including females. However, it must be emphasized at this point that these transformations in women's role were mere indicators of change and are by no means final or decisive. Despite the positive advances made by women, their major contribution in the family was still as a tool of reproduction. In addition, their status remained inferior to that of men. However, change in women's position remained tied to their social, political, and geographical background. For instance, educated and

politicized women from an urban or middle-class background responded to changes in a manner different from that of the uneducated,
unpoliticized women in remote rural areas who, in turn, were different
from those who live in the camps and have received limited education
or those who worked as waged laborers.

The Effects of the Intifada on the Palestinian Family

I sincerely believe that it is not possible to understand the shifting
position of women without taking into consideration social, economic,
and political problems facing the family as a whole. Women's return to
the home coincides with a decline in income, with the economic and
psychological impact of the Gulf War, and with other aspects of life
under occupation. The main factors affecting the family can be summarized as follows:

The economic factor. With the rise in the rate of unemployment, the
devaluation of the local currency, the introduction of new foreign exchange policies, and the eruption of the Gulf crisis, poverty started to
spread rapidly in large segments of Palestinian society, especially in
camps, small villages, and the poorer quarters of big cities. As a result,
newly married couples found it more economical to continue living in
their parents' homes where one person's income could support the rest
of the family. A newly wed young man from Rafah camp expressed his
frustration in these words: "After the intifada I lost all hopes of having
a separate home. I simply could not afford to spend on two households,
especially after my father and brothers had been laid off from their jobs.
Being the youngest brother, I could not stop my family from interfering
with my wife and my own affairs. They even went to the extent of
forcing my wife to wear the veil inside the house."[10]

In the early phase of the intifada there was an effort to replace
imported Israeli goods with local products produced in small and me-
dium-scale production centers. However, these economic projects were
too small to absorb large numbers of employees and thus to curb the
high rate of unemployment among both sexes. Further, the United
Leadership directives, which stressed the need to revive family or
home-based economies (including the cultivation of vegetable gardens
to replace dependency on imported vegetables), did not provide an
economic and agricultural model for such projects. Nor did these directives provide any information on how to successfully revive family or
home-based industries or provide a model for this type of enterprise. It
should be noted here that during this period and at all other times,
traditional family-based investments have always been an indispens-
able source of income to the Palestinian family.[11]

Relations in the Palestinian Family during the Intifada

The political and organizational factors. The new organizational patterns that existed at the outset of the intifada strongly appealed to Palestinian women regardless of their socioeconomic background. These patterns of relations became known as the "popular committees," which soon spread to every neighborhood and village. The fact that these committees were open to everyone on a purely democratic and nationalist basis and regardless of sex or age gave them special significance as tools of social change. But these committees were quickly targeted by the Israeli authorities and a military ordinance declaring these committees illegal in July 1988 nearly eradicated the committees.[12]

Despite the fact that the popular committees experience was a shortlived one, it highlighted certain major shortcomings in the organizational structure of the intifada. It showed that the leadership of the intifada lacked a clear view of how to bring about a social transformation that could meet the needs of women and other neglected segments of society, such as laborers, small traders, and peasants. And the failure of the United Leadership to recognize and to address these issues resulted in factionalism among the committees. Moreover, social issues, as opposed to national issues, were left to be tackled by low-ranking members of the cadres who often lacked the necessary social consciousness to guide the various sectors of society, particularly women. Although most committees were made up of more than 50 percent women, one committee, the "striking forces," which hurled stones at soldiers, was almost exclusively male. It was precisely the work of this particular committee that was hailed by society; their acts were glorified. Yet the very nature of this activity excluded women and a broad sector of society and appealed only to the swift in movement: teenagers and young people, sometimes including schoolgirls.

Occasionally, disorder in the ranks of the striking forces would lead to infringements on individual rights or even to mistaken killings. This created an atmosphere of alarm among the people and occasionally led to the isolation of the national movement from the people. The development had serious implications: individuals were forced to resort to the family for protection, and this in turn reinforced the traditional role of the family at the expense of the political organization and reversed the process of democratization that had started to take place inside the family. Women, in this case, had the most to lose.

The social factor. A major setback for Palestinian women was the growth of fundamentalist movements whose ideologies advocated traditionalism in family relations, reestablishing a more authoritarian attitude toward women. As a means of controlling women's behavior, these movements promote segregation of the sexes and force women to wear the *hijab* (Islamic head covering) and the *jilbab* (traditional long gown). Further, fundamentalism reinforced the traditional paternalistic setting where the father is fully authorized to control the conduct of his family members even by violent means. In some areas, watch groups were set up to observe women outside their homes or when their families failed to exert such control.

The spread of fundamentalist ideology was accompanied by a new type of oral and written literature that concentrated on revealing Israeli methods used to corrupt Palestinian women and to force them into collaboration by sexual blackmail. Although this literature was intended to alarm women to these methods, it caused a wave of panic, especially in villages and popular residential areas, where some families went to the extreme of preventing their daughters from going to school.[13] This was partly due to the excessively detailed accounts of how women were corrupted by sexual means. In a culture that places a high emphasis on the concept of family honor, which is directly associated with the sexual behavior of women, this kind of literature is bound to have a long-lasting impact on the mobility and freedom of women.

The emergence of fundamentalism provided the climate for challenging the national and democratic concepts of the new political and cultural institutions. It also provided the Israeli authorities with a great opportunity for fostering factionalism and for spreading confusion among Palestinians. Toward the end of 1988, the West Bank and Gaza Strip communities were shocked by the circulation of leaflets with fake accounts that targeted the reputation of leading female figures in the nationalist movement. One of these circulars depicted them as embezzlers and traitors;[14] another fabricated statements by political detainees, contending that:[15] "Only when our homes, wives and daughters got assaulted, robbed and even raped . . . only then did the PLO regain its moral consciousness, [only then was] an investigative committee set up by Yasser Arafat. . . ." The circular clearly targeted the leadership of the nationalist movement by questioning its sincerity in guarding the people.[16] Another circular listed names of Palestinian men and women who were said to be agents for the Israeli authority and instigated people to track them down for execution. The fifth point of the same circular calls on all Palestinian women to abide by religious modes of dress that require covering the head, and concludes by citing the words of the Prophet Muhammad: "The best women of my nation are those with the most shiny faces and least costly dowries."

The cultural factor. The closing down of universities and schools over long periods of time reinstated the authority of the family as the sole higher institution and increased its authority over its members, especially women, for whom schools and universities were the only alternative to home. Men also came to be confined to the home because of curfews or because their sports clubs and other male gathering places were partially or totally shut down. The atmosphere of constant mourning in addition to frequent strikes all led to the presence of men and children inside the house for longer periods of time, which burdened women with new housework and limited their movement.

During the later part of the intifada there was a drop in the marriage age of women to below the age of eighteen, the reasons for which are not entirely clear. Some Palestinian families may have been encouraging their daughters to marry at an early age to lessen the financial burden of the father or because schools and universities were closed and women were unable to find employment.[17] It is also possible that the reduction in the size of the dowry has made it possible for young couples to marry at an earlier age. In both cases, however, starting a family earlier will affect the ability of young women to pursue a higher education that could lead to a career.

Conclusion

The pressing economic, political, social, and cultural problems led young couples who were married during or just before the intifada to move back in with their parents' families. Another factor that encouraged this trend was personal and health security. The intifada left many people handicapped, jailed, or widowed; the extended family provided all the necessary protection at such times. However, despite the advantages of this communal system, the family placed the individual in a weaker position vis-à-vis society. This was particularly the case with women, especially because their participation was not glorified like that of the young men. Sons, on the other hand, were considered heroes for their rebellious stone throwing and could challenge the authority of the father who, in contrast, stood as a nondaring, home-bound figure. The need to protect the smaller family from the Israeli occupation or even from society, encouraged the return to family-arranged early marriages, which was more often the case with females than males. This constituted a major setback for Palestinian women, who had earlier started to break away toward more and better education.

What shape will the pattern of social relations inside the Palestinian family take in the future? The answer to this question is tied to the goals and policies of the Palestinian nationalist movement with its various sectors, especially women. More attention should be given to developments that could positively or negatively affect the democratization of social relations inside the Palestinian family—a process that benefits women above all.

ISLAH JAD

NOTES

1. To understand the changes in the role of women within the Palestinian family and against the background of the Arab Muslim family, see I. Atta, "Prospects and Retrospect on the Role of Moslem Arab Woman at Present: Trends and Tendencies," *Islamic Culture* 55, no. 4 (1981).

2. The incident at Beita refers to the blowing up of Palestinian homes in Beita in retaliation for the death of a young settler woman thought to have been at the hands of Palestinians. As it turned out the girl was killed by mistake by her guard. October 31, 1989, marked the end of siege of Beit Sahour, a small Christian village on the West Bank. Residents of this small village defied the occupation by refusing to pay their taxes.

3. "The Intifada and Some Women's Social Issues," a paper presented at a conference with the same title on December 14, 1991. The conference was sponsored by the Women's Studies Committee/Bisan Center for Research and Development. At this conference, Eileen Kuttab, a lecturer in sociology at Birzeit University on the West Bank and a coordinator of the Bisan Women's Research Committee, attributed the retreat in female participation to the lack of social programs that could articulate women's concerns and to the emergence of a reactionary sociopolitical movement within the framework of the national movement that led to a weakening of the popular democratic structure of the intifada.

4. These statements were issued by the clandestine United Leadership of the intifada in the form of bayanat.

5. For information on the Palestinian family from 1948 to the present, see I. Atta, *The West Bank Palestinian Family* (London: KPI, 1986).

6. Camille Mansour, *Les Palestiniens de l'interieur* (Washington, D.C.: Institute for Palestine Studies, 1989), p. 80.

7. Mohammad Gibriel and Sulaiman Ghassan, "Agricultural Relations on the West Bank and Gaza Strip under Occupation," unpublished manuscript.

8. Ibid.

9. Nahla Abu-Zubi, *Family Women and Social Change in the Middle East: The Palestinian Case* (Toronto: Scholar's Press, 1987).

10. Personal interviews in Rafah camp in 1990.

11. A joint evaluation report on the position of women in the Gaza Strip, 1990.

12. A statement by Metzna, head of the Middle Area, on Israeli television, July 1988.

13. Report, "Joint Evaluation of Women in the Gaza Strip," pp. 5–25.

14. From the "Striking Forces," a bayan issued by the United Leadership of the intifada and entitled "A Call to the People," May 8, 1988.

15. From a bayan by the United Leadership of the intifada entitled "The Wealthy of the Intifada—Enemies of the People," May 8, 1988.

16. Bayan signed by Hamas, the Islamic fundamentalist movement in the occupied territories, entitled "In the name of God the Almighty, Arise for Jihad," July 1989.

17. Najah al-Manasra, "Early Marriage, a Temporary Regression in the Palestinian Women's March," *al-Katib* (Jerusalem), no. 112 (August 1989).

·3·

PHILIPPA STRUM

West Bank Women and the Intifada: Revolution within the Revolution

The intifada affected West Bank women and their activities drastically, but whether it altered their status permanently remains to be seen. So many phenomena occurred at once that realities occasionally seemed to conflict. There were women doing battle with Israeli soldiers but being ordered by their husbands or fathers not to work in local political committees. There were young people of both sexes planning demonstrations and enforcing commercial strike hours, but there were girls of fifteen or even younger being married off by their fathers. The intifada involved a wide variety of women: elite women with professional degrees, knowledgeable about women's liberation around the world; poorly educated women who would have been shocked by feminist theory but gloried in the belief that they and other "real women" were the strong ones of the family; women who saw the intifada as a chance to gain gender equality; and those who, along with most men, viewed the participation of women in it as an emergency measure that would be unnecessary when independence was achieved and the women returned to their homes.

What follows is a brief examination of the status of women immediately before the intifada and lengthier analyses of the intifada's first year, December 1987–December 1988, and the period from January 1989–December 1991.

PHILIPPA STRUM

Before the Intifada

West Bank society, like many Mediterranean and largely Muslim entities, adhered for generations to the ideal of women as almost completely private and apolitical. This stereotypical woman was secluded in her home, remote from the political and paid economic spheres. It was men who went into the paid workforce, men who mingled in cafes and played backgammon after work, men who socialized outside the home.[1]

The ideal differed from reality for many women. While the genders did not normally mix outside the home, it was mainly middle- and upper-class women who were secluded and segregated from men. The majority of West Bank women were and are rural. The field work that was part of their lives did not lend itself either to seclusion or to another ideal, the veiled woman (or, in the twentieth century, one whose head and forehead are covered with a scarf). Even in rural areas, however, there was usually a clear gender-based division of labor. Rural women fetched water and men herded flocks, for example, while some seasonal jobs, such as picking olives and harvesting, were done by men and women together. Women occasionally did "men's work," but West Bank men, like those everywhere, normally played no role in the "women's work" of child-rearing, cooking, and housekeeping. Men controlled money no matter who earned it and were viewed as the primary breadwinners.[2]

Palestinian women of all classes are expected to be chaste, and men's honor has depended on their being kept that way. A woman has always been the responsibility of a man, with marriage formally transferring the responsibility from a woman's father to her husband. Couples traditionally have not met in advance. The bride was irrelevant to the marriage contract, which was signed without her presence or participation. It was her father's obligation to get the best possible *mahr* (bride price), which was both compensation to her family for loss of her labor and her means of support should she be divorced. Traditionally, a low value was placed on female literacy, considered irrelevant to marriage and the production of children.[3]

An emerging core of elite women challenged this ideology. They had studied at universities in Egypt or Lebanon or at the relatively new West Bank universities, participated in the voluntary work committees organized by municipalities after the election of 1976, and drew on both experiences for discussion of gender roles and the place of women in the national liberation effort. Beginning in 1978, they established the four women's work committees that, along with a number of leading nonpartisan women—primarily from academia—constitute the women's movement. The committees created literacy classes with newly written materials instructing women about their rights; child care centers; vocational training classes; and production teams designed to enable women to gain at least some economic independence. A governance hierarchy was established so that the committees were controlled from the bottom up. The emphasis was on bringing committee members into the national liberation movement and empowering them by making them part of the decision-making process. Thus local subcommittees were in place when the intifada began.[4]

The First Year of the Intifada

The physical involvement of women in the first year of the intifada meant a major change in activities considered permissible for women and shook the old ideas of dependent women whose honor lay in their remaining hidden from the public eye. Although the early intifada revolved in part around the demonstrations by the *shabab* and their consequent emergence as street leaders, the spontaneous nature of many demonstrations, such as those at funerals attended by massive numbers of people, meant that a cross section of the population was involved from the start. Women quickly became a mainstay of the demonstrations, both as participants and as protectors of their men when the IDF (Israel Defense Force) attempted to arrest them. The bulk of the violent casualties of the uprising—people killed, badly beaten, teargassed—came from refugee camps, villages, and poorer neighborhoods of cities, precisely the areas most highly populated by families whose men were working abroad or in Israel, as well as the places that had seen a disproportionate share of pre-intifada IDF violence. Some urban women claim that they, too, took to the streets before men did.[5]

Women from all areas rushed out to take on a public political function, throwing themselves between soldiers and the young men they were trying to seize. One day in the Old City of Ramallah, a poor village within a small city, women wielding pots and pans attacked a patrol of soldiers in order to release a youth being arrested. On another occasion a man in his early twenties was being beaten by soldiers in Ramallah. A woman rushed up with her baby in her arms and began shouting at the man, "I told you not to leave the house today, that the situation is too dangerous. But you didn't listen; you never listen to me!" She turned in disgust to the soldiers and, telling them to beat him, cried, "I am sick of you and your baby; take him and leave me alone," pushed the baby into the young man's arms, and ran away. The confused soldiers soon left the scene. In a few minutes the woman reappeared, retrieved her child, and wished the young man safety and a quick recovery. They were total strangers. The degree of women's success in protecting men from the IDF is indicated by one scholar's comment that "it has become dangerous for men to participate in demonstrations or marches in the absence of women."[6]

The women not only protected the men around them but also engaged in spontaneous demonstrations of their own, expressing their outrage at violence by soldiers or Jewish settlers, at arrests or killings, at the deaths and wounding of women and children, and at the miscarriages attributed to tear gas released from canisters thrown into homes or hospitals. By March 1988, three months after the intifada began, reactions of women in the territories to these incidents had resulted in a weekly average of 115 women's marches. Sixteen women died in them. There were numerous marches and sit-ins by women on March 8, International Women's Day. In Nablus, about 150 women marched behind Palestinian flags, carrying posters calling for the end of Soviet immigration. Close to 200 Beit Sahur women were joined by about a dozen Israeli women peace activists when they took the authorities by surprise by holding their Women's Day march three days early, carrying Palestinian flags, singing and chanting slogans. They were dispersed by tear gas. A twelve-year-old girl was struck in the head by a rubber-coated bullet and eighteen other women were injured by tear gas when police broke up another Women's Day demonstration in Jerusalem's Old City. Troops beat three girls, one of whom was hospitalized, when 400 women carried flags and anti-immigration posters through the Nablus casbah. Ten women were treated at Ramallah Hospital after rubber-coated bullets were fired at about 100 women marching near the old quarter. In Jenin, a seventeen-year-old girl was injured in the head by a rubber-coated bullet in one of four processions of women and girls. Similar marches, also broken up by rubber bullets and tear gas, were held in Tulkarem, Bethlehem, Hebron, Halhul, and elsewhere.[7]

Women were beaten and shot even when they were not participating in demonstrations. Al-Haq, the Palestinian affiliate of the International Commission of Jurists, noted that most women subjected to violence during the intifada were in their homes at the time, frequently attempting to protect male relatives from physical assault or arrest. Some of the women who died during the intifada were passers-by killed by chance, on their way home from school or market during a demonstration. By the end of 1989, sixty-seven women had been killed in the territories, and al-Haq had evidence proving that at least forty-six of them had been killed by the IDF.[8]

Some women began assuming more active roles in mixed-gender demonstrations in 1989 and 1990 as the nature of demonstrations changed. There were fewer and smaller spontaneous demonstrations. Instead, there were well-organized marches by young people, including women, who were no longer willing to subject themselves to jail and therefore masked their faces with the keffiyehs traditionally worn as head coverings by men. On the 1989 anniversary of the founding of the Popular Front for the Liberation of Palestine, for example, it was young women as well as men who masked their faces with keffiyehs or with hoods bearing the colors of the Palestinian flag and marched in Birzeit. Some of those in a women's demonstration that took place in the Nablus casbah and in which twenty-five people were shot and wounded were wearing keffiyeh masks.[9]

In a situation of war, women are always confronted with the threat of sexual violence, and men are always tempted to use such violence as a threatened or actual method of punishment and control. Traditional mores made it unthinkable that Palestinian women hearing sexual acts even mentioned by men would do more than cover their ears or shriek with horror. The intifada changed that. Al-Haq documented numerous cases of soldiers using obscene language. There were also cases of soldiers exposing themselves to women. Women probably shocked soldiers as much as themselves not only by resisting physical assaults but by returning the soldiers' sexual taunts and using explicitly sexual language to question their manhood. The reliance upon women for protection may have begun as an extension of a traditional role, but the forms it took were new. Numerous racy stories were told early in the intifada about village women "hiding" unrelated men wanted by the IDF, doing such things as bathing them and thereby convincing the soldiers that they had to be family members rather than the wanted men. Whether or not such stories were true is less important than the fact that they could be recounted, with laughter, and implicitly accepted by an insistently protective patriarchal society as appropriate behavior in a time of emergency. Palestinian women face sexual threats and sometimes fondling of their bodies by soldiers. Before the intifada, a woman "contaminated" by rape or other sexual abuse, whether by soldiers or men of her own society, might well have been ostracized if not killed by her family. Women who were prisoners during the first year or so of the intifada, however, were treated as heroines by men as well as by women. This led Birzeit professor Eileen Kuttab to suggest that "the honor of the women has a more political and nationalist context now. . . . The women feel that their honor is really in protecting people, not their own bodies." Hanan Mikhail Ashrawi of Birzeit University added, "The whole system of taboos, and the definitions of honor and shame, have changed. Now it is the national issue that determines what is shameful and what is not, not the social issue."[10]

Beginning roughly in March/April 1988, when the need for long-term planning became clear, Palestinians began consolidating and extending the new kinds of committees that had sprung into being early in the intifada. These were the "neighborhood" or "popular" committees, which gradually acquired an entire and highly specialized infrastructure. Some provided emergency medical treatment, blood-typed entire neighborhoods, or taught first aid. Education committees replaced the schools as the authorities began to close schools on the grounds that they were indoctrinating and rallying the protestors; the committees also provided an education different from that in government-run schools. There were committees to stockpile food and other necessities that were distributed when curfews, sometimes lasting for weeks, were imposed. Others collected money for families that lost their incomes because of the imprisonment, deportation, death, or wounding of wage-earning men. There were committees to aid in planting home gardens, to clean the roads, to ensure proper disposal of garbage, to provide information to the media—in short, to maintain an entire societal infrastructure.

Although these were mixed-gender committees, it was women who were most active in almost all of them. The women's committees were a model for, cooperated with, and in some cases overlapped the popular committees; and they provided a mechanism for women wanting to increase their involvement in the intifada. Women's committee activists were among the first popular committee members, marching, building barricades, smuggling food and other necessities to communities under curfew, and supplying rocks to the shabab as soon as the intifada began. The intifada also brought a dramatic rise in the variety of women's agricultural and food production projects and the number of women involved in them. Such projects, a key element of the intifada's drive for self-sufficiency and creation of an economic infrastructure, contributed to the empowerment of women.[11]

The reaction of men and women to working together in the neighborhood committees is instructive. One young woman, asked whether her activism in a neighborhood committee had led to problems, responded, "Not at all, although my community is conservative. I think that in the uprising, many people have put their conservatism aside. I am respected by my neighbors. . . . In the beginning, I felt a certain timidity from the young men who . . . believe women should take a more active role, but who also hold traditional social values. But I think this interaction between men and women will become more natural." A women's committee member commented, "Really, the shebab's [sic] respect for us increased because of our awareness, and our role in the streets and in the neighbourhood committees. Our initiatives gain us the respect of all the people, not just the young men." She added, however, "But this is not everything. We have to give more, make a stronger effort, not to lose their respect and to transfer it to their daily behaviour, to reflect the change in the position of women in the future." A third chimed in, "When we went to demonstrations or participated in clashes in the beginning of the Intifada, we met groups of young men. We didn't speak to them, because of the social customs we were raised with, and also to prove to people that we were there to confront the soldiers and not to meet boys. But later on, we would talk to them every day. We would make plans, build barricades for the streets, burn tyres, and would provide the boys with stones as well as throwing stones ourselves. So the trust between us increased and we feel now that they respect us." She, too, perceived a continuing problem: "But they still believe that we are weaker than them and sometimes we hear things like, 'You have long fingernails—give me those stones, and I will throw them for you.' But we have discussed these ridiculous comments with them," and many of the men have stopped trying to coddle the women.[12]

In the early months of the intifada, many young women fought family attempts to limit their participation in it. A young committee member reported, "My mother tried to prevent me from participating in the clashes, but after I was arrested, it became an accepted thing." Some women, especially in the rural areas, initially lied to their parents about their participation in popular committees or demonstrations, but others stopped doing so. Some young women helped distribute the Unified Leadership's *bayanat* (leaflets) setting strike days and hours and establishing basic rules of behavior. Young women in their teens, particularly adept at smuggling food to needy families during curfews, also joined young men in checking to see that shops closed as soon as strike hours began and in organizing demonstrations. Members of the working class gained positions in popular committees, which made it possible for them to tell the economically better-off what to do. It was all part of the changed social structure brought about by the intifada.[13]

A new leadership cadre developed. Before the intifada, middle-class women had moved from university-based politics into leadership positions outside educational institutions. This was facilitated by the experience women gained in mobilization, public speaking, writing, the planning of strategy and tactics, and other aspects of organizing while they were university students and members of the women's committees. A second factor was the vacuum created by the increased level of incarceration or deportation of male leaders. A good many university-trained women had achieved "middle management" positions in male-dominated trade unions and political parties before the intifada. During the intifada, this process was taken further by the removal of much of the male leadership from the public sphere by the IDF, which enabled the "middle management" women to fill positions that might otherwise have been reserved for men. The new visibility of women leaders, combined with the demands of the intifada and the resultant opportunities for female political activity, led to a radical change in the attitude of some women, and perhaps of some men. Political discussion was no longer a male preserve. Women routinely joined in or initiated conversations about politics, demonstrating that the public sphere was as much the sphere of women as of men.

The first year of the intifada, then, saw what was probably the majority of women assuming a political function. Confronting soldiers, visiting the wounded and the families of martyrs, and organizing alternative education can be viewed as extensions of the traditional nurturing role. There was a new sensibility, however, implicit in women wrestling with strange men, serving time in prisons, and, in smaller numbers, achieving a measure of economic independence.

After 1988: Reaction and Reexamination

By 1989, what had seemed to be a permanent alteration in the status of women had begun to crumble. It became apparent, in fact, that the "permanent alteration" was not that in the eyes of most men, who eagerly awaited both political independence and the return of no-longer-independent women to their homes. While many women were out of their homes, participating in the political sphere, others were once again being kept behind locked doors.

It is questionable whether women's large-scale participation in the popular committees (declared illegal by Israel in August 1988 and in rapid decline thereafter) added to their long-term political power. There was no indication that women shared in the decision making of most popular committees in the camps and villages. Meetings of the camp leadership were usually held in mosques or coffee shops, where women were rarely to be found. Most village popular committees coordinated with women's committees but retained the gender segregation that made joint meetings impossible.[14]

When Palestinian leaders held a press conference, the only faces to be seen were usually male. The occasional exceptions were invariably women's committee leader Zahira Kamal and Hanan Mikhail Ashrawi. Hanan Mikhail Ashrawi was one of the three Palestinian leaders meeting regularly with United States Secretary of State James Baker in 1991. She had no popular power base, however, and was clearly present in spite of rather than because she is a woman. The leadership outside the territories was male. As Birzeit scholar Nahla al-Assaly noted, there were no women on the Palestine National Council's fifteen-member Executive Committee which, since the PNC's 1988 Declaration of Independence, was the equivalent of a Palestinian government. The implicit message is that there was no room in the government for women.[15]

The language of the intifada was found in the bayanat issued periodically by the Unified National Leadership of the Uprising. The Leadership's composition was secret, beyond the fact that it included all four parties (Fateh, the Democratic Front for the Liberation of Palestine, the Popular Front for the Liberation of Palestine, and the Communist Party, but not the fundamentalist Islamic Resistance Movement, which was nonetheless sometimes consulted). The bayanat told the population who was to be congratulated for what deeds, the dates of upcoming strike days, and what new actions were recommended. Anyone reading them might well conclude that the intifada was essentially male, with women occasionally playing a very peripheral role.[16]

The bayanat referred to "brother workers," "brother businessmen and grocers," "businessmen, professional workers and craftsmen," "brother doctors and pharmacists," "sons of our people," "brother members of the popular committees and the men of the uprising," "our sons in the fascist jails," "heroes of the Lofty Intifada." Very infrequently, there was mention of "doctors, pharmacists, and nurses," "our people and the youths and girls of Palestine," or "male and female detainees jailed in enemy prisons and detention centers." When women appeared in the bayanat, they usually were coupled with children and the elderly, as in "women and old men will organize protest marches to the Red Cross headquarters," or "the bereaved, children, women, and the elderly who are suffering from the repressive measures of occupation." Even the bayan entitled the "Call of Celebration of the Independent State" mentioned women in only two passages: when the Leadership offered its "congratulations to the mother of the martyr, for she has celebrated only twice: when she gave her son and when the state was declared," thus defining women as baby- factories and bystanders, however enthusiastic, in the nationalist effort, and again in its "Congratulations to all our women, men, children, and the old!" which would seem to desex the elderly.

The bayanat might be regarded merely as hurried efforts that did not reflect men's altered consciousness. The November 15, 1988, Palestinian Declaration of Independence, however, was written with care after extensive debate about its content. It portrays women in a traditional, nurturing, but politically passive role: "We render special tribute to the brave Palestinian woman, guardian of sustenance and life, keeper of our people's perennial flame." The Declaration also says that "governance will be based on principles of social justice, equality, and non-discrimination in public rights on grounds of race, religion, color, or sex...." But the accompanying PNC "Political Communique" reverts to defining the "Palestinian masses" as "the unions, their vocational organizations, their students, their workers, their farmers, their women, their merchants, their landlords, their artisans, their academics . . . ," thereby excluding women from the categories of students, workers, farmers, artisans, and academics, where they could already be found.[17]

Papers presented by Palestinian scholars at a conference held in Jerusalem in December 1990 suggested both that the nature of women's participation in the intifada had changed and that the alteration in values was short-lived for much of society. The scholars pointed out that after the popular committees were outlawed, party-based "popular armies," in which women had at most a minimal role, came into existence. Many women turned their attention to production projects that were extensions of the home economy. Parents, who had ceded much of their power over their children, had begun to reclaim it by the end of 1988. The ensuing years witnessed the resurgence of forced early marriages and the old concept of shame. Marriage and the early arrival of children were viewed by many as a way of keeping single men and women out of political activities that could result in imprisonment and the subsequent unmarriageability of women, and the permanent wounding or death of men. The appalling rate of unemployment that existed after late 1990, which was exacerbated by the total curfew during the 1991 Gulf War and the replacement of Palestinian workers by new Soviet immigrants to Israel as well as the limitations on territories' residents entering Israel, made fathers eager to turn the burden of supporting their daughters over to potential husbands. The tendency toward forced early marriages moved from the villages and camps to the cities.[18]

The family desire to protect women from political activities and loss of honor led some to compel women and girls to drop out of schools and universities. Women ex-prisoners began to be treated as contaminated, regularly being denied jobs and having difficulty in finding husbands. The few exceptions were members of women's committees, which continued to be supportive. The culture of the intifada, which downgraded frivolous or costly activities, including restaurant meals, movies, parties, and family excursions, reinforced the tendency of some elements in Palestinian society to scrutinize women's behavior and dress. Clothing became even more of a political statement than usual with the rise of fundamentalism and its emphasis on "modest" apparel for women.[19]

The effect of the occupation and intifada on marriage was obviously complicated. Women who battled soldiers in the streets or earned money objected, not surprisingly, to arranged marriages. Many found prospective husbands while doing political work. The Unified Leadership requested Palestinians to limit wedding celebrations and bride prices as an austerity measure. Some women refused the mahr entirely, either as a patriotic gesture or because they had come to view it as offensive. But not all women spurned the mahr, either because they continued to adhere to the older ideas, were under pressure from their parents, or because they wanted the security a mahr offered in case a marriage ended.

It appears that marriages increased and the frequency of divorce dropped during the intifada, possibly out of a felt need to adhere to societally acceptable norms during a period of crisis—or because the combination of minimalization of wedding celebrations and small dowries lowered the cost of weddings and encouraged people to marry at an earlier age. A 1990 survey showed that the marriage rate had gone up between 20 and 30 percent, that the intifada's street demonstrations had brought people of marriageable age into contact, and that siblings of wounded or killed "martyrs" were seen as particularly desirable partners. At the same time, interviews suggest that many women were eager to produce "more children for Palestine" during the national liberation struggle. They reportedly were encouraged by sermons in the mosques calling for early marriage and a higher birthrate. This changed somewhat after the Gulf War, when the depressed economic situation made having a large number of children less attractive.[20]

Some scholars believe that by 1991 membership in the women's committees had decreased because of family and fundamentalist reaction against female political activity, the inability of the committees to articulate a specific program for women beyond participation in production projects and cooperatives, the lack of progress in the peace process and a concomitant general questioning of the utility of political activism, and the demands made on women's time by the combination of household responsibilities, child care, and participation in the drive for economic self-sufficiency through creation of home gardens.

Still, the phenomenon of women becoming active outside their homes constituted a revolution that occurred in a remarkably short time. Although some families were taking their daughters out of school early, the idea that women should receive a substantial amount of formal education had spread—its popularity, ironically perhaps, encouraged by anger at the government's long-term closing of schools and the belief that the closures were designed to render the Palestinians illiterate and ignorant. No less radical, if not as popular, was the idea that women who do not absolutely need to earn money could choose to do so without losing their respectability or femininity.

One key question that remains concerns the extent to which the hoped-for Palestinian government will recognize women's new roles. Although the Unified National Leadership appeared to include few, if any women, the leadership of the political parties and trade union movements had an increasing number. There appeared to be less resistance to a grassroots public role for women among the people of the West Bank than there was within the PLO leadership abroad. The women who have been "talking politics" are unlikely to be satisfied with a purely private persona. Their interest and experience may well be translated into support for women in a national legislature.

While it seems safe to predict that the status of women will never again be precisely what it was before the intifada began, the impact of women's role in the intifada on their status as women cannot be assessed with any finality until the intifada itself has come to an end.

NOTES

1. See Magida Salman, "The Arab Woman: A Threatening Body, a Captive Being," in *Women in the Middle East*, ed. Khamsin Collective (London: Zed Books, 1987), pp. 6–11; Amal Rassam, introduction to "Arab Women: The Status of Research of Social Scientists and the Status of Women," in UNESCO, *Social Science Research: Women in the Arab World* (New York: UNESCO, 1984), pp. 2–4; Fatima Mernissi, *Beyond the Veil* (London: Al Saqui Books, 1985); Fatna A. Sabbah, *Women in the Muslim Unconscious* (New York: Pergamon Press, 1984), esp. chap. 5, "The Omnisexual Woman," and chap. 6, "The Omnisexual Woman in Action: Subversion of the Social Order." On men's activities, see Joseph Ginat, *Women in Muslim Rural Society* (New Brunswick, NJ: Transaction Books, 1982), p. 15.

2. See Salman, "Arab Woman," p. 8. On differences among classes, see Annalies Moors, "Gender Hierarchy in a Palestinian Village: The Case of Al-Balad," in *The Rural Middle East*, ed. Kathy Glavanis and Pandeli Glavanis (Ramallah: Birzeit University; London: Zed Books, 1990), p. 201; Sarah Graham-Brown, "The Political Economy of the Jabul Nablus, 1920–1948," in *Studies in the Economic and Social History of Palestine in the Nineteenth and Twentieth Centuries*, ed. Roger Owen (London: Macmillan, 1982). On veiling (which

Margot Badran says has to do with economic standing, not Islam), see Margot Badran, introduction to Huda Shaarawi, *Harem Years* (New York: Feminist Press, 1987), p. 8; and see Ginat, *Women in Muslim Rural Society*, p. 19.

3. Shaarawi, *Harem Years*, p. 8; Moors, "Gender Hierarchy," pp. 197–98, 200–201; Halim Barakat, "The Arab Family and the Challenge of Social Transformation," in *Women and the Family in the Middle East*, ed. Elizabeth Warnock Fernea (Austin: University of Texas Press, 1985); Ibrahim Wade Ata, *The West Bank Palestinian Family* (London: KPI, 1986), pp. 58, 60–61, 66, 119, 122. A relatively small number of women was educated during the pre-intifada period. Among them were a few women from the societal elite, largely from Christian families. Some were daughters of post-1948 refugee camp families. The men, having lost their land, were unable to find adequate employment. Illiterate women were able to obtain work only as domestic laborers, and it was hoped that a basic education would enhance their chances of getting better jobs.

4. This information, like much of the rest on which this chapter is based, was obtained from interviews with women on the West Bank during the author's stays there in 1989, 1990, and 1991.

5. Islah Jad, "From Salons to the Popular Committees: Palestinian Women, 1919–1989," in *Intifada: Palestine at the Crossroads*, ed. Jamal R. Nassar and Roger Heacock (Ramallah: Birzeit University; New York: Praeger, 1991), p. 140. On the entire population, see Rita Giacaman, "Political Women in the Uprising: From Followers to Leaders?" unpublished paper, September 1988, pp. 1, 2n. 1; Michael C. Hudson, introduction to idem, ed., *The Palestinians: New Directions* (Washington, D.C.: Georgetown University Center for Contemporary Arab Studies, 1990), p. xvi; see also the discussions by Salim Tamari and Joost R. Hiltermann in ibid., and discussions by Odil Yahya and Husein Jameel Bargouti in Nassar and Heacock, *Intifada*. On pre-intifada violence, see Yahya, in ibid., p. 95. See also Joost R. Hiltermann, "Sustaining Movement, Creating Space: Trade Unions and Women's Committees," *Middle East Report* (May-August 1990), p. 34. On defiance of soldiers by women, see Giacaman, "Political Women," p. 5; cf. Palestinian Union of Women's Work Committees, Newsletter, special issue, *Women in the Uprising*, March 8, 1988, p. 2.

6. The incident was witnessed by Professor Munir Fasheh of Birzeit University, who recounts it in "Community Education: To Reclaim and Transform What Has Been Made Invisible," *Harvard Educational Review* 60, no. 1 (February 1990): 30. On the dangers for men, see Jad, "From Salons to the Popular Committees," p. 140.

7. On tear gas and miscarriages, see Report of Chief Physician of the IDF, May 5, 1988, in al-Haq, *Punishing a Nation: Human Rights Violations during the Palestinian Uprising, December 1987–December 1988* (Ramallah: al-Haq, 1989; also available in an edition published in Boston by South End Press, 1990), p. 39; on the use of tear gas canisters in confined spaces, see al-Haq, *Punishing a Nation*, pp. 35–40; and idem, *A Nation Under Siege: Annual Report on Human Rights in the Occupied Palestinian Territories* (Ramallah: al-Haq, 1990), pp. 409–511. On the number of demonstrations, see Jad, "From Salons to the Popular Committees," p. 133. On Women's Day, see Joel Greenberg, "IDF Demolishes Home of West Bank Fugitive," *Jerusalem Post* (hereafter *JP*), March 8, 1990, p. 10; Greenberg, "4 Settlers Released from Custody," *JP*, March 6, 1990, p. 10; Associated Press,

caption accompanying photograph, "Israelis Break Up Women's Demonstration," *New York Times*, March 9, 1990, p. A8; Robert Rees and Joel Greenberg, "Rubber Bullets Used to Stop Women's Day Marches in J'lem [sic]," *JP*, March 9, 1990, p. 1.

8. *Nation Under Siege*, p. 504.

9. Joel Greenberg, "Masked Birzeit Teenagers Mark PFLP's Anniversary with Paramilitary March," *JP*, December 12, 1989, p. 12. On the Nablus casbah, see Michal Sela, "Palestinians Report 25 Wounded in Scattered Clashes in Territories," *JP*, December 25, 1989, p. 8.

10. See al-Haq, *Nation under Siege*, pp. 511–20; Jad, "From Salons to the Popular Committees," p. 138; Palestinian Union of Women's Work Committees (Palestinian Federation of Women's Action Committees), *Newsletter*, special issue, "Women in the Uprising," March 8, 1988, June 30, 1988, October 1988; Sharon Rose, "Women and the Intifada: Interview with Eileen Kuttab," *Palestine Focus* (November-December 1989), p. 8; Harriet Lewis, "It Is Possible to Agree on Principles: An Interview with Hanan Mikhail-Ashrawi," *New Outlook* (June-July 1989), p. 8.

11. On mixed-gender committees and women in new production projects, see Saida Hamad, "Intifada Transforms Palestinian Society, Especially the Role of Women," *al-Fajr Weekly*, March 13, 1989. Jad, "From Salons to the Popular Committees," pp. 134–35, suggests that women were more active than men primarily in education and first aid committees, although they were active in other urban popular committees. On the overlapping of committees, see Islah Abdul Jawwad, "The Evolution of the Political Role of the Palestinian Women's Movement in the Uprising," in Hudson, *Palestinians*, p. 71.

12. All the women quoted are between fourteen and twenty-two years of age. On committee members, see "In Their Own Words . . . ," *Voice of Women* (Palestinian Union of Women's Work Committees, undated but probably early 1990), pp. 2–3.

13. Rita Giacaman and Penny Johnson, "Mother, Sister, Self: The Women of Nahalin" (Birzeit University, 1989, unpublished), p. 8.

14. On lack of involvement in camp and village committees, see Abdul Jawwad, "Evolution of the Political Role," p. 71; Jad, "From Salons to the Popular Committees," p. 135.

15. Nahla al-Assaly, "The Palestinian National Movement and Its Perception of the Women's Role," in Women's Studies Committee, *The Intifada and Some Women's Social Issues: A Conference Held in Al-Quds Al-Sharif/Jerusalem on December 14, 1990* (Ramallah: Women's Studies Committee/Bisan Center, 1991), pp. 12–13.

16. Translations of most of the bayanat issued between January 8 and November 22, 1988, through number 29, can be found in *Intifada*, ed. Zachary Lockman and Joel Beinen (Boston: South End Press/Middle East Research and Information Project, 1989), pp. 327–94. Bayanat are also reprinted in *Jerusalem* (Tunis, Palestine Committee for NGOs), which is issued monthly, and in the press bulletins released by Sanabel Press Services in Jerusalem (through 1990). Nassar and Heacock, *Intifada*, include some information about the composition of the UNLU (p. 197).

17. The PNC's discussion of the Declaration of Independence and the accompanying communique are discussed in Edward Said, "Intifada and Independence," in *Intifada,* ed. Lockman and Beinin, pp. 14–16. Nineteenth Session of the Palestine National Council, "Proclamation of the Independent Palestinian State," Algiers, November 15, 1988, in ibid., pp. 399 and 397–98; Palestine National Council, "Political Communique," Algiers, November 15, 1988, in ibid., p. 402.

18. The conference was organized by Bisan. The papers are printed in Arabic with English summaries in *The Intifada and Some Women's Social Issues.*

19. On the culture of the intifada, see Rima Hammami, "Women's Political Participation in the Intifada, A Critical Overview," pp. 75–78, 81–82.

20. Information on the numbers of marriages, divorces, and births was derived from the author's interviews; and see Ya'acov Lamdan, "Love, Marriage and the Intifada," *JP,* May 18, 1989, p. 7, reporting on the survey mentioned.

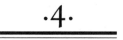

ZAHIRA KAMAL

TRANSLATION BY RAMLA KHALIDI

The Development of the Palestinian Women's Movement in the Occupied Territories: Twenty Years after the Israeli Occupation

The underlying reason for women's subordinate position in the occupied territories is the existence of a skewed structure of ownership and property. This structure has resulted in discrimination against women. Over time, while the division of ownership between men and women was transformed, their respective roles remained unaltered. The development of modern means of production as well as changes in the relations of production have caused domestic work, as compared to work carried out by men, to lose much of its value. This has, in turn, placed men in a dominant position and given them the power and authority to make the decisions, create the laws, and establish the ideological, social, and economic principles of society. In view of these developments, the discrimination that women face becomes the main target in the women's struggle, and men, irrespective of their class background, become the primary obstacle to the achievement of women's full rights.

Feminist movements around the world, by emphasizing the importance of eliminating all forms of usurpation and discrimination, have united women of diverse socioeconomic backgrounds. As with other movements, the feminist movement is influenced by the political and economic systems of the society in which it is born. Each movement therefore acquires a distinctive character. Two of the factors prominent in the occupied territories are: 1) the distorted and backward socioeconomic structure that has traditionally prevented women from potentially great contributions in the production of goods. Production is, in and of itself, an important starting point for liberation; and 2) an ideological structure that is based on ancestral traditions. This structure derives its strength from Arab religious practices and is filled with superstitions. It finds expression through specific patterns of behavior. One result of this structure is that Arab women are denied basic rights, including education and employment. They are considered weak, incapable creatures, mere shadows of their men, their main duties being toward their husbands and toward the preservation of the species.

Arab society embodies all of the characteristics of underdeveloped societies—politically, economically, socially, and culturally. Since Palestinian society is an integral part of the Arab world, it would only be natural to assume that the women's movement in Palestine resembles those in the Arab world. The Israeli invasion of Palestine, the establishment of the State of Israel in 1948, and the consequent loss of land and dispersion of the largest segment of the Palestinian population into the diaspora have, however, given Palestinian women's liberation special importance. There is a heightened awareness of the necessity for popular participation of women alongside men in confronting the imperialist, Zionist invasion of Palestine. Unfortunately, however, the importance of liberating women from the shackles of tradition and social customs that have effectively barred their participation in various aspects of life has yet to be recognized.

The rights of Palestinians in the occupied territories have been severely curtailed by the colonial policies of the military authorities. Land confiscation, establishment of settlements, continuous attempts to destroy national institutions, and suppression of civil rights and national culture are all tactics aimed at destroying Palestinian identity and guaranteeing that self-determination and the legitimate right to return are not achieved. It is thus the national and revolutionary path taken by Palestinian society—more than economic factors—that has influenced the women's movement in the occupied territories.

The Impact of Occupation on Palestinian Women

The Israeli occupation of the West Bank and Gaza Strip caused many dislocations in the Palestinian economy, including a precipitous drop in family income. As a result of the deterioration in the standard of living, many Palestinian women were forced to seek employment in order to supplement the family income. The occupations most commonly taken up have been in the traditional sphere (sewing, teaching, and nursing) as well as in industry and agriculture. But working women, whether in the occupied territories or inside the "Green Line," have experienced flagrant discrimination in terms of remuneration. In addition, they have often been deprived of the benefits of social security and health insurance. Thus, most women do not qualify for paid maternity leave or work relief for breast-feeding, nor do they have access to day-care centers and kindergartens for their children. The problems faced by women who have had to take on paid jobs in addition to their household chores at a time when the cost of living is rising have been exacerbated by the Israeli economic crisis and its repercussions for the occupied territories.

The Israeli occupation created many hurdles for Palestinian health care institutions and their efficient functioning. This in turn has led to a marked deterioration in health, especially that of mothers and children. The infant mortality rate, for example, has risen to eighty-four deaths per one thousand live births. The absence of health insurance, coupled with an increase in the cost of medical treatment and the erosion of public health facilities, has placed a heavy burden on low income families on the West Bank and in the Gaza Strip.

The Israeli policy of annexation and the deterioration of economic conditions in the occupied territories have forced a number of husbands to immigrate in search of work outside the territories. This has acutely affected the women left behind, burdening them with additional social, economic, and educational responsibilities. Over time, this has led to an imbalance in society, as witnessed by the number of early or incompatible marriages and a rising divorce rate. However, while this new situation is a burden to women, it also opens up new opportunities for them to strengthen and reinforce their role and their position in the communities.

The socioeconomic changes in Palestinian society—including a shake-up of traditions and values—and an increase in the number of Palestinian universities and institutions of learning have served to improve women's educational level. The illiteracy rate for women has declined dramatically: on the West Bank, the rate dropped from 65 percent in 1970 to 37 percent in 1983; and in the Gaza Strip for the same period, the rate declined from 65 percent to 39 percent. The number of women who have completed nine or more years of education increased form 9 percent in 1970 to 26 percent in 1983 for the West Bank, and from 19 percent to 37 percent for the same period in the Gaza Strip.

The Development of Different Types of Organizations and Work Patterns in the Palestinian Women's Movement

Until the early 1970s, the philanthropic and "semisocial" organizations were the only institutions that dealt with women's issues. Such organizations offered, and continue to offer, very important social services under the severe living and social conditions of occupation. Thus, in the absence of national Palestinian rule, these organizations have provided for the social, health-related, and educational services normally provided by national governments. For example, they have provided kindergartens, nurseries and centers for mother and child care, and they have opened centers for the eradication of illiteracy. One of the leading organizations is the Society for the Development of the Family, which has worked speedily to reorient its activities and to circumvent the obstacles created by the occupation.

The level of coordination between organizations and institutions that provide the same services has also greatly improved. The formation of specialized committees to supervise the work has been invaluable in this process. These committees include the Higher Committee for the Eradication of Illiteracy, the Committee for the Care of the Handicapped, and the Coordination Committee of the Red Crescent Societies on the West Bank and in the Gaza Strip. It is important to note at this juncture the valiant role played by the Bethlehem Arab Women's Union. Immediately following the Israeli occupation of the territories, this union began combining the various efforts of the social and voluntary organizations in Bethlehem and put forward an agenda for all these groups: "confronting" the occupation and its practices was to be the main task of the various organizations.

Since 1967, hundreds of women on the West Bank and in the Gaza Strip have joined in the national struggle in various ways. Several of them have been exposed to the harsh measures of the Israeli authorities, including arrest, deportation, and house arrest. Until 1978 the most common activities of the feminist movement were individual acts of protest. Such protest took the form of strikes, the dispatching of protest telegrams, and participation in demonstrations organized by the national movement. The most important of these activities were centered around the conditions of the detained men and women in Israeli prisons and Israeli repressive activities, including collective punishment of refugee camps, confiscation of land, deportation, desecration of religious monuments, the destruction of homes, and so on. The number of women participating in these activities remained limited, however, and in most cases involved only the wives, mothers, and sisters of detainees. The vast majority of women were in fact not involved at all in any political work.

Philanthropic organizations and "semisocial" societies remained, for the most part, the only framework within which a limited number of women agitated for change and sought solutions to some of their problems. Because of the narrow social base of these organizations and the dominance of upper-class women among the leadership, these organizations were never able to meet the demands of the majority of women, nor were they able to mobilize the mass of average women. In addition, because their activities were centered in the cities, they were unable to provide for the needs of a large percentage of women in the rural areas. For all of these reasons, the traditional women's organizations were unable to affect any qualitative changes in the status of Palestinian women.

Similarly, existing women's unions, such as the Arab Women's Union in Jerusalem and the Palestinian Women's Union in the Gaza Strip, remained closer in their methods and programs to the philanthropic societies. They lacked a broad base of support and were unrepresentative of the cross section of women. This rendered them incapable of accurately defending the rights and interests of Palestinian women.

Assuming, on the one hand, that the feminist goal is to attain full basic rights for women and, on the other hand, that the liberation of women is inextricably intertwined with the national struggle, it stands to reason that women must take their place in the front lines. Thus, the United Women's Movement must confront the repressive policies of the Israeli occupation to the best of its ability. It can, and indeed it must take its position as an integral part of the national movement. Through these channels, Palestinian women in the occupied territories could develop and establish their role in society. What is needed is a framework for the efforts of tens of thousands of women who are willing to contribute to the struggle for women's rights. New organizations should be formed that tie their programs to the national struggle as well as to needs arising from the social, economic, and cultural position of the Palestinian woman.

In March of 1978 the Union of Palestinian Women's Working Committees (UPWC) was established in the occupied territories. It has worked toward uniting the different women's groups into one united popular feminist movement. Since its founding, the organization has grown significantly and has spread throughout the occupied territories. Its expansion is proof that there is a readiness among women to organize and work on the basis of a program that ties the national struggle to the development of the woman's social, economic, and cultural position.

The experience and success of the UPWC proved to be a catalyst for the emergence of similar groups. In March 1980, the Union of Working Palestinian Women's Committees was founded; in March 1981, the Union of Palestinian Women; and in June 1982, the Union of Women's Committees for Social Work. The social basis for these four women's organizations matured, and in a few years, they boasted several thousand members, a much larger number than that of philanthropic organizations that existed on the West Bank and in Gaza. These women's unions differ from the philanthropic societies that preceded them in the following ways:

First, the women's unions present programs that link national liberation and the end of occupation with the liberation of women. This has given these women cadres the power and authority to mobilize and organize the masses of women in cities, villages, and refugee camps. By emphasizing the special and invaluable contributions of women to the national struggle, these cadres can also enhance women's political perceptions and enable them to occupy their place within the framework of our national movement. In addition, the women's cadres aim to empower working women in a professional setting by urging them to join syndicates that represent them collectively. They are encouraged to form working women's affairs committees in each of these syndicates in order to raise syndicate awareness for women's needs and to decrease the difficulties and the problems faced by women on the job. These cadres coordinate with worker's unions to defend the rights of working women, to improve working conditions, and to eliminate any discrimination between women and men performing the same job.

Second, the unions have presented alternative frameworks for organizing women. The novel methods they have used include organizing women in districts and residential areas in all cities, villages, and camps, as well as developing a national organization. This national structure is flexible enough to recruit women from all social and economic walks of life, and incorporates as many varied activities as demand requires.

Third, the unions have drafted internal bylaws with an eye to enhancing and maintaining a democratic atmosphere. Such bylaws have opened the door for the active participation of women in general. The unions have also broken with the idea that work by women should be confined to offering services and help. Instead, they are committed to involving women in the various sectors of the national struggle as well as in the struggle for the advancement of women's social, economic, and cultural status. Some of the cadres have organized seasonal and annual work programs and have held women's congresses based on popular representation through democratic elections.

Fourth, the unions have begun developing a sound foundation for the women's movement. Participation in conferences and political movements has allowed women to take the initiative and to contribute meaningfully to both national liberation and to the fight for equal rights as working women. One result is that March 8 and May 1 are now paid holidays in many institutions.

Fifth, the unions have fostered a genuine awareness of the importance and necessity of the feminist movement. In addition, there is a realization that a high level of coordination between the different cadres is essential in order to achieve progress in both the struggle against occupation and on issues relevant to women. Such an approach can pave the road toward the consolidation of women's efforts under one umbrella movement. The growth of the social base of the unions and its expansion to include all the different cadres are two primary factors that will help the feminist movement mature and bring about real unification of the Palestinian feminist movement in the occupied territories.

Sixth, the unions have devoted more attention to the dissemination of educational information relevant to women's particular concerns. This is evident from the publishing by the cadres of a number of pamphlets and journals concerned with the problems faced by women. The publications are characterized by a refreshing realism and an awareness of the conditions facing women. The topics addressed include health problems, women's legal position, problems of marriage and divorce, problems resulting from work, and the problems of motherhood.

Future Tasks for the Feminist Movement

In light of these developments, we can say that despite suppression and the terroristic practices of occupation, the women's movement in the occupied territories has been able to improve its position. It has established its role in the national struggle and guaranteed its participation in the defense of women's rights through a syndicated movement. Meanwhile, women's social role continues to grow, develop, and change. Women have confronted not only problems touching on illiteracy, health, and child care, but also in training other women for jobs, combating the high cost of living, setting up cooperative committees to help low-income families affected by the occupation, and maintaining relations with housewives and workers in the countryside. All of this is in addition to the women's role on the national level, most clearly exemplified by women's involvement in the defense of national institutions. Women have been particularly active in the formation of Land Defense Committees, and Committees for the Defense of Prisoners and Detainees, and they have bravely confronted colonization policies and defended the legitimate national rights of the Palestinian people. The Palestinian women's movement has therefore become an integral and effective part of the national movement.

In spite of the many qualitative achievements of the Palestinian women's movement in the occupied territories, and in spite of its quick development and the vitality it has shown in confronting the occupation and its repressive policies, there are several hurdles ahead:

First, the Palestinian women's movement must keep working to widen its popular base. Reports on unions of women's movements show that organized women's movements do not exceed 3 percent of the total number of women. This requires the doubling of efforts to recruit more women into the various organizations. The experience of the Union of Palestinian Women's Work Committees and the socialist campaign they launched in preparation for their fourth conference is worth noting. This campaign reflected a definite improvement in the assimilation of the organizational work plan. It was based on collective rather than individual representation, and it resulted in a significant increase in participation. It therefore acted as a multiplier. In addition, the experience points to the women's, and particularly housewives', high level of readiness for collective work.

Second, the women's movement must attempt to maintain social balance in its membership. Representation has so far been consistently skewed in favor of the cities and against the countryside and refugee camps. The deficiency in these areas is a result of the absence of local committees.

Third, there should be a greater effort to organize housewives. Housewives represent 55 percent of the total female population on the West Bank and in the Gaza Strip. Thus, while there is no doubt that the organization of women workers is of utmost importance, this should not preclude organizing the larger segment of Palestinian women in the occupied territories. A formula must be found that will guarantee increased awareness and participation by housewives in the political and social struggle. The report from the fourth Union of Women's Work Committees points to an understanding of the importance of this segment of the female population, without which no widespread mass movement could exist—housewives make up 73 percent of the members of the Women's Union.

Fourth, more attention must be paid to the problems of working women and the exploitation to which they are subject. Discrimination occurs whether they are working on Israeli projects or in national institutions. In spite of the close relationship between women and the labor movement, the percentage of women union workers is still low. Thus, a doubling of efforts is required to recruit working women into union organizations.

Fifth, it is essential to coordinate the work of unions with that of philanthropic societies. Many of the activities that are carried out by the cadres are service oriented and overlap with the work of the philanthropic societies. These functions include: mother and child health care, nurseries and kindergartens, training centers, etc. In these areas, the philanthropic societies have had more experience and can thus contribute a great deal of knowledge and information. Such coordination will help maintain the role of social welfare societies and the cadres as well as allow the women's cadres to concentrate on the improvement of the social, cultural, and political status of women.

Undoubtedly, the tasks facing the women's movement are immense. They require a concerted effort from all the women's cadres in the occupied territories. The main concern put forward by the Union of Palestinian Women's Work Committees is that an effort be made "toward the achievement of a unified popular women's movement." This would require that all women's cadres, unions, and institutions, including the philanthropic societies, work under a unified umbrella group with one program that is responsive to the needs of Palestinian women. The women's movement is an indivisible part of the Palestinian national movement. It carries with it the commitment to fight toward the right to return, the right to self-determination, and the establishment of an independent Palestinian state on national soil.

Epilogue — 1990

Like feminist movements elsewhere in the Third World, the Palestinian feminist movement has been inextricably intertwined with the national liberation struggle. The ties between the two movements stem from certain universal truths: no man is free in an enslaved land, and no nation is free when half its people are bound. Based on these principles, the Palestinian women's cadres have linked their fate with that of national liberation.

In 1990, the steadfastness of the Palestinian people in their fight for freedom, the feminist movement in the occupied territories has come to the fore in the national struggle. As the intifada took on the occupiers, women of the West Bank and Gaza Strip became more active than ever. They expended their time, energy, and dedication in an invaluable effort to bring about the success of the uprising. As a result of their activism, Palestinian women have suffered heavily at the hands of the Israelis.

Palestinian women did not await any directives to join the intifada. On the contrary, many women acted on their own initiative and assumed positions of leadership. Among the activities in which women have been involved are street demonstrations, setting up barricades, and working with committees on emergency health care and education. In addition, women have played an active role in the local popular committees and have contributed to national decision making through neighborhood and regional groupings.

While women's participation in the uprising evoked much admiration and public respect, no fundamental social change has taken place in Palestinian society. Women's social position has indeed remained unchanged despite their participation in the national struggle. At this juncture one must question why no change has taken place and what role the Palestinian feminist movement has played to further the advancement of women's rights. The feminist movement has as its primary goals to change women's traditional roles and to work toward gaining social and political equality for women. One might argue that the feminist movement cannot attain civil and political rights for women in the occupied territories given the situation on the ground and the absence of a national government and a constitution. However, the Palestinian government that was declared on November 15, 1988, must have a blueprint. The question is, What has the Palestinian feminist movement done to insure equal rights for women in a future government?

Even if one puts this question aside, there is still the question of what has been done on the ground to improve the lot of Palestinian women and to address the problems that they face as women. How many training centers have been set up to allow women to break out of traditional occupations and enter fields traditionally reserved for men? How many debates have taken place to discuss women's rights in the workplace and possible methods that could be used in organizing women? How many feminist publications are there that deal with women's issues and tackle problems from that vantage point? The fact that the answer to all these questions is "very little" leads one once again to ask why.

The only honest answer is that we do not have a feminist movement. What is meant by "feminist movement" here is one that defends women's civil, political, and social rights. The Palestinian women's movement is a national one. The women involved in it are motivated primarily by national interest. The philanthropic societies, for example, are concerned with specific issues such as child care, rehabilitating the handicapped, taking care of orphans, and training women in traditional skills. These societies have avoided dealing with the fundamental problems of women.

The development of women's cadres in 1978 was a clear departure from the traditional type of women's organization. By stating their program clearly and expressing their views on issues concerning women, the new cadres were able to attract a wide cross section of women. This was the beginning of a genuinely popular, democratic, feminist movement that worked in accordance with feminist principles. Unfortunately, however, the cadres became mere ornaments for different political groups, and political considerations began to take precedence over feminist concerns. Thus, while coordination between the cadres has improved and the uprising has offered fertile ground for launching feminist work, many obstacles remain. For example, the establishment of a Unified Feminist Council is, in and of itself, a step in the right direction. However, this council has proved to be ineffective and has not fulfilled its intended purpose. There are still many women who have not been integrated into the movement.

The reason for this is simple. Politics continues to dominate feminist work. It can be said that Palestinian women are prisoners of a concept of "women and the intifada." The emphasis on women's involvement in the national struggle has come about at the expense of all their other work. While it is undeniable that women's participation in the national struggle is invaluable, it remains incomplete if concerns specific to women are not taken into account. The uprising brought to the surface many social issues relating to women. These issues must be addressed with the same enthusiasm as national issues if we are to be a truly feminist movement. While there are some cadres that have initiated serious and honest debates on their internal problems—and this is a necessary step for overcoming the present stagnation—if these debates are not accompanied by concrete changes, they will have little if any effect on the women's movement.

It may be that the above criticism is excessively harsh. However, the time has come to be honest with ourselves and to face the truth so that we can carry out our duties to our nation and to our sex.

PART TWO

How Culture
Recorded
Women's Role

·5·

ILHAM ABU GHAZALEH

Gender in the Poetry of the Intifada

Although Palestinian women have participated in the national resistance movement for a long time, the intifada provided them with an opportunity to assert themselves through their work. Their contributions have been the subject of research by academics and by women's centers. Women's centers have focused on collecting field data and conducting interviews, some of which have been published. Many academic books published on the intifada contain at least one chapter on the role of Palestinian women. International magazines and magazines on the Middle East have all run articles describing the resilience and ingenuity of women.[1] In the Arab world and in the Arab press, Palestinian women are recognized as heroines. Their ingenuity in developing survival methods under occupation constitutes an integral part of the daily news in the Arab world.

Women's activities may be divided into two categories. The first reflects an extension of women's traditional role at home and includes such activities as establishing kindergartens, sewing centers, literacy programs, clinics for mother and child care, canning cooperatives, and in taking care of the wounded at home when they cannot be sent to hospitals following demonstrations, rallies, sit-ins, etc. The second category includes less traditional activities: participating in acts of resistance and throwing stones at the occupying forces. But the most important activity is participation in popular committees. These committees oversee all aspects of life under the intifada. These committees guard the neighborhood at night against attacks by settlers, offer food and medical relief, run a clandestine educational system, operate bakeries, plant vegetable gardens, and provide first aid and transportation to hospitals in times of curfew. Over 50 percent of the committee workers are women. In a segregated culture in which male and female roles are strictly defined, this type of participation by women constitutes a major break with traditional norms. These changes are evident in women's body movements and in the way in which they now dress: women walk more briskly and with greater purpose. More women wear pants and fewer wear tight-fitting skirts. Few women wear make-up. The attitude of women is no longer submissive. Even the topics of conversation have changed, and more women are discussing long-term plans for the community and the survival of the family.

It is to be expected that these transformations in the role of women would find their way into society, including literature. Examining poetry is one way to test the validity of this premise. In this chapter I will examine the way in which our poets, many of whom are male, have recorded these events in the lives of women. In Arab culture poets take on the role of social critics, and poetry reflects the collective unconscious of the group. In addition, in both Arab tradition and in the intifada, poetry has served as a form of recorded history. It is to be expected that this history would include the contributions of women to the intifada. In this context, the responsibility of the poet is not only to register the actions of his or her people but also to take on a historic role.

There are two reasons for the importance of research in this area. During the intifada, there were more females than males residing in the occupied territories, and this was reflected in their participation.[2] Second, research has shown that the mental images of a certain culture shape the expectations of that culture.[3] The perceptions of the role of women will surely decide gender relations and the rights of women in an independent Palestinian state. Thus, the way women are portrayed in literature and in anecdotes will lead either to positions of leadership and to involvement in decision making, or as has been the case in history, back to point zero, where the gains of the women's movement will be lost.

My analysis of the poetry of the intifada is based on the dialectical relationship between action and cognition or "praxis."[4] I would acknowledge at the outset that finding in these poems familiar images of women as weak, emotional, burdened with housework, etc., is inevitable. All these images are rooted in tradition and in the economic systems of the Arab world.[5] It will not be easy to break away from either. Furthermore, these images also occur in traditional Arabic poetry, and breaking away from literary norms or poetic canons will require some time. In this analysis, I have considered both old and new images of women. I have sought images that reflect the greater participation of women, their newly found freedom, and their perception of themselves as active partners. Since the term "intifada" means the shaking off of all forms of oppression, my working hypothesis was that poets who were fully aware of women's emergence during the intifada would also shake off the old images of women and let in the new.

I have undertaken an analysis of most of the poems written since the beginning of the intifada that deal with the popular uprising. The poems are not for women or about them, yet the presence of women in every poem is a clear reflection of women's contribution. Male poets must be commended for reflecting women's participation in this form. This study is based on seven books of poetry *(dawawin shiria)* by seven poets[6] and one hundred and ten poems taken from local literary journals.[7] I have not discussed poems printed in daily newspapers, poems written by "amateurs," or poems by Palestinians residing outside the occupied territories. I have concentrated on mainstream poets and some left-wing poets, all of whom have contributed to local journals. Most of the poems studied were written by men, and this reflects the male-female ratio among poets of the intifada. Of the seven books of poetry, only one was written by a woman; only four of the one hundred and ten poems found in literary journals were written by women. In this study I discuss separately the poems written by males and females in order to determine whether gender influences the perception of women's roles and women's rights.

In analyzing the poetry, I have developed a classification system for the images of women, a task that is complicated by the interconnectedness of images of women on the one hand and the feminization of nonhuman entities inherent in the Arabic language on the other.[8] I have chosen to treat both: the images that clearly describe women, and the images that describe nonhuman entities in female terms—the notion of the land, city, or village, for example, is treated as feminine in Arabic. The basic classification system that emerges indicates that most images of women reflect the same cultural and traditional biases that existed before the intifada.

The Portrayal of Women by Male Poets of the Intifada

With only some minor differences, Palestinian women are still seen as they were prior to the intifada. The poets of the intifada, who are also the intellectuals of the culture, continue to perceive women in terms of reactionary ideologies and pre-intifada ideas. In spite of their leading role in the streets, women are perceived as entities whose primary role is to give birth. The following images of women are listed in the order of their predominance in the poems. The image I here call "woman as a biological entity" constitutes by far the dominant image.

Women as Biological Entities

By portraying women strictly according to their biological and reproductive functions, poets unconsciously silence women. Women's mental and intellectual productivity are diminished to the same degree that their reproductive capacity or their physical characteristics are recognized. Women's participation in the political sphere is also denied. One must ask who would indeed benefit if women were to conform to these images of themselves. The answer would point to the interconnectedness between certain patriarchal norms, reflected in traditional attitudes toward women, and the mechanisms of occupation. Both systems have a vested interest in keeping women in the private sphere. I have found it useful to divide the works that emphasize woman as a biological entity into two groups: one that stresses biological images and one that stresses sociobiological images.

The Biological Functions of Women

The biological role that characterizes women—pregnancy and birth —is the basis of a great number of images. In the work of the poets studied we read: "The women in the heart of Arabism, in the beloved Palestine, today give birth to stones" (Abdul-latif Barghouti), and "to the one who arose in her ninth month, and never sat, to her mutinous delivery . . ." (Yusif Shhadeh).[9]

Both Barghouti and Shhadeh employ pregnancy and delivery as metaphors for the birth of the struggle. Pregnant women become metaphors for the country. However, Shhadeh breaks with poets such as Barghouti in that he gives women a greater degree of control over delivery; this is reflected in his giving the woman greater command of her body as "the one who arose" and in her upright position during delivery. A sense of power arises from the description of her delivery as "mutinous."

In addition to the theme of childbirth, miscarriage constitutes a dominant subject; it is used by many poets as a symbol of the suffering inflicted on the population as a whole. The percentage of miscarriages rose during the intifada as a result of stress and soldiers' attacks on women. In this respect the images in the poetry are representative of women's reality. Yet not one of these poems presents the women's reactions to the assailants. Women are viewed as silent victims—and that hardly reflects the reality of women's participation in the intifada. An equally important image is the portrayal of the homeland as a woman's pelvis "that must be defended, in order for labor to occur."[10] In all of the preceding instances, woman is seen in terms of her biological reproductive function and not in terms of her intellectual and physical activity in running the intifada.

The image of the pregnant woman or the mother is highly revered in Arabic poetry and culture. But the pedestal on which male poets place women deprives women of an active voice and a proud existence in which they can be something other than a symbolic object.[11] There are no images that represent women working on an equal footing with men to achieve a better future. Furthermore, some poets go even further and recall the fossilized images of pre-Islamic poems, choosing images that are far from optimistic even though pre-Islamic poetry is replete with images of active, progressive women. Muhammad Shraim writes: "They [the occupiers] launched a war of infanticide"[12] (the reference here is to a practice that preceded Islam and according to which female infants were buried alive).

Along with motherhood, chastity and virginity constitute further male preoccupations in these poems. While no verse refers to women as fighters or as builders of the future state, many verses address women as chaste virgins. Muhammad Shraim writes: "The singing of the birds, the secrets of the virgins belong to me." Issa Housain Rumi writes: "Oh virgin, don't go away. . . ." And Atshan Zaqtan notes "the reward of virtuous years."[13]

The importance of chastity or virginity is also reflected in the title of a poem by Issa Housain Rumi, "The Virgin."[14] Here the author uses the definite article, "al," which in Arabic refers to the absolute. Moreover, the title does not reflect the subject of the poem, which is about stone throwers. The poet might have considered giving the poem the title "The Stone Throwers [feminine form]." But by placing the emphasis on sexual chastity, the author emphasizes the traditional cornerstone that holds back the participation and development of women in Arab culture. Fear of the loss of a daughter's chastity has often prevented women from receiving an education in a coeducational system or from joining the work force. It behooves these poets to find new ways to address women that will reflect the roles women have taken on for themselves.

The Sociobiological Characterization of Women

The birth of children, miscarriage, and the presence of the hymen are biologically determining features for women.[15] But there are other aspects of women's nature which, though biological in nature, can be classified as associated features.[16] These features are culturally determined, but they have been treated by many poets as determining features of woman. One such feature is women's long, flowing hair. (I will not discuss here the socioeconomic and traditional factors that make this feature so important.) Many poets address women through this biological feature as if it were a determining feature and not a variable characteristic that is culturally conditioned and changes according to time and place. Among these poets, Sami Al-Kilani describes the village as a woman: "Her scattered hair . . . if on the asphalt rolled a braid and then another braid." In Yousuf Hamed we find: "The horizon is in her hair." Ribhi Abdul-Quader Ibrahim writes: "I saw my country as long braided hair . . . I see the long, braided hair of Khitam."[17]

Whereas the poet might have focused on his beloved's participation in the intifada, what he sees instead is her long flowing hair. This image has its source in poetry that goes back to the pre-Islamic and early Islamic periods and does not reflect any transformations in the role of women.

There is another feature that is associated with the biological and is therefore secondary. But by virtue of its social importance, it is treated as a determining feature for women. This is the waist of a woman, which must be slim. Other features admired by poets cited below include the eyelashes, the face, and the voice of women. Sami Al-Kilani writes: "Tighten the waist embroidered in silk," and Ribhi Abdul-Quader Ibrahim admires "the slim waist of Khitam." As'ad Al-As'ad writes: "Make room for me between your eyelashes," while Yousuf Hamed admires "her face, her voice," and Sami Al-Kilani describes her as "pretty and beautiful."[18]

The glorification of women's features is based on a long tradition of the segregation of the sexes in which the very sight of these features becomes an occasion for a poem. But during the intifada women worked side by side with men, and it would seem likely that these old images would make room for a more egalitarian relationship. Instead, many poets describe the women who participated in the intifada as brides— with all the symbolism of male domination that this image reflects— when they could have described them as heroines and full participants in the struggle to loosen the grip of occupation.

In a poem called "Her Wedding," Sami Al-Kilani addresses the woman freedom fighter as a bride—"to the bride whose dowry"[19]— while Al-Mutawakkel Taha entitles his poem about Sana Mheidli, the martyred Lebanese freedom fighter, "The Dancing of the Bride: A Poem to Sana Mheidli."[20]

Women as Static Entities

Part of the indoctrination of young Palestinian girls involves the idea that women should be static recipients rather than active participants in society. This indoctrination represents an extension of an economic system that is not set up to incorporate the female half of the population. Perhaps the most difficult task facing women in the intifada was to break away from this learning process and reject this form of indoctrination in order to become activated by the events around them. But the poetry of the intifada supports the system of indoctrination rather than women's rejection of it.

Women and Passivity

Most of the poems studied portray women in static, noneffective situations. In the following verses, none of the verbs that are used portray women in an active and participatory role. The descriptions all suggest the passiveness of women, which was traditionally considered a virtue. The use of verbs indicates that poets still perceive women as passive entities. Sami Al-Kilani writes: "She went on gazing at the prayer rug . . . she thanked the almighty . . . she felt with her hand." Yousuf Hamed writes: "She awaits the knight . . . he takes her . . . the sea passed her by . . . she awakened in delirium, crying like a child worn out by massacres . . . defeated by time . . . gazing." And Majed Abu-Ghosh writes: "The mothers take care of me." Harkash writes: "She slept long years . . . lonely, sad, patient, silent, thinking, she has secrets . . . crying . . . surrounded by wolves."[21]

In the preceding passages women are seen in a state of general passivity that reflects a certain acceptance of their predicament and that of society as a whole. Instead of watching the soldiers' movements, an activity that even older women engaged in during the intifada, Al-Kilani sees the woman in a static condition, gazing at a prayer rug; rather than portray women as informing youths about the movements of the soldiers, the poet depicts women's voices and relationships in very private and abstract terms: in the relationship to God, or—instead of supplying stones to the youths or throwing themselves at the soldiers—as merely feeling with their hands. The same can be said about Yousuf Hamed, who sees women waiting rather than initiating action as they did during the intifada. While these images might have reflected reality before the intifada, they do not reflect women's daily battle for survival during the intifada.

Women as Recipients of Action

In contrast to the reality of women hurling stones at soldiers, women are portrayed in the poetry of the intifada as the static recipients of action. In the poetry, women never initiate action but are often the recipients of actions by others, usually males. Yousuf Hamed writes:

"Lamis [a female name], is in the palm of my hand . . . I will deliver her [to her destination]"; elsewhere he writes: "I will let Laila in through the window . . . [I will show her that] . . . Laila is still within me." And Sami Al-Kilani writes: "He bid farewell to the beaming face."[22]

The question that must be asked is to what extent does the portrayal of women as recipients of male actions also mask denial of women's contributions. It is possible to see in these images an unconscious desire to deny women credit for their work. In this context, the glorification of passive women could also mask certain male fears that these women might some day demand total equality.

Women as Emotionally Tortured Entities

The Palestinian intifada is credited with creating in the community a sense of euphoria rooted in efforts to build a future democratic state. In the early stages, there was a feeling that this goal would be achieved sooner than turned out to be possible. Women felt very much part of this process. Yet the intifada poets continued to portray women as sad, tortured creatures in need of comfort. Yusuf Idris writes: "She cries like a child . . . the night sleeps but she does not sleep . . . immersed in nothingness." Ribhi Abdul-Quader Ibrahim writes: "Tears on her cheeks, she is afraid. . . ." And an anonymous author writes "about Jerusalem, the woman, . . . shy . . . her eyes away . . . her eyelids [as if] melting . . . crying complaining."[23]

According to Idris and Abdul-Quader, tears are the language of women and children. It is interesting to note that the beginning of the poem about Jerusalem by the anonymous author suggests strength and pride while describing the stone throwers. It is only toward the end, when the poet starts to compare Jerusalem to a woman, that the strong, proud images begin to be replaced by weak and negative images—"shy . . . her eyes looking away . . . her eyelids melting." In the poems below women are portrayed as being in need of comfort, which is provided in many cases by males. Yaser Isa Il-Yasir writes of "women's [urgent] call for help," and Sami Al-Kilani writes: "their wounded heart . . . feeling the pulse of pain . . . the pretty [women] return with the perfume of tears." Yusuf Naser tells women "don't be afraid" (suggesting that they are), and As'ad Al-As'ad writes: "Save your dear tears." Adnan Dmeiri writes: "Oh how worried I am about you [woman]. . . ." Yousuf Hamed writes: "God will inflict pain on those who inflict pain on you."[24] It never occurs to Hamed that women could perhaps inflict pain and are indeed inflicting pain on the soldiers through their daily activity; instead he takes recourse to God's assistance.

In analyzing these images I became aware that they often project a reversal of the cultural images of women with which we have become familiar. In many anecdotes of the intifada women are portrayed as strong, dominant entities capable of extracting children from the clutches of the occupation by shoving the soldiers aside.[25] The weak woman described above exists in diametrical opposition to the woman that emerged in the Palestinian intifada. Poets seek to portray the weak, fearful side of women while bringing out the fearlessness of men.

Women and Housework

According to the male poets of the intifada, housework is the only area in which women excel. While it is true that in the poetry of the intifada housework receives some degree of recognition because it is now associated with a contribution to the "National Labor" *(al amal al Watani)*, this recognition is something of a mixed blessing for women—while women's chores are given some importance, poets see no other role for women. Sami Al-Kilani writes: "Take care of the unborn child, oh mother," and "women knead the dough." Adnan Dmeiri writes: "Sumud hung her clothes," and As'ad Al-As'ad writes: "Wave to me with your scarf, I am coming."[26]

Elsewhere poets praise women for cheering to them, especially for their ululating when men go to battle.[27] These male poets praise the supportive or "cheerleading" role of women when they could be emphasizing their independent role. Furthermore, all of the preceding verses reinforce the role of women as nurturers and mothers; they do not describe their newfound sense of themselves as activists and liberated women.

Two poets provide what might have been a departure from casting women in a passive role by including women in street action. Unfortunately, the opportunity is not totally realized. While street action first includes men and women, it is soon limited to men only. Harkash writes: "They [young men and women] of the neighborhood came, this one [masculine form] with burning tires, the other [masculine form] with slingshots and stones."[28] Had Harkash continued to include women in the action of barricading the streets and burning tires, his portrayal would have reflected the true role of women and it might have initiated a new vision in the poetry of the intifada.

A similar abortive effort occurs in the poetry of Sami Al-Kilani, where the participation of Zoya (the poet's daughter) in resistance is expressed through her songs. However, according to the poem, she sings in the Ukrainian language and not in Arabic, the language of her culture. Al-

Kilani is unable to conceive of his daughter's resistance from within the confines of her culture; he must therefore transform her songs into the language of another culture. Only then can Al-Kilani accept her resistance.

Women and the Act of Speaking

The male poets of the intifada seem to think that the greatest action that women can perform is to speak.[29] Verbs that denote the act of speaking are the verbs most often used for women—she said, she says, she told, she asks, she called, she ululates. These verbs denote either the woman speaking for herself (direct speech), or the poet speaking for her (indirect speech). In both cases the poet portrays woman as speaking about things she already knows; no new experiences are recounted, in spite of the ardent transformations taking place in woman's role through the intifada. Sami Al-Kilani's work is full of references to women's past and present knowledge, but as might be expected, this knowledge is static and not an ongoing learning experience: "She said, I knew the steps, . . . I knew. She shouts preventing me. . . ."[30]

In Kayed Abu Hashish's work, the woman stands as a witness and gives testimony: "Even the old woman said . . . saw . . . testified . . . she said they [feminine form] heard . . . my mother said," etc.[31] Each one of these acts of saying is embedded in the other in an intricate web that gives the impression that, for women, the general act of speaking takes the place of action.

Speech attributed to women also appears in the form of inquiry, denunciation (of the occupation), or asking for help. Abdul-Ghani Mizher attributes the following question to his female: "She asked: 'Why were you late all these years?'"[32] Men act while women inquire about the actions of others. Such is the view of male poets, even when they write about a woman who was killed while resisting Israeli soldiers. Yousuf Hamed chooses to describe the death of Ghalia Farhat, killed by Israeli soldiers in Lebanon, by praising her last words denouncing occupation: "To the ululation uttered by the martyred Ghalia Farhat."[33] And the female voice often seeks help from the male, as in this line from an anonymous poem: "I think she said: 'Help! Antar. . . .'"[34]

Furthermore, women are told of the events taking place in the streets, and they are often informed how to interpret events. The tone indicates that women are thought incapable of making such judgments. Samih Faraj writes: "That day rubber was good, oh Khadiga [female name], and today's bullets are glory, oh Amina."[35]

The examples given above are only a small sample of the speech

Gender in the Poetry of the Intifada

attributed to women and addressed to them. However, this area deserves more research, for it constitutes one of the most pronounced qualities attributed to the female persona in these poems.

Women and Gender Relations

In the reorganization of the world according to male perceptions, the poetry of the intifada reflects a certain relationship between men and women that merits further investigation. The views can be categorized as follows:

The Nullification of Women

I have argued that in spite of women's immense contribution to the intifada, male poets view them as static entities, emotional and passive, and see their most important activity as their speech. When poets describe action, achievement, planning for the future, physical resistance, all of which are male activities, there is no place for women in these descriptions. We can infer that women are nullified in some images of intifada poetry. This nullification is complete in those verses that glorify men and action. Muhammad Hneihen writes: "My country, oh mountains of manhood. . . . Men in these times are my wealth." And Yusif Shhadeh writes: "We won. . . . All victories and glory are for the men."[36]

It would seem that these poets are writing in accordance with poetic traditions in the Arab world that associate men with wars and with victory, and not in response to the present scenes of women defiantly struggling against the army of occupation. Some poets, for example, Husain Barghouti, manifest a greater degree of sensitivity to the present; yet the total picture has changed very little. Barghouti writes: "When streets are flooded with women."[37] Here the nullification of women stems from the verb used; in Arabic the word denotes streets being filled basically with nonhuman or animal forms. It also derives from "streets" being made the subject of the sentence and not women. The alternative would be to describe women as agents of action, to write, for example, "when women take to the streets."[38]

Women as Nonactualized Entities

In the poetry of the intifada women are actualized in an abstract way only. In verses where they are not nullified, women are mentioned as nonconcrete entities. Issa Housain Rumi writes: "I dreamed, my darling, that you descended from heaven, a houri, a bride in white, a virgin." Yusif Shhadeh writes: "I named you [feminine form] many names in discrete whispering."[39] There is a nonspecificity to the woman's persona in Rumi; she is a houri, a bride, a virgin. Here, woman is an abstraction, one that takes its meaning from the poet. Furthermore, the woman is not one of flesh and blood but a dream, part of the imagination of the poet. For Shhadeh as well the woman is named by the poet in a whisper, not in public, and the nonspecificity of women is thus reiterated.

Women as Semiactualized Entities

Male poets seem to be unable to perceive a woman as existing on her own. They always see her as dependent on a man for all her needs. Such dependence must be distinguished from the mutual support that constitutes positive relations. Here, support is given in the form of guardianship, subordination, which presupposes a hierarchy in human relations; as such it must be deemed negative. In the poems under consideration, the woman is treated as a semiactualized entity in need of guardianship. Al-Mutawakkel Taha writes: "Oh Handala [male name], who will care for Fatima [female name] after you depart?" Ribhi Abdul-Quader Ibrahim writes: "How will she survive if I die?" And Jamil Mikhel writes: "A widow is walking behind me."[40] In this verse, "widow" is used as a term of dependency; there are few poems that portray the male in a state of dependency on the female. In these cases the man is ridiculed and made fun of, as in the following verse by Harkash: "Your husband, oh sister, the name of God be on him."[41] Defining the male through the female, "your husband" is reason enough to make fun of his manhood.

Women through Blood Relations

When women attain full recognition and respect from male poets, it is only as a result of blood ties to men. When women's achievements are celebrated, women are referred to as sister, mother, or daughter. They thus become part of the male world and system of blood relations in which the position of the mother is the most highly revered. Al-Mutawakkel Taha speaks of "the sister of my soul," and Samih Faraj writes: "Sister wrap . . . and spray him. . . ."[42]

As part of the extended family system, women are an appendage to men. In the verse cited above, Taha describes women prisoners, who are very highly regarded in the culture. His esteem is expressed by linking women with the male persona through the term "sister." Faraj is referring to female activists, also recognized in the culture. Esteem is translated here into a physical association with the male, also based on blood ties. All these descriptions reflect the ideological position of the male, who dominates the culture through patriarchy.

Women and Sadistic/Masochistic Relationships

Many male poets see their relations with women in terms of a masochistic/sadistic relationship in which woman is the torturer. Arabic literature is replete with images of women who torture their lovers by their absence. Here we see images of women whom the poets love and admire for their long history as sufferers. Why is it that these poets are not able to portray love as a relationship of equals, in which both men and women are quite happy?[43] Yousuf Hamed writes: "I love a woman whom sleep has forsaken, while I sleep through the nights. . . ." Al-Mutawakkel Taha writes: "We curse women in the morning while we walk on their bosoms. . . ." Il-Hayja writes: "The lady of pain engraved in the depth, the way to her is the violin of my bleeding . . . your love surrounds my neck like a rope . . . stabbed in the depth with the sword of desire." Ribhi Abdul-Quader Ibrahim writes: "All that remains are my tears and my wounds." While Yousuf Hamed writes: "How could love come to a mad person . . . all that he desires became unlawful."[44]

These verses indicate that the male poets are dissatisfied with the segregation dictated by tradition. Hamed sums up this view by saying that madness is the result of the restrictions when all that is desired is unlawful.

Women and Uneven Relationships

Rarely do we find a relationship of equality between men and women in the poetry of the Palestinian male poets. A woman is often perceived either as a superior entity and placed on a pedestal—where she quickly becomes a metaphor for the country, the symbol of giving and selflessness—or she is considered subordinate to the male. In the following verse Ali Al-Khalili elevates the woman by giving her the position reserved for men; he writes, "My lady, my female master."[45] But there are numerous instances when the poet places himself in a position of authority over women, assuming the role of guardian or father, as in the following verse by Husain Barghouti: "I am the Sheikh, . . . my daughter.[46] The same kind of authoritarian relationship is also expressed through the use of the imperative form of the verb with women (see below).

Ilham Abu Ghazaleh

Women as Targets of the Imperative Verb

The imperative verb is used to issue orders or requests. Orders indicate a hierarchial relationship in which the person receiving the orders is lower in the hierarchy. The poetry of the intifada is replete with examples in which the imperative is used in addressing women, with all the hierarchical structure this implies in terms of male-female relations. Very rarely is the imperative verb used by poets in addressing other men. Samih Faraj writes: "Sister, here we come. . . . Wrap . . . sprinkle . . . shake. . . ." Yusuf Naser gives the following order to a woman: "Don't be afraid . . . stay by my tomb. . . ." Yousuf Hamed writes: "Do not be afraid." Sami Al-Kilani writes: "My little girl: follow . . . tighten the waist . . . get up . . . baptize me . . . bestow on me . . . absorb my spirit." Husain Barghouti orders the woman to "brighten up . . . open. . . ." Hamed orders a woman to "come back," and As'ad Al-As'ad writes: "Leave . . . ask . . . keep."[47]

The patriarchal hierarchy is clearly manifested in the use of the verb form. By using the imperative the poets have placed women in an inferior position. It should also be noted that the kinds of action required of women are an extension of their traditional role.

Positive Attitudes toward Women

There are some positive images of women in the male poetry of the intifada. However, in quantitative terms the preceding categories far exceed this one. What constitutes a positive image? Obviously it must be a new image that reflects the new roles that women have taken on. It must also be an image that recognizes cultural oppression and seeks to eradicate it. It must be an image that supports women's struggle to assert themselves. Empathy with women is a good start. Finally, this image must be one of a woman of flesh and blood, an image that reflects women's current desires and aspirations. The following verses come closer to describing this new female persona. Yusif Shhadeh writes: "She is the sun, the shores, honey and olive trees"; while it is fairly common to see a woman equated with all these qualities, it is the next line that sets Shhadeh's work apart. This is because he condemns in it all "those who resort to [writing about] the long eyelashes and the lean body." Wasim Al-Kurdi writes: "We fill the heart of life and the heart of women with fresh pure air."[48] Al-Kurdi recognizes the double circle of oppression exercised against women when he recognizes the need to allow women to breathe freely fresh and pure air. Here he makes reference to the oppressive conditions that women endure under occupation and also under a patriarchal system set up to make life easier for men.

Furthermore, he calls for transformations that will make women breathe more freely, equating their freedom with the freedom of life itself, "the heart." He makes himself—the male—responsible for making this happen, thus acknowledging the role of the dominant male in such female transformations.

Taha writes: "Shall I ask your soul how the mountains erupted in it?"[49] In Arabic poetry the image of the mountain symbolizes pride and strength, and Taha deserves mention for recognizing these as female qualities.

Husain Barghouti addresses a female, saying, "Light your Babylonian window with the old candle, engraved with old designs."[50] Barghouti uses Babylonian civilization, an image of a rich culture, to describe the contributions of women. Babylonian culture is known to have given the world one of the first alphabets; the laws of Hammurabi; and the Hanging Gardens, one of the Seven Wonders of the World. The poet is here asking women to step out of the darkness and to light up these qualities, making them visible to the rest. It is a positive image that reflects his deep concern for the periods in which women were dormant in Arab culture and an acknowledgment of their rich past history.

Most of the verses in this category describe women through images and symbolism. Yet these are positive images that encourage women's development. What we have not seen yet is a woman who really reflects the desires and aspirations of the woman in the street.

The Portrayal of Women in the Work of Female Poets

Far fewer women than men were writing poetry during the intifada. While there have been many female poets, poetry has traditionally been a male domain in Arab culture. During the intifada in particular women's activities focused on the basic need for survival in committee work and in the more traditional women's institutions. Their work made the intifada possible. It is therefore disappointing that women poets do not show a marked difference from men in their perception of themselves. The image of women in poetry written by women can be classified roughly in the same categories as those defined above. It is possible to conclude that these women poets still perceive themselves through the eyes of the male other.

The poems mentioned below were written by women. Yet in spite of the gains made by women during the intifada, the female voice in these poems reflects the same sense of alienation and dependency that characterizes male poetry about them. It is possible that women activists are not the ones writing poetry, yet it is also possible that women have not begun to free themselves from the poetic standards set before the intifada.

The Annulment of Women in Women's Poetry

The grammar of Arabic exhibits gender inflection of the noun, the adjective, and the verb. This means that a speaker can indicate his or her own gender as well as that of an addressee and a third person. The gender inflection for the male, however, is employed by some as generic. One might expect that women who are trying to assert themselves would be sensitive to the use of the female gender in denoting females. But the women poets discussed often use male gender as generic. I consider this to be a manifestation of self-annulment. Such examples can be found in the following verses: "Loving you, my country, taught me to be strong [masculine form] and enduring [masculine form]" (Najla Shahwan); "My veins bleed Palestinian, Palestinian [masculine form]" (Hanan Awwad; elsewhere she writes: "To the mothers of lovers [masculine form]"). Khadija Abu-Arkoub writes: "I [masculine form] am leaving."[51]

In the verses cited above, female authors address themselves in the masculine voice. It would seem that in order to break the silence in which women were engulfed for so long, they must use the male voice. This also indicates that when women take on an active role, the female poet sees them through the cultural prism of male behavior.

The Annulment of the Personal

Female poets do not treat the problems women face. Instead, they focus on national issues. There are two reasons for the absence of the personal voice. First, the occupation is taking a severe toll on the population as a whole, and women's first priority is to be rid of occupation. However, fewer women now believe that they should postpone their struggle until the national struggle is completed. The second reason has to do with traditional attitudes to women, which dictate that women should deny their own feelings and conform to the perception of them in the culture as selfless, giving entities, demanding little for themselves. Few women live such a selfless life. Palestinian women poets are complying with literary canons created by men when they reflect an outdated perception of women. The following are some examples of such verses: Khadija Abu-Arkoub writes: "My people are under siege."[52] By the same token she is excluding herself from the siege.

And Hanan Awwad, whose book is dedicated to Palestine, writes: "I am the daughter of the struggle, I fight the hurricane for your [mascu-

Gender in the Poetry of the Intifada

line form] sake." Thus, she is only fighting for the sake of the male in her country and not for other women too: "I love you [masculine form], oh Palestinian flag, ... Palestinian man."[53] In Awwad's work, the male she is addressing is equated with the symbol of the country, the flag, leaving women totally out of the picture. Hanan Awwad, the head of PEN in Palestine, is a committed woman and a qualified spokesperson for women in the occupied territories; yet her poetry negates women and speaks only of men.

Alienation

Women's verses reflect a feeling of being lost or unsure of women's proper role in the world around them. This feeling characterized women's poetry before the intifada. But there is a sense in which these poems also reflect the alienation of women who no longer trust the political future; and the present does not provide the security they seek either. What is disturbing, however, is the sense of dependency on the male reflected in the use of the masculine noun. Khadija Abu-Arkoub writes: "Where am I? ... A traveler [masculine form] ... gasping." Fatma Anabusi writes: "The dumbness of time ... the thirst of years ... the revolt of the silent self ... I went on suffering the day you left."[54] These images reflect the situation of women at the crossroads. For economic reasons, the traditional roles of women as mothers and wives must give way to a future that seems unsure. These verses question both the political future of the country and the future economic role of women in it.

Women as Dependent Entities

Writing poetry is a process of self-assertion. Yet little of this self-assertion is translated into women's poetry. In the following verses women create an image of the male other as teacher, moral guide, and overall authority over women. This relationship is patriarchal; the male other is the father figure on whom women depend. Equal partnership does not constitute part of this scenario. Fatma Anabusi writes: "I learned from you [masculine form] the way to struggle." Hanan Awwad writes: "I came to this world under your [masculine form] shadow" (implied is a relationship of dependency on the male); elsewhere she writes: "I see my road in your eyes. ... Oh my supporter."[55]

Women's Pain and Sadness in Other Literary Canons

Arabic poetry was influenced by the European Romantic tradition, which is replete with images of women who are emotionally tortured, sad, pensive, and depressed. Women who view themselves in these terms reflect the absence of control over their own lives. Khadija Abu-Arkoub writes: "I yearn . . . with sadness." Fatma Anabusi writes: "Did they understand the pain in my heart . . . my great pain . . . and the fire that burns my inside . . . ?"[56] Hanan Awwad goes so far as to speak of herself as "a wound." But her pain is not the physical pain inflicted on some fighting women. Rather, it is reminiscent of the victimized woman.

Women's Time

Poets seem to evaluate the way in which time has been spent. Time is always perceived as negative in terms of its devastating effect on youth, a woman's most valuable asset. Hanan Awwad writes: "I might lose some of my youth." Fatma Anabusi writes: "All my coming days are of waiting," and elsewhere she notes: "I started to count what remained of my life."[57]

In these verses women seem to be constantly waiting in a world where death is the reference point of life. Here women are passive participants in the passage of time that constitutes their lives. The passage of time as a source of enrichment is not considered.

Conclusion

Analysis of the body of intifada poetry discussed above reveals very few changes in the images of women. I believe that the poets remained bound by literary canons and images that characterized pre-intifada, noncommitted poetry. It is clear that while women's role has changed markedly in the "outside world," this transformation is not reflected in the poetry of the intifada. The inability of poets to question fossilized images of women and poetic canons has its roots in the inability of the same male poets to consider as individuals a challenge to the patriarchal system, to their authority and autonomy, in the text. The ability of poets to question literary norms is a reflection of their ability to challenge and question the superstructures of the culture, including the patriarchal paradigm and the semitribal institutions that reflect this paradigm. The poetry analyzed here indicates that although the poets are using their poetry as a tool for resisting foreign occupation of their country, they have not yet resisted their own reactionary acculturation toward women.

It is not within the confines of this analysis to investigate the extent to which novels have reflected the changing role of women. Yet it is possible to point out several novels that have focused attention on the double burden of oppression facing women, that is, the novels by Sahar

Khalifeh that deal with precisely this issue. Further research is necessary to investigate the differences between the novelistic tradition and
the poetic tradition under the intifada.

The inability of poets to challenge poetic canons and fossilized images has been linked to their inability to challenge the system of patriarchy. However, this conflict has its roots in the conflicting situation under
occupation. The most patriarchal institution, the extended family system, is the very system that protects the individual and makes the
intifada possible. The family provides security that is generally provided by the state in the form of welfare and unemployment insurance.
For example, family members must rely on relatives for temporary
help. It can only be surmised that a serious challenge to the central
paradigm on which patriarchy rests could presently rend the fabric of
society. Consequently, occupation constitutes a retarding factor in the
overall liberation of women.

Through their work, women forced a reconsideration of such notions
as dowry, arranged marriage, the inherent weakness of women, and so
on. But in order to preserve the badly needed protection of the family
structure, women have generally hesitated to challenge the central notion of patriarchy, which is the power that men have over women and
which is one of the cornerstones of the culture.

There are other related problems that must also be considered in this
light. None of the political groups in the Palestinian national movement have so far clearly outlined their theoretical understanding of the
marginalization of women. No particular group has called for freeing
women from the oppression of traditions. The Palestinian women's
movement has not done enough in this regard.

The solution to all problems related to women's issues must come
about as part of a theoretical framework provided by the national
women's movement. Their program could include discussion of the
effect on progress toward equal rights of portrayals of women in fossilized images. And a timetable must be drawn up for the implementation
of this program to free women from cultural and social constraints.
Women constitute one half of our human resources—no country can
afford to waste such a valuable commodity.

NOTES

1. *Time Magazine* (July 13, 1990) chose a Palestinian woman for the cover of a
special issue on the intifada, while the *Philadelphia Inquirer*, in an article entitled
"Liberated by the Struggle" (May 19, 1990) described many crucial transformations in women's lives in the territories occupied by Israel.

ILHAM ABU GHAZALEH

2. *Statistical Abstract of Israel* 38, 1987, p. 702, gives a percentage of 50.04 for women. The statistics exclude Jerusalem.

3. See Howard Margolis, *Patterns, Thinking, and Cognition: A Theory of Judgement* (Chicago: University of Chicago Press, 1987), p. 110, for an illustrative diagram of the process of transmitting knowledge in society.

4. See Paulo Friere, *Education for a Critical Consciousness* (London: Sheed and Ward, 1985) for a treatment of the concept of "praxis."

5. Many countries in the Arab world are consumer societies and have no industries to speak of. Women are therefore socialized into the role of mothers and housewives because the economic sector cannot absorb them in the work place.

6. The seven Dawawin are:

Al-Kilani, Sami. 1989. *Qabbal Al-Arda wa Starah* (He kissed the land and rested). Jerusalem, Union of Palestinian Writers.

Al-Muhmud, Yusef. 1989. *Zagharid ʿala Bawwabat is-Sabah* (Ululations at dawn). Jerusalem, Union of Palestinian Writers.

Al-Asʿad, Asʿad, et al. 1988. *Maqaliʿ* (Slingshots). Jerusalem, Union of Palestinian Writers.

Awwad, Hanan. 1988. *Ikhtartu al-khatar* (I chose danger). Jerusalem. Union of Palestinian Writers.

Harkash, Sidi. 1988. *Hulm is-Sabi.* Jerusalem.

Taha, Al-Mutawakkel. 1988. *Zaman al-suʿud* (Time of ascending). Jerusalem, Union of Palestinian Women Writers.

7. *Al-Kateb,* vols. 92–102 (40 poems); *Al-Fajr Al-Adabi,* vols. 89–92 (10 poems); *Ibdaʿat Il-Hajar,* vols. 1–2 (39 poems); *Al-Bayader Al-Adabi,* vol. 11/1–4 (21 poems).

8. See M. Sawʿaie, "Discourse Reference and Pronominalization in Arabic," Ph.D. diss., Ohio State University 1980, for a comprehensive treatment of the issue.

9. Abdul-latif Barghouti, "Sarat in-niswatu fi qulb il-ʿuruba, fi filistina al-habiba, talidu al-yawma hijara" (*Ibdaʿat* 1:29); Yusif Shhadeh, "li allati qamat wa lam taqʿud fi shahriha al-tasiʿ, li makhadiha l-mushagheb" (*Al-Kateb* 126:80).

10. "Wa thalika min ʾajli ʾan yajiʾa at-talq" (Anonymous, *Ibdaʿat* 1:88).

11. Placing women on a pedestal is a universal practice. See Dale Spender, "Constructing Women's Silence," in *Man Made Language* (New York: Routledge and Kegan Paul, 1980) pp. 52–75.

12. "Hatta tatayyara haʾulaʾ . . . watajashamu harban li ʾajli walidatin" (*Ibdaʿat* 2:88).

13. Majed Abu-Ghosh, "li zaqzaqat ul-ʿasafir . . . asrar ul-ʿathara" (*Al-Kateb* 99:88). Issa Housain Rumi, "ʿathraʾu la tarhali" (*Al-Fajr Al-Adabi* 89/90:66). Atshan Zaqtan, "Thawabu as-sinin al-ʿafifa" (*Al-Bayader Al-Adabi* 2:24).

14. "Al-ʿadhraʾ" (Issa Housain Rumi, *Al-Fajr Al-Adabi* 89/90:66).

15. Robert de Beaugrande and Wolfgang Dressler, *Introduction to Text Linguistics* (New York: Longman, 1990), p. 97.

16. George Dillon, *Introduction to Contemporary Linguistic Semantics* (Englewood Cliffs, NJ: Prentice Hall, 1977), p. 14.

Gender in the Poetry of the Intifada

17. "Sha'ruha al-mantur . . . 'in tadahrajat 'ala l-'isfalti jadilatun tumma jadilatun" (Sami Al-Kilani, Diwan 32). "Al-mada sha'ruha" (Yousuf Hamed, Diwan 47). "Ra'aytu biladi dafirata sha'rin tawila . . . 'atalammahu sha'ra Khitam at-tawil" (Ribhi Abdul-Quader Ibrahim, Al-Kateb 95:91).

18. "Shiddi l-khasra al-mutarraza bi l-harir" (Sami Al-Kilani, Diwan 44). "Khasra Khitam an-nahil" (Ribhi Abdul-Quader Ibrahim, Al-Kateb 95:91). "'utruki li matrahan bayna rimshi l-'ayn" (As'ad Al-As'ad, Al-Kateb 92:67). "Wajhuha . . . sawtuha" (Yousuf Hamed, Diwan 47). "Jamila . . . maliha" (Sami Al-Kilani, Diwan 44).

19. "'ursuha . . . li l-'arus l-lati mahruha" (Sami Al-Kilani, Diwan 13).

20. "Jalwat l-'arus: zajaliyya'ila Sana' mhidli" (Al-Mutawakkel Taha, Diwan 113).

21. "Shakhasat 'ala sijjadatin . . . hamadat l-'aliyya al-qadir." "tahassasat bi kaffiha" (Sami Al-Kilani, Diwan 18). "tantaziru l-faris . . . ya' khudhuha . . . fataha l-bahru," "kanat tuwqazu fi l-ghaflati, tabki kat. tiflati, hattaha l-thabhu,'aslamat li zamanin . . . tuhaddiqu" (Yousuf Hamed, Diwan 67). "tasharu 'ala rahati al-'ummahatu" (Majed Abu-Ghosh, Al-Kateb 107:88). "Namat . . . snin itwilih, wahidi, hazini, sabra, samta, tufakkir, ladayha 'asrar, tabki, muhata bi th-thi'ab" (Sidi Harkash, Diwan 52).

22. "Lamisun 'ala kaffi . . . sa' wsiluha . . . Sa'udkhilu Laila min an-nafitha . . . sa'uriha 'an Laila lam tazal fihi" (Yousuf Hamed, Diwan 49). "Wadda'a l-wajha l-muda'a" (Sami Al-Kilani, Diwan 18).

23. "Tabki katiflatin hattaha l-thabhu . . . yanamu l-laylu wa la tanam . . . tughilu fi faraghin" (Yousuf Hamed, Diwan 19). "'ala wajnatayha dumu'un . . . Kha'ifatun" (Ribhi Abdul-Quader Ibrahim, Al-Kateb 97:91). "maksufa . . . 'uyunuha zaghat . . . jufunuha thabat . . . tabki . . . tashku" (Anonymous, Ibda'at 1:17).

24. "'istighatatu l-nisa'i" (Yaser Isa Il-Yasir, Ibda'at 2:22). "fu'aduha l-jarihu . . . tuhissu nabda al-'alami," "ta'udu l-hisanu bi 'itri d-dumu'i" (Sami Al-Kilani, Diwan 20). "la tajza'i" (Yusuf Naser, Ibda'at 2:94). "'iddakhiri min 'azizi dam'iki" (As'ad Al-As'ad, Al-Kateb 92:67). "awwahu, awwahu, awwah . . . lahafi 'alayk" (Adnan Dmeiri, Al-Kateb 99:85). "'allahu sayubki man 'abkaki" (Yousuf Hamed, Al-Kateb 99:89).

25. See Sharif Kanaana's discussion in this volume.

26. "'uhrusi l-janina ya'ummuhu," "ta' jinuhu l-nisa'u" (Sami Al-Kilani, Diwan 28, 25). "wa nasharat Sumudu tiyabaha" (Adnan Dmeiri, Al-Kateb 99:85). "lawwihi bi mindiliki . . . 'atin 'ana" (As'ad Al-As'ad, Al-Kateb 92:67).

27. See Sami Al-Kilani, Diwan 36; Yusef Al-Muhmud, Diwan 42; Yousuf Hamed, Diwan 6, 16; Asad Arabi, Ibda'at 2:134; Azmi Najjar, Ibda'at 2:148; Abdel Naser Saleh, Al-Kateb 102:91; Al-Mutawakkel Taha, Al-Kateb 106:85.

28. "Ja'at sibyan il-hara, hadta bi'jal u sharara, wu thaka bimiqla' u hjara" (Sidi Harkash, Diwan 12).

29. The perception of women as "chatterboxes" is universal. See Cate Poynton, Language and Gender: Making the Difference (Oxford: Oxford University Press, 1989), p. 66.

30. "qalat . . . 'ariftu l khatwa . . . 'ariftu . . ." (Sami Al-Kilani, Diwan 19).

31. "taqul: hatta'ajayiz 'ahl ir-ridda qalin . . . shafin . . . shihdin . . . shafin . . .

ILHAM ABU GHAZALEH

hilfin 'inhin shafin . . . qalat . . . qalat . . . qalin 'inhin sim'in . . . qalat 'ummi" (Kayed Abu Hashish, *Al-Kateb* 102:93).

32. "sa'alat: limatha ta'akhkharta hathi s-sinin" (Abdul-Ghani Mizher, *Ibda'at* 86).

33. "'ila hutaf ish-shahida Ghalya Farhat" (Yousuf Hamed, Diwan 30; see also pp. 6, 16, 22, 33, 42, 43, 44, 65, 81, 89, 93).

34. "'azunnuha qalat: ya 'antara l-absiyy" (Anonymous, *Ibda'at* 1:17).

35. "mattatu thaka l-yawmu khayrun ya Khadija, wa rasasu hatha l-yawmu majdun ya Aminah" (Samih Faraj, *Ibda'at* 2:20).

36. "biladi ya jibala r-rujula . . . thakhirati hatha z-zamanu rijalu" (Muhammad Hneihen, *Ibda'at* 2:74). "'intasarna . . . kullu majdin wa intisarin li r-rigal" (Muhammad Shhadeh, *Ibda'at* 2:122).

37. "lamma ta'ijju sh-shawari'u bi n-nisa'" (Husain Barghouti, *Al-Kateb* 105:91).

38. "'indama tanzilu n-nisa'u 'ila sh-shawari'."

39. "halimtu ya habibati 'annaki tahbitina min as-sama', huriyyatan, rahibatan, 'arustan bi l-'abyadi, 'athra'" (Issa Housain Rumi *Al-Fajr Al-Adabi* 89 / 90:66). "ba 'idatan 'asmaytuki l-'asma'a bi l-hamsi l-khafiyyi" (Yusif Shhadeh, *Al-Kateb* 106:80).

40. "ya hanzala, liman tukhalli Fatima" (Al-Mutawakkel Taha, Diwan 106). "kayfa satahya law 'anni rahalt" (Ribhi Abdul-Quader Ibrahim, *Al-Kateb* 97:91). "tamshi wara'i . . . 'armala" (Jamil Mikhel, *Al-Kateb* 94:94).

41. "jawzik yakhti ismalla 'alih" (Harkash, Diwan 41).

42. "'ukhta ruhi" (Al-Mutawakkel Taha, Diwan 35). "'ukhtahu luffi . . . rushshi" (Samih Faraj, *Ibda'at* 2:12).

43. For a discussion of the historical, socioeconomic reasons for such an attitude, see Germain Tillon, *The Republic of Cousins* (London: Zed Press, 1983).

44. "'uhibbu imra'atan fataha an-nawmu tawilan . . . wa'ana 'anamu layalin tawilah" (Yousuf Hamed, *Al-Kateb* 99:89). "nasibbu n-nisa'a sabahan li namshi 'ala sadrihinna . . ." (Al-Mutawakkel Taha, Diwan 19). "sayyidatu l-waja'i l-mahfurati fi l-'a'maq . . . 'at-tariqu' ilayha qitaratu nazfi . . . hubbuki yaltaffu 'ala 'unuqi . . . 'ana l-mat'unu bi sayfi r-raghbati fi l-'a'maq" (Basam Il-Hayja, *Al-Bayader Al-Adabi* 3 / 4:48). ". . . wa tabaqa d-dumu'u wa tabaqa l-juruh" (Ribhi Abdul-Quader Ibrahim, *Al-Kateb* 97:91). "Kayfa yaji'u l-hubbu li majnunin sara haraman ma yashtahih?" (Yousuf Hamed, *Al-Kateb* 99:89).

45. "Sayyidati" (Ali Al-Khalili, *Ibda'at* 2:11).

46. "'ana shaykhu hathi l-nawasi . . . ya ibnati" (Husain Barghouti, *Al-Kateb* 107:82).

47. "'ukhtahu luffi . . . rushshi . . . hayya zalzili" (Samih Faraj, *Ibda'at* 2:21). "la tajza'i . . . 'aqimi fawqa qabri" (Yusuf Naser, *Ibda'at* 2:94). "la takhshi" (Yousuf Hamed, Diwan 50). "ya saghirati . . . 'ilhaqi r-rab' . . . shddi l-khasra . . . 'inhadi . . . 'ammidini . . . tasharrabi ruhi" (Sami Al-Kilani, Diwan 44, 53). "'adi'i . . . 'iftahi" (Husain Barghouti, *Al-Kateb* 107:82). "'udi" (Yousuf Hamed, *Al-Kateb* 99:89). "'utruki . . . 'is'ali . . . 'iddaxiri . . . lawwihi" (As'ad Al-As'ad, *Al-Kateb* 92:97).

48. "hiya sh-shamsu wa sh-shut'anu wa al-'asalu wa z-zaytun . . ." "'aththahibina 'ila rafifi l-hadbi wa l-jasadi t-tariyyi" (Yusif Shhadeh, *Al-Kateb*

Gender in the Poetry of the Intifada

106:80). "wa namla'u qulba al-hayati wa qalba n-nisai'; hawa'an 'alila" (Wasim Al-Kurdi, *Al-Kateb* 107:89).

49. "'a'as'alu ruhaki kayfa tashaqqaqa fiki l-jibal" (Al-Mutawakkel Taha, Diwan 41).

50. "'adi'i nawafithiki l-babiliyyata bi sh-sham'adani l-qadimi, fa' inna 'alayhi nuqushun wa fi sh-shamii; hafaru" (Husain Barghouti, *Al-Kateb* 107:82).

51. "Allamani hubbuka ya watani 'an 'akuna salban qawiyya" (Najla Shahwan, *Ibda'at* 2:125). "'anzifu min sharayini filistini filistini" (Hanan Awwad, Diwan 20). "'ila 'ummahat l-'ashiqin" (Hanan Awwad, *Ibda'at* 1:25). "musafirun" (Khadija Abu-Arkoub, *Ibda'at* 2:119).

52. "wa 'ahli ma' surun" (Khadija Abu-Arkoub, *Ibda'at* 117).

53. "'ana bintu s-silahi 'uqatilu l-i 'sara min 'ajlika," "'uhibbuka 'ayyuha l-'alamu l-filistini . . . , ayyuha r-rajulu l-filistini" (Hanan Awwad, Diwan 5).

54. "'ayna'ana . . . musafirun 'alhatu" (Khadija Abu-Arkoub, *Ibda'at* 2:117). "samtu z-zamani . . . 'atashu s-sinin . . . tawratu n-nafsi s-samitah . . . yawma rahilikum bittu 'uqasi" (Fatma J. Anabusi, *Al-Fajr Al-Adabi* 91/92:73). "musafirun 'alhatu khalfa l-'ahl" (Khadija Abu-Arkoub, *Ibda'at* 2:119).

55. "minkum ta'allamtu darba l-kifah" (Fatma J. Anabusi, *Al-Fajr Al-Adabi* 91/92:74). "ji'tu l-kuwna fi zillak," "'uhibbu intima'i 'ilayka," "min 'aynayka 'ahtallu tariqi," "ya sanadi" (Hanan Awwad, Diwan 17, 5, 53, 73).

56. "'alhatu bi l-huzni'" (Khadija Abu-Arkoub, *Ibda'at* 2:118). "hal 'adraku hurqata qalbi . . . 'alami . . . wa n-nirana allati takwi a'maqi" (Fatma J. Anabusi, *Al-Fajr Al-Adabi* 91/92:75).

57. "rubbama 'afqidu shay'an min shababi" (Hanan Awwad, Diwan 55). "kullu 'ayyami intizaru," "ruhtu 'ahsibu ma tabaqqa min 'umri . . . bada'a l-'addu t-tanazuli" (Fatma J. Anabusi, *Al-Fajr Al-Adabi* 91/92:75, 73).

Sharif Kanaana

Women in the Legends of the Intifada

The Arabic word *intifada* literally means the act of shaking off something. In the case of the Palestinian intifada, it refers to shaking off the
Israeli occupation, which was about twenty years old when the intifada
erupted in December 1987. At the time of this writing—December
1990—it had entered its fourth year and was still going strong. Due to
the unique and persistent character of the Palestinian struggle, the
highly violent and oppressive character of the Israeli response, and the
high casualty rate among the Palestinians, the intifada captured a great
deal of local, regional, and international attention, and influenced resistance and liberation movements the world over.

As a result, a large number of books and articles have been written
about the intifada since 1987, both locally and internationally.[1] The bulk
of this literature deals mainly with the political, military, and economic
implications of the intifada. The psychological effects of the intifada on
Palestinian children is a topic that has also attracted a good deal of
attention. Opting for a different approach since the early days of the
intifada, I have concentrated on an area that has been of little concern to
local scholars and of no concern at all to international scholars: the
reflection of the intifada in folk and popular Palestinian culture and,
more specifically, the portrayal of social life in Palestinian folk narratives generated by the circumstances of the intifada.[2] In the present
discussion, I intend to look at the role of Palestinian women in the
intifada as portrayed in contemporary intifada legends.

Women in the Legends of the Intifada

Theoretical Background

Contemporary legends, also referred to in the literature by such terms as modern legends, urban legends, rumor legends, and urban belief legends, can be defined as narratives, tales, or stories set in familiar locations in the recent or historical past. They are circulated by word of mouth in contemporary society and focus on a single episode related to socially important and controversial themes. The episode is usually presented as true but miraculous, bizarre, or otherwise improbable.[3] Unlike other narrative forms, for example, the folktale, the modern legend has no standard form and no beginning or ending formulas. It exists in multiple forms and is usually re-created with every new telling. The persistent and important aspect of the legend is its content or message rather than its form or narrative structure. Actually, the form of legends is so recessive that a legend may not be easily distinguished from the conversation in which it is embedded, and a legend widely circulating in a given area often has to be pieced together from several conversations or tellings.[4] The authors of a recent article on the topic described the legend as a "solidified rumour" (Degh and Vazsonyi 1989:26).

Legends, as far as we know, exist and have always existed in all known human societies, although the degree of prevalence does vary from society to society as well as over time in the same society. Legends are there because human beings need them; they fulfill a function and, like other forms of narrative, arise in response to psychological and emotional needs. Such needs are inherent in human nature, but their intensity fluctuates with changes in the physical and social conditions that impinge on the capacity of a social system to cater to the physical, social, psychological, and emotional needs of its members. Legends, in particular, seem to be more responsive than other narrative forms to such changes. As Linda Degh puts it, "social and historical changes may influence the nature of the legend more than they do any other genre of folklore" (Degh 1971:60).

Two types of sociopsychological conditions or climates, when they prevail in a society or community, seem to be especially conducive to the emergence, growth, and persistence of modern legends. The first of these conditions is that of collective stress, fear, and anxiety. Carl Jung, for example, contends that the belief in UFO legends is rooted in "an emotional tension having its cause in a situation of collective distress and danger, or in a vital psychic need. This condition undoubtedly exists today" (Jung 1969:24). Max Lüthi specifies some of these sources of collective fear and distress when he states, "the legend looks fixedly at the inexplicable which confronts man. And because it is monstrous—war, pestilence, and especially often a numinous power, be it nature, demons, or spirits of the dead—man becomes small and unsure before it" (Lüthi 1976:24). Under such circumstances, legend explains, rationalizes, confirms, denies, negates, distances, derides, ridicules, or in some other way helps man in coming to terms with the monstrous powers that cause the collective distress.

The other type of climate conducive to the emergence of legends is the climate of rising nationalism, especially when accompanied by struggle for national liberation against an outside invader, occupier, or oppressor. Under such circumstances, most legends tend to portray local or national heroes accomplishing extraordinary feats against the enemy. At times, these feats are accomplished with the help of supernatural forces. More often, though, the heroes triumph by carrying out heroic, courageous, clever, or imaginative deeds that are extraordinary but realistic, and without appealing to supernatural forces. Such legends provide symbols that embody the social aspirations of the group and help in welding the varying elements of the group into "something like a common consciousness," as Paredes puts it (Paredes 1971:101). Paredes thinks that such "legends are ego supporting devices. They may appeal to the group or to individuals by affording them pride, dignity, and self-esteem: local or national heroes to identify with, for example, or place name legends giving an aura of importance to some familiar and undistinguished feature of local landscape" (ibid., 98).

Whatever the circumstances that give rise to a legend may be, a legend always functions as a wish-fulfilling fantasy. But, as Alan Dundes points out, there is something special about the fantasy of the legend: "One does not escape the real world into legend; rather, legend represents fantasy in the real world, an important point psychologically speaking. It is 'true' fantasy, not to be confused with the 'false' or fictional fantasy of folktale" (Dundes 1971:24).

The Palestinian Context

The climate among Palestinians in the occupied territories under the intifada combined both the element of collective stress and that of rising nationalism. On the one hand, the intifada marks the culmination of the Palestinian nationalist movement, which started at least as far back as the second decade of this century. It is the highest point of the Palestinian struggle for national liberation thus far. The Israeli occupation authorities, on the other hand, responded to the intifada by increasing their oppression, terrorization, and victimization of the Palestinian people under occupation.[5]

Women in the Legends of the Intifada

Details of Israeli terrorization and intimidation of the Palestinian people dominated news broadcasts all over the world for a large part of the period from 1987 to the end of the intifada, and the scene of Israeli soldiers breaking the bones of Palestinian children on the outskirts of Nablus, which was photographed secretly by a CBS newsman, has become a classic. It is sufficient here to state that Israeli practices resulted in a great deal of fear, stress, pain, and sorrow to the approximately one and a half million Palestinians under occupation. More than one thousand people were killed between 1987 and 1990, tens of thousands were injured, maimed, deformed, and handicapped, and tens of thousands were arrested, detained, and imprisoned.[6]

Considering the presence of all these elements—collective distress, rising nationalism, and sustained struggle for liberation—it is no wonder that thousands of rumors and rumor legends—heroic, horrific and humorous—emerged among Palestinians in the occupied territories during the intifada. Clearly, not all of these legends were original, new, or unique to the intifada; many of them were adapted to the intifada situation from previous Palestinian uprisings, especially that of 1936 against the British Mandate and the Zionist invasion in the twenties and thirties. Many of the legends about martyrs and those containing religious or supernatural elements are recognizably derived from publications of, or about, the Islamic resistance movement in Afghanistan. Yet others derive from oral or written Arabic and Islamic traditions that are thousands of years old. However, as they circulate now among Palestinians by word of mouth, all of the legends carry distinctive Palestinian and intifada flavor. This flavor comes from the mention of familiar names of Palestinian individuals, families, or places, or by some form of association with some familiar but factual incidents of the intifada. Thus, legendary child-heroes, who carry out extraordinary feats against the Israeli soldiers and whose bodies are immune to penetration by Israeli soldiers' bullets, live in familiar Palestinian refugee camps such as Balata or Nuseirat; the ghosts of recent martyrs attend Friday prayers at known mosques such as the Abdul-Nasser Mosque in Ramallah; and infants, who speak to people the moment they are born and assure them that the intifada will succeed, are born in such existing hospitals as Shifa Hospital in Gaza. The actual live burial of three Palestinian youths from the village of Salem near Nablus by an Israeli army bulldozer stimulated hundreds of similar, but even more sensational, reports all over the country.

At least three characteristics of the legend can be highly irritating when one is trying to study the legends of a whole society or community rather than one legend of a specified collection of legends. One characteristic "concerns quantity and generative power." There are literally

Sharif Kanaana

countless legends. As Wayland Hand phrased it, "For the systematizer, folk legends seem endless. . . . there are an infinite number of legends, especially local legends as opposed to migratory legends. . . . Legends, in contrast [to folktales], can spring anew whenever an appropriate personage, place or event is deemed legendworthy by a folk group" (see Dundes 1971:24–25). Another characteristic, which is somewhat related to the first, is the fuzziness of the borderlines between legend and neighboring narrative genres such as the rumor, the jest, the tall tale, the anecdote, the memorat, the joke, the family story, the explanatory tale, and the humorous tale.

The third problematic characteristic of the legend is one that we have already mentioned, namely the large number of versions of the same legend usually circulating within the same community at the same time. As Herbert Halpert phrases it, "where the legend-making process is alive we get infinite variety that cannot, or rather should not, be standardized" (Halpert 1971:48). When folklorists try to select a version to use in a discussion, they are faced with the fact that "it is one of the cliches of folklore that there is no one right version for the folktale item. All variants of a folk song or a folktale have equal validity, assuming that the singer or storyteller is a competent performer in good health and memory" (ibid., 47). As we have previously mentioned, this problem is exacerbated by the lack of any fixed form for the legend which, if it existed, could be helpful in selecting the best version.[7]

Taking into account these three characteristics of the legend, it is clear that my collection of intifada legends can in no way claim to be exhaustive, nor can I guarantee that any one of the narratives I use here will be accepted by all narrative scholars as legend. In addition, I cannot give all the versions I have collected whenever I mention a legend; I have had to select the "best" version for inclusion in this article. Since, as we have repeatedly mentioned, a legend has a message rather than a form, and since I cannot prevent myself from having an explicit or implicit hypothesis about the message embodied in each of the legends I study, my definition of the "best" version will, consciously or unconsciously, hinge on my understanding of which version communicates the assumed message most completely and accurately. In some cases I will supplement my choice with some comments about other variations on the same legend. The collection of Palestinian intifada legends I am concerned with consists of about two hundred and fifty "best" versions and several hundred variations. These narratives were collected from all parts of the occupied territories and from all three types of Palestinian communities—towns, villages, and refugee camps.

All the material used here was collected between 1988 and 1990 by

Women in the Legends of the Intifada

myself and some of my students from folklore classes at Birzeit University on the West Bank. Most of the narratives were collected on tape during simulated legend swapping sessions, each consisting of either a group of young males or members of both sexes of an extended family and close relatives. The tapes were transcribed in handwriting by the person recording the session. Some legends were heard in natural settings and written down later from memory.

The same young males who contributed many of our narratives also form the backbone of the intifada, at least the more active and publicized aspects of it, such as demonstrations; tire burnings; stone, bottle, and firebomb throwing, and other forms of active confrontation with Israeli soldiers. Other members of Palestinian society are involved in what may be called passive or peaceful resistance, such as striking; abstaining from going to work in Israel; refusing to pay taxes; boycotting Israeli products; and so on. I assume that these narratives are told not only by these young males but also from their point of view.

I have referred to this group as "young males" because as a group, they do not coincide with any traditionally known class or age group with a linguistic designation of its own, either in English or Arabic. In Palestinian culture, the most salient and meaningful folk classification of males in the society would look roughly like the following:

1. *Tifl*, plural *Atfal* = Birth–6 years
2. *Walad*, plural *Awlad* = 6–13 years
3. *Shab*, plural *Shabab* = 14–25 years
4. *Izlam* or *Rejul*, plural *Rijaal* = 25–60 years
5. *Khitiariyeh* = 60+ years

According to this classification, the actual age of the youth groups that form the active elements of the intifada cuts across two of these stages. This situation has actually created a language problem for Palestinians when talking about this group. In Arabic newspapers, political speeches, social science articles, and other formal settings using classical Arabic, the term *atfal* is used as the officially recognized translation of the English "children." It is defined to cover both males and females from birth to sixteen years of age, and it therefore covers the young males we are discussing. Thus, in formal Palestinian culture, especially in poetry and other literary forms, such terms as *atfal el-hijareh* (literally, "children of the stones," meaning stone-throwing children) are in vogue. These poetic forms have great appeal for Palestinians and Arabs in general because, even here, the term "children" has connotations of a younger group of adolescents than it denotes in actuality. As a result, the Israeli enemy is portrayed with all its armies and military power as failing to subdue the mighty little Palestinian children after several years of intifada. On the other hand, Palestinians, using colloquial language and discussing their daily affairs under the unstable conditions of the intifada, are usually confused about how to refer to these youths and often vacillate between the three terms *atfal, awlad,* and *shabab;* but they do not feel comfortable with any of them. *Atfal* and *awlad* would be insulting particularly to older youths, because of their age, and to all youths because it detracts from the seriousness of the role they are playing in the intifada. *Shabab,* which is the term preferred by the youths themselves and which causes many of the adults within earshot to snicker, is suitable for the role but too dignified for the ages of most of them.

A compromise solution has been reached by some people in an attempt to resolve the contradiction between the ages and roles of these youths; they refer to them as *shabab izghar,* or "little shabab." This, I expect, will become the permanent colloquial linguistic designator for the new perceptual category created by changes in the reality of Palestinian society.

A body of narratives, like ours, can be analyzed in many ways and can produce a variety of answers depending on the angle from which we approach it, the dimensions along which we classify it, and the questions we pose about it. In this discussion I am interested in the types of characters that appear in these legends and the types of roles these characters perform in the legends. In particular, I am interested here in the Palestinian female characters appearing in my collection of intifada legends.

In folk legends, as with all traditional genres of folk narratives, there is always "the tendency for only two characters to be on stage at one time or even for a complete tale to have no more than one or two characters" (Williams 1984:217). The legend, as one of the shortest narrative forms and usually having only one episode, tends to be of the latter kind. The major reason for this tendency in folk narratives in general, and in the legend in particular, is that folk narratives typically convey a struggle or conflict between two parties or forces, each represented on the stage by one person at a time. When more than two characters appear simultaneously, two of them are usually the major characters of the narrative, while the others are supporting characters on either side.[8] When a complete tale has no more than one character, it is usually because the other party to the struggle is an intangible or supernatural force.

The legend normally consists of one single episode that takes place in one location or within a small area. The episode typically ends with the resolution of the struggle in favor of one of the contestants, usually the party by whom or among whom the legend was created. In such cases the resolution is of the nature of wish fulfillment. When a legend created by a group shows the enemy emerging victorious, it usually serves as a warning to the group members of what may happen if the enemy wins, and it also helps them to come to terms with a bitter reality. The tragic endings of such legends are sometimes replaced by humorous ones—often of the black humor type—at the hands of some individuals. Such individuals use humor in order to relieve their anxiety by distancing themselves from the course of events and by making the terrifying events look outlandish and ridiculous and thus more acceptable (Ballard 1984:12).

In Palestinian intifada legends the contestants are clearly the Palestinians and the Israelis. The Israeli side is invariably represented by one or more male military personnel—a soldier, an officer, the military governor, or a group of soldiers or border policemen—but never by civilians, not even the settlers who in reality play a significant role in the Israeli effort to put down the intifada. However, in this discussion we are interested in the representatives of the Palestinian side of the conflict as portrayed in the legends.

The Legends

Of the 237 narratives in my collection, the Palestinian representatives or contestants are exclusively male in 148 of them and exclusively female in only 15. In 23 cases the Palestinian side is represented by an entire community, and in 8 cases by an animal belonging to a Palestinian. The remaining 43 cases have each a cast of both Palestinian males and females.

In the 148 narratives with exclusively male actors on the Palestinian side, the actors consist mainly of members of the group we have described above—the young shabab—although some older men and infant males also appear in a small number of incidents. I will leave the discussion of these particular narratives for a future essay and will limit my discussion here to the female characters of the 58 items involving a Palestinian cast that is partly or exclusively female. I will be investigating the questions of who these females are and what kinds of roles they play in these narratives.

From a purely quantitative viewpoint, we may note that male characters appear in about 93 percent of all the narratives in which Palestinians are not represented by a community, a crowd, or an animal, while females appear in only about 28 percent of these cases. In other words, there are approximately 3.3 male characters for each female character. The comparison, however, is more meaningful when we turn to qualitative analysis. The male characters consist primarily of one age group, namely the young shabab, while the females are mainly adult or elderly women. The male characters are restricted essentially to one kind of role: that of direct confrontation with Israeli soldiers, while the females are given a much wider range of roles to play in these narratives. Female characters often come to the aid, support, or protection of the males, but the males never reciprocate. Most of the credit given to female characters comes from their association with male heroes, while males are glorified for their own acts of heroism.

After this very short comparison of the male and female characters in this collection of narratives, we can now turn to the analysis of internal variations within the female sample. The female characters that appear in 58 narratives can be divided into two main categories: adult women (marah, plural nisswan), who appear in 45 cases, and young girls of marriageable age (bint, plural banat), who appear in 15 cases. Two cases have both a woman and a girl. The adult women are portrayed as having a much more significant role to play than that of the young girls. Adult women, in the 45 narratives where they appear, represent the only or the major character on the Palestinian side in 26 cases, and a supporting character to a male hero in the other 19 instances. As the major or the central Palestinian figure in these 26 narratives, the adult woman plays one of two roles: the heroine or a naive peasant woman.

As a heroine, the adult Palestinian woman may confront the Israeli soldier, involve him in a physical fight, and defeat him. Following are two such cases. The first was collected from the town of Jenin in the northern part of the West Bank in April 1989 and the other from the city of Gaza in May 1989.[9]

> A woman was participating in a demonstration in Jenin when she got into a shouting argument with an Israeli soldier. The woman shouted to the soldier that if he was to put his gun aside, she would show him who was the more courageous of the two. The soldier accepted the challenge and put his gun aside. The woman attacked him and with one blow knocked him down on the ground, sat on him, and continued to beat him until the other soldiers came and saved him.

> One time, a woman went out during a curfew. Some soldiers met her and asked where she was going. She answered that she was going to get food for her children. They told her to go home. The woman told the officer, "I'll hit you if you don't let me go!" The officer said, "Let me see you do it!" The woman rushed at the officer and started hitting. One of the soldiers hit her with the butt of his rifle. She fell to the

ground. The soldiers left; only one of them stayed behind. He took off his uniform and helmet (wanting to rape her). When he came close to her, she grabbed him by the neck and tried to strangle him. He started to scream. Other women came and released him from her grip and sent him, naked, back to his officer.

The adult woman can also become a heroine by showing great courage and by setting an example for other Palestinians of how to behave at the time of great stress when weaker people may feel defeated and crushed. Such is the message of one narrative that was collected in the town of Ramallah in June 1990:

> One time there was a woman from the village near Jenin. This woman's son threw a firebomb at the [Israeli] soldiers. The soldiers came and blew up her house [as a punishment]. When the woman saw what had happened, she started to sing joyfully. The officer asked why she was so happy. She answered, "The streets of our village had almost run out of stones [to throw at the soldiers]. Now that you have blown up my house, [I am happy because] we have lots of them."

Most often, however, the heroic feats carried out by courageous adult women consist of protecting the young shabab and saving them from being harmed by the Israeli soldiers. In order to achieve their goal, women have to be creative, courageous, and willing to make heavy sacrifices. Hence, a woman may have to put on a big act in order to save a young man from being arrested, as was the case in this narrative, which was collected in Ramallah in July 1989:

> A group of soldiers stopped a young shab in the marketplace and were about to take him away. A woman who was shopping in the vicinity saw what was happening. Immediately, she threw herself at the soldiers and started shouting and screaming, telling the soldiers to let her son go because he had not done anything but was simply walking with her while shopping. She kept pulling and tugging at the boy until she got him loose. As she walked away with him hand in hand, one of the passers-by heard the woman ask the boy, "Which family are you from, dear?"

A woman may also have to go through some awkward and embarrassing moments in order to prevent the arrest of a young shab. The following narrative was collected from a forty-year-old woman from Gaza in July 1989:

> One time, a young shab threw a Molotov cocktail at the soldiers and ran into Shifa Hospital, and the soldiers followed him into the hospital. He ran into the reception room. He was so scared that he became

confused and did not know where to hide. There was a woman there from Khan Yunis with a *dayer* [a long, flowing, black skirt]. She called to him and hid him between her legs under the dayer. And she said to him, "Stay there, you are like a son of mine." The soldiers came after him to the reception room but couldn't find him. When they left, he came out.

This scenario is a very popular theme, and variations on this narrative were collected in several parts of the occupied territories. In several cases, the story, mercifully, specifies that the young shab was only eight or nine years old. A test that is harder to go through in trying to rescue a young man involves a woman's coming close to compromising the family honor. The following story was collected from a twenty-year-old woman from Nablus in April 1989:

One time, there were troubles in the streets of the Old City [of Nablus]. One young man ran into a nearby house, which had only a woman and her young daughter living in it. The girl was, at the time, sleeping in her own room. The woman closed the door behind the young man, but the soldiers were chasing him and started pounding at the door. She said to the young man, "Go into that room, change your clothes, put on this pair of pajamas and get in bed next to my daughter. Please hurry up and don't hesitate." The young man did what the woman told him to do, while she went and opened the door for the soldiers. They said, "We believe that a young man just ran into the house, where is he?" She answered, "There is no one in the house except me and my daughter and her husband. You can go in and see for yourselves." They went in and there was no one except a man sleeping with his wife, so they left. The young man got up, put on his clothes, thanked the woman, and left. Two days later the young man came back and told the woman, "You trusted me with your daughter, and I lived up to your trust, and now I have come to ask for your daughter's hand to be my wife."

We are left to assume that the mother and daughter agreed to his proposal and the couple lived happily ever after.

However, try as they may, women cannot rescue all the young shabab, and some of them inevitably get killed and become martyrs (*shahid*, plural *shuhada*). But even in the case of a shahid, the woman can still try to prevent the body from being taken to the Abu Kbir Medical Center, where it would be dissected by army doctors, or worse yet, have some parts of the body stolen for organ transplants. The following is a story in which a woman's efforts paid off and the body was rescued. The story was collected from a twenty-five-year-old housewife from Gaza in July 1989:

One time, one of the shabab was killed. One of his friends carried the body on his shoulders and started running and shouting, "Shahid! Shahid!" He did not know where to take the body [to hide it], and bullets were falling all around him like a hailstorm. A woman saw him and called to him. He went to her and said, "Hide him! Hide him! We don't want the soldiers to take him to Abu Kbir." The woman had *tabun* [an outdoor clay oven] for baking bread, and next to it there was a large pile of dried branches [used for fuel for the oven]. She made an opening in the branches, placed the body in it and piled more branches on top of it. In a little while, the soldiers came into the house and searched for the body but could not find anything, so they left.

According to the narratives in our collection, besides the heroic role portrayed in the narratives thus far, a woman occupying the center stage as a representative of the Palestinian party in the struggle may play only one other role: the role of a simple, naive peasant woman. This role is similar to that of the "wise fool," which is usually portrayed by the lovable character of "Hodja" in Turkey, "Khuja" in Persia, and "Joha" in the Arab world. The "wise fool" character usually makes naive or foolish statements that turn out to reveal, unintentionally and unknowingly, some wise and profound truth. In the following narrative, a village woman from the Ramallah district, naive and inarticulate, gives an answer that on the surface appears to be ignorant and meaningless. At a deeper level, however, it seems to portray the essence of the new order of things in the occupied territories after the outbreak of the intifada:

In the early eighties the Israeli authorities sealed off a house in one of the villages near Ramallah because one of the family members was involved in anti-Israeli military activity. In the early days of the intifada, the young shabab reopened the house, fixed it up, and returned it to the family. One day, the soldiers realized what had happened. They came to the house and asked the housewife living in it, "Who gave you permission to reopen this house?" The woman answered, "Our village military governor [meaning the shabab] gave me permission."

In another narrative, this time from the Jenin area, a woman ignorantly directs insults at an Israeli officer by giving him a name that to most Palestinians conveys a great deal of truth:

In Jenin, when children want to tease the soldiers, they shout at them, "Ya Homo! Ya Homo! [from English through Hebrew]" One time, a boy was caught by the soldiers and taken to prison. The boy's mother went to the Israeli officer and begged him, "Please Mr. Homo, release my son."

In other versions of this story, the term used is *memzare* ["bastard"], or *zonah* ["whore"].

Finally, an old woman from 'Askar refugee camp, again unintentionally, brings out the basic contradiction between being a collaborator with the Israeli authorities and a decent person. In the occupied territories, those who collaborate take bribes from local Palestinian residents in return for such favors as getting them a driver's license, a car license, a travel permit, and so on. Understandably, the collaborators often take the bribe but do not deliver the goods. Here is a narrative collected in Nablus in January 1990:

> An elderly woman from 'Askar refugee camp went to get a travel permit. She stood in the middle of the crowd waiting in front of the military governor's office and shouted at the top of her voice, "Ya naas! Oh people! Who knows of any decent collaborator to get this travel permit signed for me?"

We come now to the nineteen cases in which an adult woman appears in a supporting, rather than leading, role within a team that represents the Palestinian side of the conflict, or opposition, in our narratives. In all these cases the Palestinian team consists mainly of a mother and son. It is the son rather than the mother who is the central figure of the narrative, but the mother gets some of the credit or glory by association by being the mother of the hero.

The son-mother team appears in two basic situations: when the son is born and when he dies as a shahid. To start with, it is no mean feat to give birth to a male Palestinian infant who, it is assumed, is destined to become a *mulathem* (one of the shabab who wears a headdress mask, plural *mulathemin*), as can be seen from a humor narrative collected in East Jerusalem in June 1990:

> Two women, a Palestinian and an Egyptian, were in the maternity ward of a hospital. The Palestinian woman was shouting and screaming while the Egyptian woman stayed very calm. Then, the doctor came and said to the Palestinian woman, "What is all this screaming about? Here is another woman right next to you, and she is in the same situation but is not screaming!" The Palestinian woman replied, "Well, giving birth to a *mulathem* is not as easy as giving birth to a belly dancer."[10]

A Palestinian woman can be proud of simply giving birth to Palestinian male children because, even when they are little children or infants, they are equal to adult men:

> A woman from Gaza had seven sons, two of whom became shuhada, and she had five left. One time the soldiers pounded at the door and

Women in the Legends of the Intifada

shouted, "Where are the men? Are there any men in the house?" The woman raised her hand with her fingers spread out making the sign of the number five and said, "Yes, I have five men in the house!" The soldiers barged in to arrest the five men only to find out that the five men she referred to were her five sons, whose ages ranged from one to four years.

A Palestinian woman naturally has the right to be proud of her male infants because they are known to start the struggle against the Israeli soldiers even before leaving their mothers' wombs. From Gaza comes the following story, which was collected in June 1989:

> One time when the town [Gaza] was under curfew, a pregnant woman started to have labor pains. The soldiers took her to a military hospital to give birth there. It turned out that she was pregnant with twin boys. The head of one of the babies came out, he looked around and saw all these [Israeli] military uniforms, turned back to his brother and shouted, "Ahmed! Ahmed! We are surrounded, get some rocks!"

Anyone who, after hearing all these stories, still doubts the courage of these Palestinian male infants may check with the enemy's own soldiers. They acknowledge this fearlessness, as happens in the following story from Gaza:

> A woman was going home after having given birth at the hospital. There was a curfew, and she wanted to get home. A doctor who had a permit [to drive during the curfew] took her with him. On the way home a group of soldiers met them and stopped them. They asked the doctor, "Where are you going?" The doctor said, "A woman has given birth and is going home." The officer turned to the woman and asked her, "What did you give birth to?" "A boy," she replied. He said, "Oh, a boy! Where are his hands? Let me see them." She asked, "What for!" He replied, "I want to find out if there are any rocks in them!"

The second standard situation in which the mother-son team appears in the narratives is one in which the son, who is the major character, is a shahid. The mother comes into the picture through several types of relations or associations with the shahid, all of which spring from the implicit assumption that the strongest ties a young shab can have are with his mother. In our narratives, the shahid is often portrayed as having previous knowledge of his death, sometimes down to the exact time and location. He faces his death intentionally, knowingly and heroically. The shahid usually does not reveal this secret to others, and it becomes known only after his death through retrospective analysis of the shahid's behavior or comments during the last days or hours of his life. But if any shahid is ever to give away his secret before his death, it is to his mother, as did this shahid from Gaza:

There was a young man whose sister had just returned from outside the country and had brought him some new clothes. He put on the new clothes and in the evening did not take them off. He came to his mother and told her, "Mother, I have a feeling that I am going to die tomorrow, and therefore I would like to sleep next to you tonight." The mother exclaimed, "May the name of Allah protect you! What is going on with you?" He answered, "As I told you, tomorrow I must become a shahid." He slept next to her that night. In the morning he had his breakfast, washed up and stayed in his new clothes. He said to one of his friends, "Today we will show them [the Israeli soldiers]." The confrontation started, but despite the heavy shooting none of the shabab was injured except for the young man. He was hit and became a shahid. During the funeral procession, the coffin started to move on its own [showing that he was a real shahid], and people started running after it.

However, even if the shahid fails to inform his mother about what he knows is "written" for him, the whole community, including the shabab, know that the one person the shahid would want to see and be seen by before his death is his mother. The following anecdote was heard in Ramallah in July 1989:

Shahid Muhammad Sammi from Qaddurah refugee camp [near Ramallah] died on the tenth of May 1989. The shabab confirmed that he was dead. The shabab took the body to [the shahid's] home so that his mother, the family members, and close relatives could see him. His mother, his relatives, and some of the shabab who were then in the room confirmed that [the shahid] opened his eyes and looked at his mother for a few moments, then closed them again.

Clearly, the closest and dearest person to a shahid is his mother. The shahid, however, seems sometimes to be torn between wanting to live for the sake of the real mother or to die for the sake of the figurative mother—his country. The mother in the following narrative, collected from East Jerusalem in January 1990, resolves the problem for her son by devising a symbol that incorporates both mothers almost equally, a symbol the shahid-son can take with him into the second world:

One time, a shahid brought his mother a large [Palestinian] flag and said to her, "There is a demonstration in town [in which I am going to participate], and if I die do not forget to wrap my body in this flag. As soon as he left, his mother tore up the flag and burnt it because she was afraid the [Israeli] soldiers might come into the house [and find the flag there]. About half an hour later she heard of the death of her son. She wondered what to do [about replacing the flag]. She gathered some of her own personal clothes, tore them up into pieces and sewed a [Palestinian] flag out of the pieces, and she used the flag as a shroud for her shahid-son.

The communication and communion between a mother and her son does not end even after the shahid is buried; death is not a strong enough barrier. The soul of the shahid-son keeps in touch with the mother in her dreams, as is the case in this short narrative collected in Nablus in April 1988:

> A shahid's mother [from Nablus] relates that the morning her son died he got up, bathed, put on his wedding suit, splashed on some perfume, chatted with his wife and other family members, then left home [for the downtown area]. It was not long before he was hit by the occupation [forces'] bullets and killed. The mother says that a few nights later he appeared to her in her sleep and told her that he was happy and doing fine and that if she wanted to see him he would be available every day at four o'clock, but he did not mention where he would be available.

The shahid can be seen by his mother even in her waking hours, as happened to another woman from Nablus:

> A shahid's mother went to the cemetery to visit the grave of her son. When she got there she saw him together with a group of his shuhada friends walking toward the mosque to perform their prayers. She called to them, "Come [back] with me!" They answered her, "No! Here, we are in the house of ultimate truth and we are much happier here!"

Testimonies to the effect that a shahid is happier in his second life in heaven than on earth are reported by hundreds of shahid stories circulating in the country, and it is almost invariably mothers who bring back such reports. It is true, of course, that only the soul goes to heaven, but in the case of the shahid, the body reflects the new happiness by staying fresh and smiling even after several months:

> The mother of a shahid felt that she was not given enough time [by the Israeli authorities] to say good-bye properly to her shahid-son. She kept asking the village sheikh [religious leader] to give her permission to have the grave reopened in order to see her son. Finally, the sheikh agreed, and the grave was opened. It was already several months since her son's death. She found her son looking exactly as he did when he was alive. A sweet smell came from his body, and a smile was on his face. At the time of death, a friend of the shahid had placed a rose under his arm, and when the grave was reopened, the flower had grown into a rose bush in full bloom.

Lastly, we come to the fifteen narratives that include a young female character. In four of these cases, a girl or a group of girls appears at the center of the narrative, and it is possible to say that these are stories about one or more girls. In the other eleven narratives a girl appears among the cast, but she is not in the leading role. Altogether, however, the young girl, as she appears in all these narratives (including the first four and in all other version and variations with which I am familiar), is a weak, passive, and ineffectual figure.

Young girls appear as the central figures in the first four narratives not because of any courageous or heroic actions, but because society assumes that young girls are weak and vulnerable and thus can be used to symbolize the feebleness and susceptibility of a group that one may wish to tease or insult. Thus, when village or refugee camp residents of the West Bank want to make fun of the residents of East Jerusalem for supposedly not participating as strongly as they should in the intifada effort, they may tell humorous stories like the following:

> One time, there was an army roadblock at the entrance to Jerusalem. One of the soldiers made the passengers get out of a cab and wait by the roadblock for a couple of hours, then frisked them and checked their identity cards. After the soldier turned his back and walked away from them, one of the spoiled [*nawaim*, literally, "soft"] Jerusalemite girls was so "courageous" that she looked at the soldier's back and said, "Oh, you are such a cruel person!"

The remaining eleven narratives are those in which a young girl appears in a role secondary to that of a shab, who is occasionally supported by an adult or elderly woman. In all of these cases, there is a transparent message related to how or how not to behave under intifada conditions. The message is delivered through the portrayal of the behavior of a shab who is the central figure of the narrative. A young girl appears in the narrative not because she is significant on her own, but because the setting needed to deliver the message requires the simple presence of a young girl.

Two types of message seem to be intended from these eleven narratives. One of the two messages concerns weddings under intifada circumstances. Traditionally, weddings in Palestinian society are occasions for a great deal of celebration and feasting; it may last up to a week or more and may involve several thousand people, including family, relatives, clan members, local community leaders, and friends and acquaintances from all parts of the country. At the beginning of the intifada, instructions were given several times by the intifada Joint Leadership that weddings should be carried out without any celebrations. It was explained that since so many people had been killed, the mood of the nation was one of national mourning, and it would be improper to celebrate and be merry in the midst of suffering and death. People were also urged to save all their resources for the intifada effort, and consequently, the splurging that usually accompanied wedding celebrations was highly discouraged.

Several of our stories simply deliver this same message, but in narrative form. A young girl appears in each of these narratives because a wedding requires the presence of a bride. The message is quite clear in the following narrative, collected in Ramallah in April 1989:

> In Hebron, a young man was to get married. The bridegroom's family decided to sing while taking the bride from her family to the groom's family. The young shabab had come to see the groom's family several days before and warned them against singing, out of respect for the prevailing [intifada] conditions. The groom's family refused to listen, so the shabab decided to teach the groom a lesson he would never forget as long as he lived. After the bride had been brought to the groom's family, some of the shabab pretended to be coming to congratulate the groom. They asked him to step out of the house with them and took him to a faraway place, beat him, tore up his wedding clothes, and kept him all night long, while the bride stayed at his parents' home. The next morning, they brought him back, and he went in to his bride with his clothes all torn up.

In this case it was the groom who paid because his family refused to respect "the prevailing conditions." In another narrative it is the bride's mother who is inconsiderate and the bride who suffers. This time, the punishment comes at the hands of the Israeli soldiers, but the message remains the same:[11]

> A bride in Jalazoun [a refugee camp near Ramallah] did not want to wear a white [bridal] dress, but her mother insisted that she had to wear a white dress. Finally, the bride agreed, bought a white dress and wore it. They gave a small party and invited [only] the neighbors. While the bride was on her way to the bridegroom's house [on foot], three army jeeps came by. They told the bride, "The strike forces of the intifada forbid people to have [fancy] processions with [decorated] cars, but we are going to give you a big one, to spite them. They sat her [by force] on the hood of one of the jeeps and drove around the streets of Jalazoun until they got all the way to the UNRWA school [outside the camp].

These two cases tell us what should *not* be done in a wedding during the intifada. What, then, should an intifada wedding be like? Well, we do have a couple of examples in our collection. Here is one:

A young man from ed-Duheisheh [a refugee camp near Beit al-Lahm], was instructed to come to the military governor's office for questioning. It was his Henna Day [the day before the wedding]. They kept him there until one o'clock. Immediately afterwards, a big demonstration broke out. He went out to look for his little brother [among the demonstrators]. The soldiers caught him and put him in jail. By that time it was two o'clock. The people of ed-Duheisheh found out that the groom had been arrested. They also knew that on three previous occasions he had been arrested on the day before the date set for his wedding [causing it to be postponed]. So they decided to go to the military governor and ask him to release the young man because it was the eve of his wedding. After a lot of arguing and haggling, the jail authorities agreed to release him for that night only. It was already seven in the evening. Ed-Duheisheh's people intervened and got the bride's family to agree to have all the formalities taken care of at the same time. They brought a large metal tray with some sweets, coffee, cakes, and cigarettes [to treat those present] and carried out all the necessary official ceremonies. After one hour, everything was completed. The bride and the groom went to Jerusalem to spend the night so the groom wouldn't be arrested during the night. The next morning, they returned to the refugee camp, and the groom was soon arrested.

The other message contained in the stories in which young girls appear concerns the behavior of the young shabab toward young women who may participate with them in intifada activities. Palestinian society is predominantly conservative and Muslim, and there is normally a distinct division of labor and almost complete separation of the sexes. With the beginning of the intifada, many young girls, particularly those from high schools and colleges, started to participate in demonstrations and other intifada-related activities. Muslim fundamentalist groups were against this aberration, and Israeli authorities used it in anti-intifada propaganda.

The dominant message in the few available and relevant narratives seems to be: any relationship should lead to marriage. This was the message in the previously quoted story about the woman who hid the shab in her daughter's bed; the young man returned a few day later and asked for the girl's hand in marriage. The same message comes across in the following narrative:

A girl from a refugee camp, eighteen years of age, lost one of her eyes when she suffered a direct hit to her eye by a rubber bullet during a confrontation with the soldiers. This caused her to lose her beauty, which in turn led to her fiance leaving her. The shabab in the refugee camp came to ask for her hand, thus causing her fiance a great deal of embarrassment. So he went back and apologized to her, and they married shortly thereafter. Now they are always seen together during confrontations with the Israeli soldiers.

Conclusion

The intifada-related, contemporary narratives that were circulating by word of mouth among Palestinians in Gaza and on the West Bank portray sons as both the major characters of the narratives and as heroes in the conflict. Mothers in the leading role appear as either heroines or "wise fools." As supporting figures to their sons, the mother's role is to bring sons into this world; to train, socialize, and protect them; and to offer them as sacrifices for the common cause of Palestinian society. Daughters are weak and vulnerable. Fathers are almost completely absent from the whole picture. In the few cases where they appear (no such cases appear in this discussion), they are pitiful, cringing figures, defended by their wives or young sons against verbal or physical abuse by Israeli soldiers.

Despite the fact that sons and young males appear in the largest number of these narratives and play the role of the heroes who challenge the enemy and engage him in deadly battles, it is the adult women or mothers who, upon surveying the whole collection of intifada narratives, appear to be the strongest figures, the pillars of the Palestinian Arab family. Thus, young men often need the moral and physical support of their mothers or mother figures. The mothers gladly and capably offer such support to their sons and to all the other members of the family but never seem to need help or protection from the others. It is a Middle Eastern/Arab—if not universal—rule of social interaction that one who gives is stronger than one who receives. In this sense it is the Palestinian mother who seems to be the strongest and most solid member of the family.

However, there is yet another aspect to these narratives. It is true that young men are the army of the intifada; they pay with their very lives to keep the struggle going. But in another sense they are tools used by society to guarantee the survival of the group in a manner reminiscent of the juvenile males who make up the outer circle of a feeding primate group. In other words, they are the most disposable.

It is the adult mothers who give birth to mulathemin, raise them, and train them to be men from an early age, offer them as martyrs when society needs them, and even makes sure they are happy in the "house of ultimate truth." Thus, ultimately, it is the mother who guarantees the continuity of the group.

NOTES

1. Nasser and Heacock, eds., 1990, is a very good source for references to the literature of the intifada.

2. See, for example, Kanaana 1989b, 1990, 1991.

3. This is a compound definition derived from definitions by Georges (1971: 5), Degh and Vazsonyi (1989:31), Nicolaisen (1984:170), and Oring (1986:125).

4. This notion incorporates ideas from discussions by Oring (1986:121–26), Georges (1971:10), Degh (1971:60–62), and Hand (1965:441).

5. For some of the victimization strategies, see Kanaana 1989.

6. The most reliable figures on Palestinian victims can be found in the occasional reports issued between 1987 and 1990 by the human rights organizations al-Haq in Ramallah and B'tselem in Jerusalem.

7. For further discussion of these and other problems related to defining, classifying, and indexing legends, see Georges 1971, Friedman 1971, Degh 1971, Hand 1971, Halpert 1971, Williams 1984, and Ben-Amos 1976.

8. For more on structural opposition in folklore, see Kongas and Maranda 1962, Maranda and Kongas-Maranda 1971, and Dundes (1978, chap. 6).

9. All the narratives included in this article were collected in Arabic and translated by the author.

10. Egypt is believed to have the best belly dancers in the Arab world.

11. In order to appreciate this story, we need to know that the Israeli soldiers often forced Palestinians to do things in ways contradictory to the instructions of the shabab.

REFERENCES

Ballard, Linda M. 1984. "Tales of the Troubles," in *Perspectives on Contemporary Legends,* ed. Paul Smith. Sheffield: University of Sheffield, Center for English Tradition and Language.

Barghouti, Abdul-latif, ed. 1990. *Folk Literature under the Intifada.* Taibeh, Israel: Society for the Revival of Arab Heritage.

Ben-Amos, Dan, ed. 1976. *Folklore Genres.* Austin: University of Texas Press.

Degh, Linda. 1971. "The 'Belief Legend' in Modern Society: Form, Function, and Relationship to Other Genres," in *American Folk Legend,* ed. Hand.

Degh, Linda, and Andrew Vazsonyi. 1983. "Does the Word 'Dog' Bite? Ostensive Action: A Means of Legend-Telling," *Journal of Folklore Research* 20, no. 1.

Dundes, Alan. 1971. "On the Psychology of Legend," in *American Folk Legend,* ed. Hand.

———. 1978. *Essays in Folkloristics.* Meerut, India: Folklore Institute.

Friedman, Albert B. 1971. "The Usable Myth: The Legends of Modern Mythmakers," in *American Folk Legend,* ed. Hand.

Georges, Robert A. 1971. "The General Concept of Legend: Some Assumptions to Be Re-examined and Re-assessed," in *American Folk Legend,* ed. Hand.

Halpert, Herbert. 1971. "Definition and Variation in Folk Legend," in *American Folk Legend*, ed. Hand.

Hand, Wayland D. 1965. "Status of European and American Legend Study," *Current Anthropology* 6, no. 4, pp. 439–46.

———, ed. 1971. *American Folk Legend; a Symposium*. Berkeley: University of California Press.

Jung, Carl G. 1969. *Flying Saucers: A Modern Myth of Things Seen in the Skies*. New York: New American Library.

Kanaana, Sharif. 1989a. "The Effect of Israeli Violence on Palestinian Children." Paper presented at the Third Annual Meeting of the International Popular Committee of Artists and Intellectuals for the Support of the Uprising and Struggle of the Palestinian People in Occupied Palestine, Athens, Greece, December 16–17, 1989.

———. 1989b. "Humor of the Palestinian Intifadah." Paper presented at the AFS Annual Conference, Philadelphia, Pennsylvania, October 18–22, 1989.

———. 1990. "Folk Narratives from the Intifadah," in *Folk Literature under the Intifadah*, ed. Abdul-latif Barghouti. Taibeh, Israel: Society for the Revival of Arab Heritage.

———. 1990. "Humor of the Palestinian Intifada," *Journal of Folklore Research* 27, no. 3.

Kongas, Elli-Kaija, and Pierre Maranda. 1962. "Structural Models in Folklore," *Midwest Folklore* 12.

Lüthi, Max. 1976. "Aspects of the Marchen and the Legend," in *Folklore Genres*, ed. Dan Ben-Amos. Austin: University of Texas Press.

Maranda, Pierre, and Elli Kongas-Maranda, eds. 1971. *Structural Analysis of Oral Tradition*. Philadelphia: University of Pennsylvania Press.

Nasser, Jamal R., and Roger Heacock. 1990. *Intifada: Palestine at the Crossroads*, New York: Praeger.

Nicolaisen, W. F. H. 1984. "Legends as Narrative Response," in *Perspectives on Contemporary Legends*, ed. Paul Smith. Sheffield: Center for English Tradition and Language, University of Sheffield.

Oring, Elliott, ed. 1986. *Folk Groups and Folklore Genres: An Introduction*. Logan: Utah State University Press.

Oring, Elliott. 1986. "Folk Narratives," in *Folk Groups and Folklore Genres*, ed. Oring.

Paredes, Americo. 1971. "Mexican Legendary and the Rise of the Mestizo: A Survey," in *American Folk Legend*, ed. Hand.

Smith, Paul, ed. 1984. *Perspectives on Contemporary Legend*. Sheffield: Center for Tradition and Language, University of Sheffield.

Williams, Noel. 1984. "Problems in Defining Contemporary Legends," in *Perspectives on Contemporary Legends*, ed. Smith.

·7·

SUHA SABBAGH

An Interview with Sahar Khalifeh, Feminist Novelist

Sahar Khalifeh was born in 1941 in Nablus, a town on the West Bank that is considered quite conservative and staunchly patriarchal. It is not surprising, therefore, that Nablus is known for its strong-willed women. Nablus has produced a number of women poets and academics, among them Fadwa Tuqan, Raymonda Tawil (who lived in Nablus during her married years), Salma Khadra Jayyusi, and Ghada Talhami. The most outspoken is Sahar Khalifeh, who deals with the denial of women's rights under occupation and in a traditional culture. In her novels, Khalifeh portrays the interrelatedness between these two forms of oppression. She has shown the same courage in her personal life as in her writing. After graduating form a parochial high school in Amman, she was forced into a marriage that turned out to be an unhappy one. After giving birth to two daughters, she sought to divorce her husband, a step rarely taken by women in Arab culture. She then continued her education at Birzeit University while raising her two daughters and pursuing her vocation as a writer. After obtaining her B.A. degree, she continued her education in the United States, where she received her M.A. from the University of North Carolina and in 1988 a Ph.D. in women's studies and literature from the University of Iowa, where I first met and interviewed her. Since then, Khalifeh and I have met several times, both in the United States and in the Middle East. This interview was conducted at different stages after our first meeting in 1988.

An Interview with Sahar Khalifeh

Her first novel, *After the Defeat* (Ba'd al Hazima), dealt with the impact of occupation on a number of characters who lived in the same apartment building in Nablus. It was also an existential novel about Arab intellectuals. Her early writings did not, however, project her feminist concerns.

Her Second novel, *Wild Thorns*, was submitted in lieu of a senior thesis at Birzeit University and was considered controversial even in the relatively tolerant atmosphere of that academic institution. It was rejected because parts of it were written in colloquial or street Arabic, not a common practice in Arabic literature. However, Khalifeh received the staunch support of a female professor, Hanan Mikhail Ashrawi, who recognized her uncanny ability to penetrate the life of the most politically and financially deprived strata of society. Khalifeh's book was subsequently accepted by Birzeit University and was soon translated into nine languages.

Khalifeh continues to write novels, and she is now head of the Women's Affairs Center in Nablus. One of the functions of the center is to document women's participation in and contributions to the intifada.

Was there a specific political factor that motivated you to write, and what impact did the experience of growing up in a conservative town have on your feminist thinking?

I began writing after the 1967 invasion of the West Bank. I was married then and living in Libya. The tensions in my marriage had stifled my creativity. As a child I used to paint and write poetry. But my marriage consumed all my creative energies and left me feeling powerless to direct the course of my life. Even in those difficult years, I never abandoned reading. I consumed all the books that came to my attention, but Simone de Beauvoir's writings had a great influence on me. Ironically, the occupation of the West Bank had a liberating effect on me. The year 1967 became a watershed year for me in a political and a personal sense. I felt that I could no longer remain an alienated housewife. I had to participate in the predicament of my people and contribute through my writings. First I wrote poetry, but I soon felt that poetry could not convey the reality that I sought to project. I was especially dismayed at the glorification and romanticization of women in poetry. Very few poems expressed the reality or the hardship of a woman's life. I felt that poetry did not convey the reality of life in the streets of Nablus.

My father was a fine man and my parents had a happy marriage. Yet, when my only brother was paralyzed in a car accident, my father felt compelled to remarry in order to have a son who would carry on the name of the family. My parents had six surviving daughters, but my father succumbed to social pressure. My mother was devastated by the experience, and her pain was transmitted to us. She was a woman who had much to offer, and yet society had mockingly called her "mother of daughters" until my brother, her son, was born. Unlike my sisters, who felt comfortable with the culture, I internalized all these messages about women and resented them. I was constantly crying without then realizing the reason. I can now say with confidence that I was reacting to all the restrictions imposed on women. My marriage did not do much to change my opinion about the situation of women. My way out of the marriage came about when I found employment as a secretary and was able to save enough money to return from Libya to the West Bank with my two daughters. My life as a student and as a divorced woman did not improve my status.

Some of these bitter childhood memories are recounted in *Memories of an Unrealistic Woman*. But the agony of women has become the main issue and the main theme of all my recent novels. I now divide my time between my work with women in the Women's Center and writing about women's issues.

Could you give the reader an idea of the topics you have chosen to write about and of the reception of your books?

The only copy of my first novel, *After the Defeat* (Ba'd al Hazima) was confiscated by the Israeli authorities as I was crossing the bridge from Jordan to the West Bank and my belongings were being searched. No specific reason was given then, and all my efforts to recover the manuscript were futile. I never tried to write the same novel again. My second novel, *We Are No Longer Your Slaves* (Lam Nauda Jawari Lacoum), also about the occupation, is currently out of print, but efforts are being made to reprint it in Beirut. My third novel, *Wild Thorns* (Al Subar), immediately received publicity in Israel and was translated into Hebrew. It deals with the plight of laborers who work in Israel. Because of the timeliness of the topic and because it is about a problem facing men rather than women, the book was translated into eight languages, including Dutch, French, Russian, and English. It did not appear in the Arab world until after the French edition. I think that is because I criticize those who would prevent the laborers from working for the benefit of the Israeli economy without offering them an alternative for feeding the many mouths that depend on them. In time, the political climate in the Arab world changed, and the book was published in Lebanon.

My first feminist novel was *Sunflower* (Abad El Shams), which deals with the lives of women laborers working for the benefit of the Israeli garment industry, and it is a sequel to *Wild Thorns*. While working on *Wild Thorns*, I became aware that women face different problems under occupation, and this was to become the theme of *Sunflower*. I did not mean to reinforce the segregation of the sexes by creating in two consecutive novels a women's world and a men's world. This was simply the outcome of my late arrival to feminism. My fifth book, *Memoirs of an Unrealistic Woman* (Mouthakarat Imra a Ghair Wakia'a) deals with the boredom of a so-called "happily married woman" who is well provided for by her husband but whose life does not allow for growth or fulfillment. I generally write about the dispossessed; but this novel, more autobiographical than the rest, is about the woman in a gilded cage. It sold extensively to women in the Arab world and was translated into Italian—Mediterranean women share some cultural similarities. My sixth and last novel, *Gateway to the City Square* (Bab Al-Saha, 1990), is about the role of women in the intifada. It describes the life of a prostitute in a strongly patriarchal culture who shows great wisdom and generosity to the culture that has shunned her. She is finally understood and appreciated.

In the Arab world you have gained the reputation of being a courageous writer who seeks to expose social problems. How are your novels different from those of male social critics, and do you consider yourself courageous?

My primary task is to liberate women from the confines of an image imposed on them by male writers. In political poems and novels written by men, women are a symbol for the land; for procreation; for endless and unconditional loving and giving. The woman is a mother, she is the beacon lighting the darkness for ships in the night and a shoulder for the tired to rest on. Motherhood in our culture is a cult that has its origins in literature. No matter how poetic these images are, they cannot lift the burden from the shoulders of women or change any of the attitudes that confine women. Rather, these symbols are gilded frames that help preserve the old female roles while making them seem more acceptable. The duty of all committed authors is to take the ax to these frames and to the pedestals on which women are placed in poetry. In their writings, women authors must replace the old images with vibrant new realities. They must portray new women who are closer to real women and who can relate to men on an equal footing.

In my novels I have sought to portray a new and different woman: a woman who is capable of giving without being exploited. A woman who is aware of her rights to the same degree as she is to her responsibilities. A woman who is self-critical and critical of society. This does not mean that I have set up one mold for women. In *Bab Al-Saha*, I empathize with many characters, although I do not support their views. I empathize with Zakiya although I do not endorse her traditional perceptions. I understand Nazha despite her excessive radicalism. I worry about Sahar and the consequences of a tarnished reputation. I admire Sahab's balanced life without exaggerating her influence as a role model.

What you call courage is, in my opinion, the only way to treat the subject of women long shrouded in lies, illusions, and falsification. I simply unveil these lies and reveal the reality beneath them. Some may find my style confrontational. Revealing the truth is the first step toward liberating women. I see my task as that of a doctor who must first undress and then examine the patient before arriving at the cure. I expose in order to examine the situation of women and not as an act of provocation. I do not see this as an act of courage but as a necessary and unavoidable step.

Your novels have caused some controversy because you use "street language" or colloquial instead of classical Arabic. How do you defend yourself against these charges?

As a novelist I am prepared to experiment with different forms and to use colloquial language when it serves my purpose. Colloquial Arabic is closer to the heart because we all grew up using this language. In addition, the use of the Palestinian colloquial creates a bond between Palestinians in the occupied territories and Palestinians in the diaspora. In this sense language becomes a shared bond that, under conditions of occupation or dispersal, can replace the homeland. The novel also becomes the means of keeping the diaspora informed about linguistic evolution. New expressions are constantly being formed in the colloquial, especially in times of crisis, and the Palestinians have had more than their share of intense political moments.

It is legitimate to ask whether the colloquial is capable of the same range of expression as the classical language. The colloquial is most suited for dialogue since it represents the way in which people actually express themselves, whereas the classical language is best suited for analytical and descriptive passages. I employ both in order to convey all levels of meaning.

How were your books and your views received in Nablus? Did you notice any change in attitudes to women after your first feminist work, *Sunflower*?

I have a love-hate relationship with Nablus, the city that formed me. I know and can relate to the many faces of Nablus. In my memories I can evoke the sounds and sights of the old city. At the same time I hate some of the intransigent, conservative attitudes toward women. In any case this is my city and I have to live with the fact that it will always be the place that dominates my writing.

An Interview with Sahar Khalifeh

The intifada lured me back to Nablus. In the early stage, the uprising had a mesmerizing effect on many Palestinians. It was a promise for a better future and it offered each the possibility of being part of that process of change. I came back to open the Women's Center in a place where it was most evidently needed. Now that I have earned a doctorate, something generally reserved for men, the attitude of Nablus toward me has changed. I have become accepted as one of the circle of established writers about which the city boasts. Mothers appreciate the work of the center and do not feel threatened when they send their daughters to work with me. Change is coming to Nablus.

What are the main functions of the center?

The Women's Affairs Center (previously the Women's Resource Center) was established in 1989 to gather information and statistics on women and women's issues. Its purpose is to document women's participation in the intifada so as to avoid the fate that Algerian women met after liberation. It also collects data on women since we do not currently have accurate information on most subjects that relate to women.

We have trained a number of local researchers in methods of collecting and evaluating data. One research project focused on the role of women nurses during the intifada and on the attitudes of hospitals toward them as employees. These findings, along with many interesting papers on women's issues, were published in the spring 1990 issue of *Shoun Al-Mara,* a journal published by the center that deals with women's issues.

Are women the only ones whose rights are denied in Arab culture?

The freedom of men, women, and the land are connected on the West Bank and I have written about all three in my novels. Often the oppression of women unwittingly benefits the occupation. Immobilization of the female population weakens by 50 percent the ability of the society to resist. We are unwittingly discarding half of our human resources. A weakened body cannot resist the attack from the outside because it is internally weak and ailing. Consequently, the liberation of women impacts in a very direct way on the liberation of the land.

Women are not the only ones who are oppressed in a given society. A healthy society must ensure the rights of the sick, the old, of children, and of the individual—including women.

I am more interested in the rights of women because I have a vested interest here. A society that oppresses the individual, including women, will not be able to produce a people capable of resisting occupation. The subaltern who has accepted diminished status is incapable of revolt. Let me give some examples from *Bab Al-Saha.* The female protagonist, Sahar, is hindered by tradition from expressing her political right to resist. Traditional cultural ties paralyze her. The mother has the right to restrict her mobility, the older brother abuses her, and the younger brother is satisfied with being an observer of her predicament. This typifies the situation of many young women who might otherwise have contributed much more to society. Palestinian women who, before they go to a demonstration, must first overcome patriarchal authority are less likely to get there. Not only the immediate family but the neighborhood, the aunts and uncles, the extended family all have the right to impose their will on these young women eager to demonstrate.

I am not asking for a redirection of energies that are badly needed for resistance. I am simply questioning the principle that governs internal relationships between people. The intifada is a process of reorganizing these internal relationships as much as it is a form of resistance to occupation. If no new social relations emerge, then, unfortunately, we will have fought in vain. After all, the future homeland that we seek is not an abstract idea. It is a concept based on the relations that we aspire to have with one another.

If I measure all women's progress in terms of their contribution to the intifada it is because there is no other reality right now on the West Bank and in Gaza. It is not possible to discuss the right of women to pursue a career or an education when the universities and high schools are shut down for years. There are many educated women, but job opportunities will continue to be few as long as we do not control our economy.

Can you foresee the agenda for social and political change on the West Bank?

This is a very important question. Unfortunately, on the West Bank today we do not have a group that is working for women's rights as there is in Egypt, although there are many charity organizations run by women who are doing a remarkable job. I don't have a base with which to work as does Sadawi, and I don't think that the issue of women's rights will be given priority under the current conditions of occupation. The following should happen: women's participation should be recorded at the present time; when a political solution has been reached, we could then negotiate for greater rights in much the same way as the numerous political factions. We will simply say we helped with the national agenda and now we need to participate in the decision-making process. Unfortunately, no one is recording the activities of women, and I am afraid that all the work done by the charity organizations will be forgotten in time and women will lose what few strides they have made so far (statement made July 1988).

An Interview with Sahar Khalifeh

This trend is similar to what has happened in most Third World countries. Khadiga Abu Alli wrote in 1974 that during times of national struggle, women go out and participate in the national agenda. However, when liberation has been achieved, they invariably return to the home. Their actions do not translate into greater rights or more jobs. I believe that this situation can be avoided on the West Bank if women do not isolate themselves but join existing cadres and structures, trying to change them from within in preparation for things to come. Right now women's organizations are exclusive and this trend may have a serious backlash.

What are some of the differences, in your view, between feminist concerns in this country and on the West Bank?

Most feminists in this country who emerged from the liberal tradition fail to see the relation between political structures and issues concerning women. In the Third World this relation cannot be ignored. In my writings I have tried to show the extent to which the two are interrelated. In addition, in this country there is a feeling that men are somehow responsible for all the problems facing women. I believe that in Arab culture it is the system of values that should be blamed for being unfair to both men and women. One of the positive aspects on the West Bank is the relation that binds society together—we cannot afford to turn this into a confrontation between men and women or we will destroy the very fiber of society. Ideally, I would like to see a situation in which men help raise women's issues on the West Bank.

The number of women who have gone out to work has not increased very markedly, and one cannot conclude that the status of those who do work has changed. Very often women come home and hand their earnings to the male head of the family. Their work does not automatically translate into greater power in the home. Even in families where women seem to enjoy equality, men make the big decisions, for example, concerning the purchase of property.

Would you say that the role of women changed during the intifada?

During the intifada women were seen on TV screens beating soldiers, throwing stones, pouring into the streets in demonstrations. Many saw this as a radical transformation of the role of women. But the spontaneous nature of these actions prevented women from achieving any serious political gains. Women's participation should have been the product of organized activity.

This spontaneous outpouring of reactions may be the cause of the current religious fundamentalist backlash that has caused women to lose many more rights. We must be leery of spontaneous actions because they can bring about reactionary responses. And we must also be leery of making sweeping generalizations about the gains that women made during the intifada. While it is true that several women emerged as political leaders, we must ask ourselves whether the situation of the majority has changed as a result. We must rely on field research rather than fleeting impressions. Many young women and many women from all walks of life became conscious of their rights and responsibilities during the struggle, but the majority has not translated their participation into gains at home. Preliminary field research has shown that the early optimistic assessment of transformations in gender relations were premature. This research poses the question of how we can expect women to struggle for national liberation when they are oppressed in every other way in society. As women, we are currently in a crisis situation, and we must reevaluate the courses of action that we must take.

Intifada implies the revamping of a social structure from within as well as resistance to occupation. It may be too early to come to any conclusions regarding the changes that the intifada will bring to the lives of women. But we must begin to pose certain questions. Has the intifada delivered the social transformations that it has promised? Did it liberate the individual? What has it done for women? And why did the participation of women diminish during the last phase of the intifada? Is it because women feel that they have no role to play, or is it because society is torn by contradictions? All the intifada slogans call for the liberation of the individual as well as the land. Is there a double standard when this individual is a woman? My role as a committed writer requires me to raise these questions in my writings.

HANAN MIKHAIL ASHRAWI

Two Short Stories
by a Palestinian Feminist

The Gold Snake

I pick up a stone. Clutching it tightly in my fist I raise my arm. The impulse to hurl it with all my strength rises in my body, through my veins, like a viscous substance—cold and deliberate—starting with my cracked feet and up through my womb, beginning to wither with prolonged childlessness, and my breasts, dry of milk, to my veined arm, for once raised in a clenched fist. The mid-morning sun reflects off the bracelet on my wrist, and the blinding glare freezes all motion. A gold snake, its scales worn by years of scrubbing and cleaning, of embracing and releasing, of dressing and undressing, stares at me blindly with two ruby eyes. I was only fourteen when the snake, with new scratchy scales, was wound around my wrist as part of my dowry—the *mahr*—in partial payment of the bride's price. Along with it came a heavy gold *halabi* chain from which dangled an intricate *iczeh*, a filigreed almond that was even bigger than the one my mother wore hanging from her neck in between her dry and wrinkled breasts. Both almonds were empty. On my other wrist, a thick coin bracelet with genuine 'Osmalli and *Inglizi* coins completed my engagement wear. I felt rich and cherished then, entering the mysterious cult of womanhood fully adorned in the tradition of my sex and race. The coin bracelet was the first to go in that year of drought, when the olive harvest failed and our grape-vines withered in early summer. Next the *lozeh* went to pay for the schooling of Walid—my only born, the joy of my life, the hope of my future—while he lived. But the snake remained. I wore it on my wrist all those nineteen years until it wore me—winding itself around my thick-ening flesh, its tail meeting its head in a tightening double circle that refused to slacken. Not all the soap or oil greasing my hand could make it slip off my wrist, until I stopped noticing its existence. We became one.

The same ruby eyes stared coldly at me on my wedding night, as I clutched the bedpost frantically praying for the pain to stop, for that monster heaving on my innocent body to disappear, for the comforting embrace of my absent mother to reclaim me. I bit my lips with a fierce determination not to scream, and the sheets turned ruby red with blood of my twice torn body. It was my duty, my fate and pride as a virgin bride, I was told. But no one warned me or armed me against the pain. On that same bed Walid was born. At fifteen I watched my body being taken away from me again as the *dayeh* poked and prodded between my thighs and kneaded my swollen stomach like leavened dough with a calculated impersonality that was even more terrifying than my pain. For a whole day and night my body refused to give up its inhabitant, while I prayed and prayed for a boy in order to spare this unknown child a woman's fate. I cursed my husband then for his unbidden forays inside my body and my mother for the forbidden secrets that she never divulged. "You'll forget," she had said. "All women do, or the race would end." I never forgot. And as the screams welled up from the depths of my stomach through my parched throat, I froze at the dispas-sionate stare of the ruby eyes and in silence and blood gave birth to Walid. At fifteen I became Im Walid, and Abu Walid strutted about with pride of fatherhood, having sired a son, while I silently cursed my fertility and worshipped its fruit. That was eighteen years ago.

Walid's eyes were open when I got to him. Staring blindly into an empty sky, they did not recognize me. With all my pent-up pain and the million silent screams I could not release, I pressed my palm to the open gash that the bullet had made in its passage through his head. Blood and brains mingled as I cradled his head in my lap and drenched my *thoub* with the warm thick liquid that seeped through to my breasts and thighs. I knew the bracelet was uncomfortable in its cold hardness and I tried to remove it from beneath his head. But he felt nothing. I wrapped his tortured head with the *hatta* he had worn around his neck ("It's our national symbol, Yamma") and cried searing hot tears, silently, gently, singing a broken lullaby, "Nam ya habibi nam."

Abu Walid, the *waled*, now stares into space; no longer a father, he fingers his beads and murmurs, "la illaha illa Allah." I am the *waledah;* having once given birth, I claim my right over life and death. The pain of the latter, I swear, is greater and more unforgivable.

The soldiers appear and the snake coiled around my wrist glitters wickedly, like an obscene signal. With my free hand I pull at it, twist it back and forth, but it refuses to let go. I pick up a stone; resting my wrist on a rock, I strike at the snake with an almost insane strength. My wrist is bloody but I feel no pain. The snake breaks off. With my mangled hand I grasp the stone damp with blood and with all my strength hurl it at the pointing guns.

A Pair of Shoes

I can't remember where I left my shoes. I remember taking them off— spike heels, patent leather, Italian import—and carrying them in my hand as we climbed the hill through a cloud of tear gas. My feet are torn and bleeding, my sheer French hose a mess, but never mind. Strange, this delightful, delicious sensation of freedom, to be able to wriggle my toes and feel the roughness of the earth, the jagged sharpness of bare stones sending shocked messages of recognition through the soles of my bare feet. Those same stones I pick up now, rough and heavy, and pile deliberately with uneven thuds onto the makeshift barricade. My soft, smooth hands are blistering, blessed beautiful bubbles that will gradually turn into rough callouses. My husband had spared no expense in preserving the cool smoothness of my hands—a dishwasher, a maid, and expensive hand and body lotions. These hands now hauling rocks were trained to do nothing more arduous than arrange on a silver tray the appetizing *kubbeh* spheres and delicate spinach *fatayer* that the guests at our bridge parties used to enjoy so much. Sami always made a point of complimenting me on the delicacy of my ringed hands as well as on my aesthetic abilities at preparing the *maza* trays. I always made a point of smiling back, dutifully, mechanically, like the cherished and pampered wife that I was, basking in the glow of my husband's pride of possession. Our guests smiled back, looking knowingly at one another (how lucky Leila was), secretly envious of my (or his) good fortune.

A captive of this chain of painted smiles, with words floating like colorful balloons over the green bridge table, I turned inward and cursed myself for my ungracious lack of gratitude. A strange and heavy sensation like a cumbersome rock settled in my chest until I could hardly breathe. Sisyphus rolled his rock uphill in an exercise in futility, while I harbored mine inside with an ever-increasing heaviness that only I could feel.

HANAN MIKHAIL ASHRAWI

I reach for a rock too heavy to lift. Najwa sees me and quickly comes to my side—in her faded jeans and "sensible" shoes—and helps me roll it, then pile it on a rising barricade. We exchange a knowing, somewhat conspiratorial smile, and I feel a lightness of spirit, a sensation of breathlessness, like a delicate silk thread weaving a safe and warm cocoon of recognition to engulf us. How I used to envy her, with a sulky, sullen, deliberate silence, as Sami and "our friends" spitefully gossiped about her. She dared live alone, openly flaunting her state of singlehood (bachelorhood, she called it), wearing unfashionable clothes (even pants and jeans for work), unashamedly educated (a Ph.D. scares away potential suitors), and clearly oblivious to the dictates of social ritual and decorum (conspicuously absent from weddings, funerals, and bridge parties). I used to look down at the ruffled front of my silk shirt, ever on the lookout for that slovenly wrinkle or spot that might betray me, passionately resenting all "dry clean only" labels on the designer outfits with which my husband's export-import (mainly import) business supplied me. Particularly her shoes—how I longed with the hidden desire of the physically deprived for the indulgence, the pleasure, of "sensible" shoes to walk in. Not the leather vice and stilts that my husband found "so very sexy" but those soft, firm walking shoes that would enable a woman to stride confidently and surely on her way to a specific destination. My shoes made me hesitant, tentative, and ever so feminine in my husband's eyes; and I never walked anywhere.

Which is why he blamed me for Lina's beating. "It's all your fault," he said. "You should have taken her to school and back every day, like I told you." But how could I know that it would be that one fateful day, the one time I gave in to her constant entreaties to let her walk home from school with her friends, to release her from that abnormal mechanical prison that transported her from one confinement (at home) to another (in school) without the joy of sunshine and fresh air? I knew about the intifada and the soldiers' bone-breaking brutality, bullets, and tear gas—more than my husband ever dreamt I knew—and yet I dared release my ten-year-old butterfly for a few minutes of freedom. I drove behind them, schoolgirls growing wings, and in that split-second between the raised truncheon in the soldier's hand and my braking and opening the car door, I lived through an infinity of terror. I wobbled on my high heels and clutched her to my breast, blood and streaming hair, taking the blows on my arms and shoulders, shielding that precious vulnerable head with an obstinate imperviousness to pain that can transform a mother into a rock. For two days and a night I sat by her hospital bed, holding her hand, staring at the closed eyes beneath the bandaged head, and willing her with all my might to live. She lived, my

Lina with the hair of light brown silk. My Lina, who always used to start her drawings with a rainbow and a smiling sun, now draws a Palestinian flag, below which a girl faces a gigantic figure in uniform brandishing a blood-stained club. Her laughter does not tinkle any more but reverberates with a knowledge way beyond her years.

It is this knowledge that I share with Najwa now. On top of the hill, behind the barricades (Sami does not know where I am), I look down at the soldiers who look like the armed robots Lina used to play with, and I laugh. I don't give a damn about my lost shoes!

PART THREE

The Double Burden of Women: Tradition and Occupation

·9·

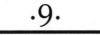

ROBIN MORGAN

Women in the Intifada

In 1986, I spent more than six weeks with Palestinian women in the UNRWA (United Nations Relief and Works Agency for Palestine Refugees in the Near East) refugee camps of Egypt, Jordan, Lebanon, and the occupied territories of West Bank and the Gaza Strip. That experience—and the intensely moving first-person stories of those women—is detailed at length in my book *The Demon Lover.*

I wrote then that "I was to meet victims and survivors, women who by their mid-fifties were already great-great-grandmothers, women who bear the societal scars of having refused to marry at all, women who dare to love other women. I was to meet Palestinian women whose sole means of resistance is to wear keys on strings of chains around their throats, keys to homes bombed or razed forty years earlier. I was to meet highly educated Palestinian women, sophisticated in the ways of patriarchal politics, who had risen as far as possible within the PLO, only to hit the glass ceiling of male supremacy." But the focus of the journey was on the women in the refugee camps who suffer with every breath they inhale. They are former peasants, teachers, ex-guerrillas, artists, nurses, manual laborers, social workers, housewives, doctors, organizers, students, mothers, secretaries, factory workers.

I had insisted on women interpreters, knowing that the kind of communication I hoped to inspire would be impossible through male interpreters. This had never been done before; UNRWA had no female interpreters but did manage to find Palestinian women among its own personnel who, although employed as educators, medical staff, or social workers, were able and eager to translate, never having been given the opportunity to do so before. These women were extraordinary, and together we asked questions no journalist had ever bothered to ask of Palestinian women. And we heard answers of such honesty and anger as to shock even the translators. Not surprisingly—although contrary to everything I'd been told—I found an omnipresent, open feminism, sometimes raw, often polished, albeit fortunately not so narrow as Western definitions of it. These women's lives were also dramatic testimony to the indomitable and affirmative spirit of female human beings surviving in unspeakable conditions.

But if the conditions were virtually unspeakable in 1986, they were almost unthinkable in 1988 when I returned to the region—this time focusing on the occupied territories, specifically to investigate the impact of the intifada on Palestinian women.

The intifada had begun in 1987 as a series of spontaneous street demonstrations and general strikes to protest the Israeli government's treatment of Palestinians, especially those on the West Bank and in the Gaza Strip. By March of 1988, the occupying army (the Israeli government's term is "Administrative Authority") had posted an additional ten thousand troops on round-the-clock patrol in the two territories; for three days at the end of that month, all 650,000 residents of the Strip—the most densely populated, poorest place on earth—had been confined to their homes under an "Iron Fist" policy of "collective punishment" curfew.

There were over four hundred deaths and severe injuries in one week in Gaza alone. UNRWA, already overworked and understaffed (most UNRWA personnel in the field are Palestinian), moved to take emergency measures—keeping some clinics in Gaza open twenty-four hours a day, organizing special feeding programs, and more than doubling the international staff that directs the field offices. These temporary emergency measures were to become permanent, however, in response to the spiraling escalations of both the intifada and the Israeli government's reaction to it. By August of 1988, almost nine thousand Palestinians were in makeshift prison camps awaiting trial (including two thousand who were being held under "administrative detention" orders, which allow a suspect to be jailed for continuous, renewable, six-month periods with no judicial review). Having already seen how Palestinian women not only share the conditions and anguish of their men but, in addition, bear the crushing burden of being female in a doubly intense patriarchal context (both Arab and Israeli) I could only imagine what the impact of even greater brutality on their lives might be.

Women in the Intifada

What I had found in 1986 was a cauldron simmering with male violence and female suffering. When I returned in 1988, the cauldron had boiled over. The following essay is extracted from chapters in my books *The Demon Lover* and *The Word of a Woman* based on what I witnessed, heard, and felt in 1988, interspersed with my recollections of 1986.

The first people I see, after the many khaki-clad, heavily armed soldiers clustered at the checkpoint of the border with Israel, is a four-block-long column of men in Gaza Town. They are kneeling on the cracked and broken sidewalks, hands on their heads, backs to the street, with faces pressed to the shuttered fronts of little shops. Some are bleeding, many have ripped clothing. Behind them stand soldiers, Galil rifles pointed at the back of the kneeling men's heads. I am told that "an incident" has just taken place—a stone throwing. These are the suspects, some caught in action, others merely picked up during a broad "sweep" of the area.

The second sight is of women—forty or fifty, perhaps—also on their knees, in the middle of the street itself. No, not on their knees; they are on all fours. Some are pregnant; some are old women; a few appear to be little more than girls. All of them are weeping—some silently, some loudly. Other soldiers stand over them, semiautomatics at the ready. That is when I learn about the new policy: after demonstrations or "incidents," Palestinian women are rounded up and forced to clear the streets with their bare hands, made to pick up broken glass; chipped bricks; stones; still-smoking, noxious tear-gas canisters; spent bullets; sometimes a live Molotov cocktail. No brooms are allowed.

I know I am back in the Gaza Strip.

January nights remind me how close the Strip is to the savage cold of the desert in winter and to the damp of the Mediterranean Sea. A muscle-cramping chill settles in every evening. It is impossible to get the clamminess out of one's clothing, still damp from having been soaked through earlier by the daily rains. The sand—as roads, as pathways, as the floors of camp shelters approximately nine by thirteen feet and housing as many as fifteen family members—has become churned mud. It sucks vigorously at my sturdy boots, almost pulling them off; what must it do to the rubber clogs or cheap sneakers worn by most camp residents? Open sewers in Rafah Camp overflow with rainwater, with run-off, with human waste. There is no heat in the shelters, and very few have any electricity at all. Punitive power cuts by the army, ordered with no advance warning, make even that unreliable.

I inquire about an impressive half-built edifice I've seen on the drive into the Strip—a tall, modern building close to the beach. It turns out to be a pilot project for the government's plans to turn the Gaza Strip into a Mediterranean tourist playground.

No news report can communicate the atmosphere of palpable fear, everyone tensed in apprehension of the next eruption of rage from one or both parties to the conflict. The ear quickly learns to interpret no shout as a greeting, no crackle of explosive as a car backfire; the eye learns to trust no scene as tranquil; there is no such thing as relaxing the alert, even for a second.

The faces of the men have changed. Relentless, intense emotions seem to have distorted them into ritual masks. That reassuringly ill-disguised panic and confusion I had glimpsed on the faces of many Israeli soldiers in 1986 has vanished, replaced by a smooth expression of contempt—though whether it is contempt for those they fight or for themselves no one can say. But it is clear that these young men have grown calluses over their feelings—over having any, much less showing them—and now wear their discipline with tragic ease. Some do so with the indifference of professionals, others with the relish of fanatics. These expressions are strikingly twinned in the faces of the *shabab*—the young male Palestinian militants. Except for the soldiers' array of weapons and the blue jeans, T-shirt, and black-and-white-checked Palestinian *keffiyyeh* (neckerchief/scarf) worn by the *shabab* one could not tell them apart.

I suddenly understand the real reason why uniforms were invented.

In 1988, each one of the 400,000 adult Gazans are forced to exchange her or his old green identity card for a computerized, magnetic one issued by the army. The thousands of Palestinians standing in line to exchange the cards are herded past soldiers carrying automatic rifles toward rows of secretaries who punch the identity numbers into banks of IBM computers that instantly reveal all data such as outstanding tax obligations; each Palestinian must "clear up" such "problems" before being issued the new card—without which it is impossible to receive rations, register a marriage, obtain a driver's license or a birth or death certificate, accept a paycheck, do any banking, pass through the omnipresent army checkpoints along the roads, or go to seek employment or work in Israel.

There is an "official policy" of no beatings. Yet everywhere in the camps now I see wounded, bandaged, and badly bruised men, women, and children. Each woman has stories: she—or her sister, her daughter, her mother, her aunt or cousin or friend—was beaten by soldiers: women in labor, old women, nursing mothers, toddlers, babies. Many point to the bullet holes in the walls of their shelters. The rate of miscarriages has risen precipitously—the result of beatings, running after children or away from soldiers, of rising rates of hypertension and anemia due to malnutrition (because of food shortages), possibly as a result of the effects of toxic elements in the tear gas, certainly from acute and unremitting stress. The UNRWA clinics, many housed in decrepit buildings, their courtyards even more overcrowded with waiting women and children than in 1986, are as immaculate as they were then—with one exception: the smell of antiseptic has been overpowered by the stench of tear gas. It is a common occurrence for the army to lob gas canisters into the clinic courtyards and into the clinics themselves. UNRWA formally protests such acts; the Palestinians denounce them as harassment; the army calls them, alternately, punitive action during the pursuit of a provocateur who may have taken shelter there, or simply "mistakes."

Used canisters—still reeking acridity—are commonplace sights. One sees them on the dirt roads, along the highways, in the muddy narrow lanes that pass for streets in the camps, in the city thoroughfares of Arab East Jerusalem. The United States officially states that it stopped shipping tear gas to Israel in the early 1980s. The canisters I see are clearly marked: USA 1987 Issue.

Most of the intifada's daily "incidents" seem to constitute a war between children and adults. Confrontation after confrontation is between Palestinian boys, many as young as six and seven, throwing stones at Israeli patrols—each member of which is bedecked with a helmet, a pistol, a Galil rifle, an ammunition belt, a truncheon, a gas mask, and tear-gas canisters.

At Al Ahli Hospital in Gaza, a haggard-looking doctor tells me that these days, when she enters the emergency room, she often thinks for a moment that by error she is in the pediatrics ward.

But the little boys no longer see themselves as children; they identify with their older brothers, the shabab, their dead or living heroes. The little boys say they are "training for manhood." When one of them has been killed, the others speak admiringly of him as having become "a little man."

The women—both mothers and teachers—openly deplore this. At Nuseirat Camp, home to almost thirty thousand refugees, I have a reunion with teachers I had met two years earlier; I am surprised and touched that they remember me.

"Oh yes," Wafa smiles, "you are the American woman who cried with us. How could we forget that?"

Embraces, little cups of the ever-present strong Arab coffee, shared confidences. The teachers lament that they can no longer control their male students of any age: "The army is not supposed to enter the camps.

But you see how, at the gates of every camp, there are soldiers—entire encampments, tents, tanks. Just waiting. And they come in and patrol. They swagger through, even though they know it will provoke an incident. Sometimes the *shabab* do the provoking; they stand at the entrance and shout curses across the road."

I nod, saying that I have already noticed how proficient the young men—both Israeli and Palestinian—have become in each others' languages, although their vocabulary is restricted to insults. "If they studied more, they would know more," one woman dryly interjects. These are, after all, teachers. I am reminded of the Palestinian obsession with education; the pride that Palestinian women have the fastest growing literacy rate of women anywhere in the Arab world.

Bassimah continues: "The moment anyone sees them enter the camp, news spreads. All it takes is four words—'The soldiers are coming'—and the boys run out of the classroom. We cannot stop them."

More than one teacher had physically interposed herself between the boys and the door—and literally been run over.

And the girl students? "They rush to the window to try and see what's happening," is the response. "Sometimes they join in—sometimes they lead the demonstrations because the boys have become more afraid of arrests. But basically the tragedy of the girls is different. Do you remember what they used to answer a few years ago when you asked what they wanted to become as grown-ups?"

I remember well. They had said they wanted to become teachers, doctors, nurses, lawyers, architects. Their faces shining with intelligence and hope, they had said they didn't want to have more than two children—not like their mothers, who have an average of six to eight. Some had said they wanted no children at all; others said they never intended to marry or, if they did, it would be for love, not an arranged match. This, in the context of Arab tradition, had struck me as an incipient revolution.

Bassimah goes out briefly and returns with a student about twelve years old. The child is solemn, wears the *hijab* (head covering), has dark circles under her eyes. "Ask her that question now," says Bassimah.

I do, and the response comes swiftly, in a flat voice: "I want to be the mother of a martyr."

"But what if there is no need for martyrs by the time you are grown?" Wafa puts in. "What if there is peace, freedom, statehood? Then what?"

"I want to be the mother of martyrs," comes the answer in monotone.

"You once wanted to be a writer, remember? You were so good with your essays. Remember how much you wanted to write books?"

The child looks confused.

"Try to remember," the teachers urge gently. "It is still possible for you. Your people need books, too, scholars, poets, storytellers. What will you do with your life after peace?"

For a moment there is a flicker in the little girl's eyes. Then the present closes down again, erasing past and future.

"I want to be the mother of martyrs," she intones.

The teachers and I exchange glances. The eyes I look into brim with tears.

Mary Khass is a widely respected Christian Palestinian educator; her specialty is preschool child psychology and education; she is in demand as a speaker on the subject at international conferences. A woman in her late fifties, she looks ten years older than she did two years earlier. Her hands twist with anguish as she speaks to me: "The children. My god, the children. You saw them before—their games, their laughter—even in the camps, even in the midst of poverty, crowding, danger, humiliation. They were still children. But now? Now their favorite game is 'intifada.' They take turns playing soldiers and Palestinians—like cowboys and Indians. They play at gassing, arrest, detention, beatings, roundups. They are brutal with one another; it has become their fun. Nothing dissuades them—not coaxing or promises, not talkings-to or discipline. They are saturated with violence."

I ask about the pride the intifada has undeniably given the Palestinians, a pride in fighting back, in ceasing to be victims. In response I am told: "The adults may feel the pride. The men, certainly. But what is happening to the children is forming a legacy we will have to live with for generations. The leadership must be brought to understand this, to comprehend that these children are being drenched in violence and vengeance. Many can no longer imagine any other way of living. The adults know that in five years, ten years, there *will* be a two-state solution. Any sane adult—Palestinian or Israeli—admits that. But how will these children deal with peace? They no longer have any context for relating to it. These children will carry the scars—scars of euphoria at bloodshed—for the rest of their lives. And infect *their* children. We are creating Northern Ireland all over again, here and now."

But the pride is there, too, and fiercely cherished as the sole possession of a desperate people. It differs in its expression. For the men, it is pride in manhood—best expressed in martyrdom. For the women, it is pride in keeping alive what little they can.

Everywhere they have organized into neighborhood women's committees. The women manage to secure and share food even under curfew. They care for the wounded. They try to rescue and hide children about to be arrested. They help one another survive—the newly widowed, the deserted and abandoned (by men who have disappeared—to detention or deportation, or to fight or to flee). They share their already overcrowded shelter homes, giving refuge to families whose shelters have been bulldozed (the policy of collective punishment permits the destruction of a shelter if the soldiers think a family member has thrown a stone).

In 1986 the just-budding women's committee had focused on adult literacy, on skill-sharing, on small, income-generating projects. Now they are full grown. But now they focus on community survival.

And the intifada has had its own effect on the women. The boldness that was evident in private, with only other women present, has gone public. They no longer ask permission of their men to receive a guest or to go out—even at night. They say that the men don't like this but can do nothing about it. Even the men know that women are the lifeline of survival.

The women are excited by their newfound relative freedom and amused by the men's reaction. They seem on the whole to have retained a sense of humor that the men appear to have lost. Rula, in Kalandia Camp on the West Bank, is witty in her description of women's plight under the intifada: "Well, of course there is the terror, and the special hardships in getting food, water, basic necessities. But I sometimes think that the worst of it is the presence of the men. Before, the men would leave after breakfast and not return until dark. If they had employment, they'd go to work; if they were unemployed, they'd be out looking for jobs. And there was always a coffee house, no matter how dilapidated, where they'd sit for hours and talk. Meanwhile, the children would be in school. This of course meant that the women could get on with life—the washing and cleaning and cooking—and maybe even have a minute to sit with a friend and talk. But *now . . .*"—Rula rolls her eyes in mock despair—"now, between the curfews and school closing and job firings called for by the Israelis, and the general strike days and school closings called for by the intifada leadership, there are sometimes days on end when all the men and children are home. *All day long.* It's a nightmare: they're underfoot all the time, wanting this, demanding that, whining about something else. The woman must cook three full meals a day—when and if there's food. She has no peace, even for a moment."

The neighborhood women's committee near her, Rula says, organized an ingenious solution. There was one battered black-and-white television set in the area and, whenever the power was on, the women marshalled all the men and children, parked them in front of it, and then went on about their lives.

Women in the Intifada

On my first trip to the region, mobility in and between camps had been difficult at times but always possible. I could start out talking with women by 6 A.M., spend the entire day at one camp or visit two or even more, and continue until late at night, sometimes "changing shifts" of exhausted interpreters.

This time, mobility is severely restricted. Camps are "sealed" with absolutely no notice, leaving one at the entrance trying to get in—or inside trying to leave—for hours, or days. Absolute curfew in the occupied territories is lowered at dusk; the streets in Gaza or in East Jerusalem look like ghost towns. Any vehicle caught driving—even with UNRWA credentials—may be subjected to thorough stop-and-search tactics, harangues, threats, and frisking of the occupants.

In some of the tiny Palestinian villages, to move at night is to risk yet another danger—the assumption is that car headlights presage an army vehicle. A shower of stones is likely to greet such a vehicle.

But there are women I promised to see in one such village, and the only time to do that is at night. Under cover of darkness, they conduct now-illegal literacy classes for adults and for children who have fallen behind in their school work because of forced school closings.

I do not travel in an UNRWA car. A Palestinian woman drives me in a borrowed, battered private car. And as we pass through the villages, she blinks her headlights in a particular signal.

"Why don't the authorities pick up on the signal?" I ask. I cannot see her smile in the dark, but I can hear it in her voice: "They try. But the signal is changed from day to day." I do not ask how.

On the West Bank, I go to Ramallah, to the Ramallah Women's Training Center, which I had written about earlier as "an oasis of sanity and hope." Two years earlier, the spacious grounds, the spotless classrooms, the tidy dormitories—were all filled with young women (288 vocational students, 350 teacher training students), talking animatedly, laughing, walking arm-in-arm, proud and beautiful. This is the first vocational training center for women in the entire Middle East, and it is a source of enormous pride to Palestinian women.

In 1988 the grounds are deserted, the classrooms and dorms empty. I learn from the school's principal, Ms. Lamis El Alami, that the school had been closed by the occupying authority for over a year. "All the Palestinian institutions of higher learning—like Birzeit University, like this one—have been forcibly closed," she tells me, "accusations that they were hotbeds breeding student radicalism, you know. The irony is that here, the girls glimpsed a peace they had never known—peace not only from occupation, but from the constraints of their own fathers and brothers. Here they learned skills for the future, and how to pass on those skills. From here they would go home questioning everything: violence, religious fundamentalism, multiple pregnancies, arranged marriages, all the patriarchal traditions. For that kind of consciousness, yes, we were a hot bed, a breeding ground. Now. . . ."

I ask when the school might be permitted to open again. She sighs. "Who knows? We petition regularly. It could be next week, next year, never. We try to use the time constructively, even with a skeleton staff. We are fundraising to build a new department, to train women physical therapists." Her eyes begin to gleam with excitement. "There is discrimination against female patients who need physical therapy, you see. And, as you know, there are many in need of physical rehabilitation, many wounded, paralyzed—from beatings, from bullet wounds, even from the so-called merciful rubber bullets. All the Arab physical therapists are men. But tradition has it that women's bodies ought not to be touched by men other than their husbands. So the male patients get rehab and the female patients usually go without. It's tragic. But this new department will begin to address the problem."

Together she and I stroll slowly through the deserted grounds. I comment on how beautifully they are still kept up—the flower beds neat, the grass mowed, the bougainvillea still cascading its crimson brilliance, the climbing white roses perfuming the air, indifferent to whether Arab or Israeli or U.S. visitors breathe in their fragrance.

"Oh yes," Ms. Alami smiles, "volunteers. Mostly women, of course. We will not fold up and go away. We will out-wait this, so the girls have us to come back to someday." Her face clouds over. "But I grieve for the ones we've lost. Some of the girls refused to leave the dorms. The soldiers dragged them out. They were desperate not to return to the camps, to their families—they knew they were of marriageable age and that their fathers. . . . Many of them are already lost now, married, pregnant, trapped in reliving the lives of their mothers and grandmothers. Still," she sighs, drawing herself up again by sheer will, "we will out-wait this. We will not go away."[1]

In an attempt to meet the demands of "the emergency," UNRWA has created a new post in the camps: Refugee Affairs Officer, or RAO. These RAOs, staffed by internationals, not Palestinians, have no actual legal authority to intervene in an altercation, but they exert a "moral presence." Totally unarmed, working in two-person teams with Palestinian RAAs (Refugee Affairs Assistants), wearing only UN armbands and carrying a two-way radio to alert field headquarters about a crisis, an RAO drives or walks through the camps. An RAO may, for example, stand between advancing army patrols and bands of shabab; try to dissuade soldiers from making an arrest; try to calm an enraged crowd;

rush a bleeding child to the nearest clinic if the camp is sealed and no ambulance is permitted in.

The previous year, when camps in the Strip had been sealed for as long as a month, with no fresh food supplies permitted in, the deputy field director of the Gaza Strip at the time, a remarkable Englishwoman, Angela Williams, defied the army and ordered in a truck convoy of good supplies on her own authority. She is now based in Vienna, as Director of Relief and Social Services, which means she travels regularly to and through the camps in the field. It was a subtle diplomatic solution. One of Williams's first acts in her new post was to increase the number of Women's Program Centers in all the camps and to create special Women's Program Officers in each field. As of 1992, the number of centers had tripled and the number of women attending them had quadrupled.

And in January of 1989, UNRWA got its first woman RAO—a Swede, who worked in the Gaza Strip. Today, ten of the twenty-one RAOs in the occupied territories are women.

Western newspapers regularly decry the "rise of religious fundamentalism" among Palestinians, formerly the most secular of the Arab peoples. This rise is said to be most pronounced in Gaza. Yet what I find in Gaza makes this "rise" eminently explicable. The Israeli government has outlawed any large political meetings of Palestinians, just as it outlawed any flying of the Palestinian colors. (Yet the colors appear mysteriously, overnight, waving from the lamppost here, a street sign there.) The Israeli government prides itself, however, on freedom of religious expression. Is it surprising, therefore, that hundreds suddenly congregate with impunity in the mosque?

To be sure, Hamas—the fundamentalist Muslim group—is delighted at this, takes credit for it, and boasts about attendance. Hamas has tried to challenge the secular leadership (both indigenous and PLO) of the intifada with its own strikes, hazings, demonstrations. But the bulletins from the intifada secular leadership—which also mysteriously appear as daily handouts—denounce the monoreligiosity of Hamas, reminding readers that this is not a *jihad*, not a religious war; that there are Christian and Druse and agnostic Palestinians; and that the fight for liberation is for all Palestinians.

I ask woman after woman if she believes fundamentalism is on the rise. And woman after woman admits that Hamas is feared—but as for the reported rise in the number of its adherents, one woman after the other laughs.

As I write this, two bullets lie in a shallow dish on my desk. These are the much-publicized "rubber bullets" that the occupying authority claims are used—even at risk to Israeli soldiers—rather than live ammunition. Because they are so "safe," they are fired at point-blank range.

The bullets are not light, as one would expect from rubber. This is because they are not rubber through and through. I have taken a razor blade and cut slices from each so as to see into the interior. In one, the interior is a solid steel core. In the other, there are hundreds of tiny iron fragments.

It becomes clear why a tour of any hospital or clinic in the occupied territories reveals such patients as a woman blinded by a rubber bullet that was shot into her throat when she opened her mouth to scream.

How I came by the bullets is simple: in some camps, they litter the ground, there for the taking. How I got the bullets past security at Ben-Gurion airport so that I could show them on television in the United States is another story—one that will have to wait for a day when I never intended to return to Israel/Palestine.

In Dheisheh camp on the West Bank, south of Jerusalem, I arrive to find I have been invited to a wake. A young man, eighteen years old, was shot and killed the day before. Both my interpreter and I demur, expressing misgivings about imposing on a family's privacy and grief. But we are pressed, and it would be rude not to accept the hospitality.

The family home is a two-room concrete shelter. In the outer room, about thirty men are congregated, some sitting in rickety chairs, others standing, all of them talking, smoking, drinking coffee served by young boys of the family. A large photograph of the dead son—the martyr—is taped to the wall, framed by paper streamers of green, red, black, and white, the forbidden colors. Under it sit the father and the *mukhtar*—the camp elder. The grieving father is being lionized by the visiting men who file past him, slap him on the back, embrace him, pump his hand in congratulations. The father is now beaming: he has prestige.

We are ushered to and through this room, into the second room. It is filled with women, sitting on the floor, backs to the wall, all around the edge of the room. At the far wall sits the mother, flanked by her daughters and other female relatives. There is an explanation of who we are, and through the interpreter I offer my condolences. The mother accepts them with dignity and thanks us for coming to pay our respects. Then she falls to talking about her son. Suheyla, my interpreter, whispers the translation.

The mother and other women are sharing memories. How lovely a child the dead boy was, how his name, Jamal, meant "beauty," how he had laughed with joy the day he took his first halting steps—remember?—how smart he had been at school, how handsome he was becoming, how he never balked at helping his mother, how he worked with his sisters on their homework, how hard he studied, how joyful he had been on winning the scholarship, how he had planned to become a lawyer someday. . . .

It is so simple and natural a thing to weep that I don't notice we are all crying softly. This woman's son and my son—safe as a student back at his music conservatory in Boston—are the same age. Suheyla and I sit cross-legged, like the rest of the women, on this cold floor strewn with threadbare blankets, holding hands.

The mukhtar bursts into the room, his rheumy eyes flashing, his bony finger pointing accusingly at the mother, his voice loud in furious denunciation. Suheyla is transfixed at his ranting; I tug at her sleeve for a translation. Rapidly, in a low whisper, she tells me that he is berating the women for mourning, reminding them that this is a day for great celebration, that they should be honored to have known a glorious martyr, that female tears scald the soul of one so elect, that they insult and dishonor his memory by their womanish sorrow. All the women fall silent; all of them except Suheyla and I dutifully draw fixed smiles across their faces. Satisfied, the mukhtar leaves.

There is a silence after his departure. Then, with a look of contempt at the door by which he left, the bereaved mother tears open the front of her dress, snatches the veil from her head, rends it in two, beats at her bare breast with her fists, and keens in wild grief, "My son, my son! See how I am not even permitted to mourn you. . . ."

And then all the women are free to cry.

Later, Suheyla, still trembling, as I am, says to me, "What we saw is the intifada *within* the intifada."

Zahira Kamal has violated curfew to come and see me at my West Bank lodgings, in a Jerusalem convent just outside the gates of the Old City. It is very good to see her again. In her early forties, she is one of the new generation of Palestinian grass-roots women leaders. No men appointed her to a formal post heading a "women's auxiliary," nor does she spend her time doing charity work, winding bandage rolls, or organizing parcels for men in prison. She proudly calls herself a feminist, and her work is with women—in prison, in the camps, in the villages.

In 1986, when we first met, I had been impressed by the Women's Work Committee that she and five women friends had been building for a decade—a network of more than nine thousand women in over seventy groups across the West Bank and Strip. The WWC, mindful that most women couldn't come to any center because fathers or husbands forbade it, made a practice of going to where the women were. Literacy classes ensued, sewing classes, knitting and embroidery instruction, typing classes—all aimed at skill-sharing, all aimed toward empowerment, toward an economic self-sufficiency that might be gained through paid employment. A fluid, semivisible, dynamic network. "If a woman doesn't show up for a meeting, we visit her where she lives," Zahira had told me. "We prod her, gently, to find out why. Usually she is being beaten and is ashamed to tell us. We talk together with all the women of the family, to build support for her—and we suggest ways in which the women might argue tactfully with the men. For instance, if the men use Koranic texts to justify beating women, we suggest that the women question whether the texts have been correctly interpreted. We try to get women to challenge the power structure in the family. And they do."

Zahira had then been under town arrest for six years; this had not changed years later. She is still refused travel papers and cannot get permission to leave the country to attend international women's conferences. She has never married, was trained as a physicist, has put all of her younger sisters through school and college. Now, during the intifada, she and I sit together again. All of the contradictions inform her conversation and show in the new lines of her strong-boned face: pride at the uprising; frustration at Palestinian fragmentation; rage at the Israeli government; fury at the PLO leadership for not always acting wisely; heartache at the violence, the counterviolence, the glorification of death. But now the WWC has expanded into the Palestinian Federation of Women's Action Committees, and she radiates pride about "her" women. Even more excitedly, she tells me that she and other women have already begun meeting to draft articles for the proposed Palestinian constitution, toward the someday-state of Palestine. "Oh it will be a while yet, I know. But it *will* come. And when it does, it is vital that women are covered by secular law, not by the *shariah*, or religious law."

The full impact of this is borne in on me slowly. Such a new state would be the first Arab country in which women were totally protected by secular law. She follows my train of thought: "Yes. There will be tremendous pressure brought to bear by the entire Muslim world for Palestine *not* to do this. The other Muslim countries will be terrified that it will be contagious. Even in Israel, as you know, divorce and marriage and custody are all under the authority of the rabbinical courts. But this is the moment to begin, so that the revolution cannot use us and then betray us, as it did in Algeria and everywhere else. That is why we are working on—and already lobbying for—such legislation *now*."

We are joined by a shy woman a little over five feet tall, in her late twenties, whom Zahira wants me to meet. Amal tells me her story quietly, without drama: how she was detained without charge but knew it was because her husband had been politically active; how she was kept for six months in solitary detention; how when she refused to give information on his whereabouts she was tortured—hung by her wrists and beaten on the soles of her feet until she could not stand; how she was kept for ten days and nights in "the cabinet," a compartment so small that even a woman of her size was unable to lie down full length or stand up straight; how they broke her arm; how they would not let her mother bring her baby daughter to visit.

As always, there are tears, and laughter, and embraces. They implore me to "write about us, tell the world we exist." Eventually, they take their leave; and I watch them go into the night, risking their safety during curfew to have met with me.

But as I turn to go to my room—perhaps because the intifada has now already numbed even me, the visitor, with its atrocity stories—I find I am thinking not of the woman who suffered torture for the sake of her husband and her people, much as I stand in awe of her courage and endurance. Instead, I find I am thinking of the women who are, against all the odds imaginable, already organizing to ensure the secular, legal freedom of female citizens in an eventual new state—right in the heart of the Middle East.[2]

Rita Giacaman, only in her thirties, is the leading Palestinian scholar on women's health and an autonomous feminist who has dared reject alliance with any political faction of the male Palestinian leadership. She receives me in her West Bank apartment, despite being late on her deadline for a scholarly paper. She comments humorously on how much time she has on her hands, now that Birzeit University, where she teaches and does research, has been closed by the Israeli government.

She speaks with her characteristic rapid energy—about the sometimes cynical use of women's neighborhood committees, women's life-saving actions, women's devotion, by the various male leadership factions: "There must eventually be a totally autonomous women's movement of Palestinian women, or—no matter how we prepare for 'after liberation'—we will be betrayed."

Such a radical position leaves her very far out on a limb, with virtually no support. "Well," she shrugs gamely, "a feminist is used to such a position, no? After all, if women on both sides of this conflict held real political power, we probably would have had peace a long time ago. I prefer to recognize the truth and speak it, no matter how painful or unpopular. Perhaps I'm just a little ahead of my time. . . ."

Indeed. It will not be until December of 1990—in the heat of the Persian Gulf crisis—that Palestinian women activists from all four factions will meet on West Bank to convene the first conference toward the birthing of such an autonomous women's movement.

Events in the Middle East seem to move at once in slow motion and with the rapidity of a vertical curve. But while "experts" debate the outcome of the intifada—Has it run its course? Can it be contained? Who are the emerging leaders? Has it become counterproductive? Has it degenerated into mindless bloodletting by self-proclaimed militants against accused collaborators?—I think of the women and how for them there is no going back. The experts still overlook them, ignoring their deaths as they have ignored their lives. Yet in this oversight resides the real hope for any lasting peace in the region.

—1990

Postscript

I have not written here about the way the Gulf War bore down on the already barely endurable lives of these women; how the Israeli government did not send warning sirens about SCUD attacks into the occupied territories; how Palestinians on the West Bank could at least rely on principled Israeli peace activist friends to ring them up (those who had telephones, that is) and warn them that the sirens were wailing and they should take shelter—but how there was no such alternative in Gaza at all. Or how even after the Israeli High Court overruled the government's position that gas masks should not be distributed to Palestinians, the masks were not forthcoming. Or how, after two children had died, Palestinian teachers and UNRWA personnel in the Strip fanned out even after curfew to warn panicked women in the camps not to put plastic bags over the heads of their children in the hope of protecting them from the rumored SCUD gas.

I have not written here how, at the height of the SCUD attacks—when Israeli and Palestinian male reconciliation activists broke off dialogue and returned to their respective adversarial positions—Palestinian and Israeli women held a peace march together . . . and were gassed—not by Iraqi missiles, but by U.S.-manufactured chemicals thrown from Israeli army vehicles.

I have not written about the much praised Israeli airlift of Ethiopian black Jews—who were immediately housed beyond the Green Line, where they are both out of sight of white Israelis and in sight (and stone-throwing range) of Palestinians outraged that these newcomers are being planted in soil from which they themselves, after generations of living there, have been uprooted. (The black Jews, of course, have no idea of the game in which they are the pawns.) Nor have I written about how the recent influx of Soviet Jews—also much heralded—has strained an already fever-sick economy; how peace-oriented Israelis worry that these emigres may constitute a new voting block for the sabre-rattling conservatives who would permanently annex the Territories for a "Greater Israel"; how more than half of the "dirty jobs" in Israel, once reserved for the Palestinians, are being taken away from them and given to the new arrivals; how Palestinian employment in the Territories now is between 35 and 40 percent; how hunger is a daily fact of life; how there is a growing number of women begging in the streets.

I have not written about Rashideyeh Camp in Lebanon, where the hunger became so great that, after the rats had been caught and eaten, the men petitioned the mullahs for dispensation to eat human flesh. No one asked who would cook it. Everyone knew that was the job of women, who were already "unclean."

I have not written about what Palestinian feminists are calling a new male backlash in their own communities: men who, frustrated at unemployment, powerlessness, and continual chaos, and irritated at the newfound independence of their wives and daughters during the intifada, are taking out their rage on those women; how domestic violence and battery have risen precipitously in the past year; how men are now taking second wives (previously a rarity among Palestinians); how fathers are selling their daughters to be second wives "because of the shortage of eligible husbands" due to death, detention, and deportation; how "honor murders" have been spreading in both Gaza and West Bank—cases of brothers killing sisters they suspect of having an affair, or even of dating a man without family knowledge. Whether or not these young women have actually done so is irrelevant; the mere suspicion was sufficient to justify one young man slitting his sister's throat in Nazareth, and another—in Gaza's Maghazi Camp—locking his sister inside a large freezer for five hours while he sat outside and waited for her to die.

But I also have not written of how the women are rising to meet this backlash: of how a new group, Al Fanar, formed in 1991, has marched publicly to denounce these killings. Such a march by women—in the context of the tradition of "family honor," and furthermore in the context of required Palestinian solidarity during the intifada—is itself a startlingly radical act.

I think of Miryam, in Beach Camp, who is congenitally blind, the offspring of an arranged cousin marriage, who grinned and told me, "Women? We are as realistic as yesterday and as inevitable as tomorrow."

I think of Rita, who has recently given birth to a baby girl, laughed in the face of death, and announced proudly, "Another Palestinian feminist in the world!"

Robin Morgan

And I think of Ablah, secretly teaching women and children to read under cover of darkness in a West Bank village, smiling up at me across the frail glow of candlelight and saying, "This is the intifada, my sister. And beyond it, next, comes the real one—the *women's* intifada."

—1991

NOTES

1. The Center reopened in 1991 and some women who had been married and were now pregnant (or even had borne children) in the interim were readmitted to complete their studies; this was "a first": married or pregnant women attending college is almost unheard of in the Arab world.

2. In 1991, Zahira Kamal would be part of a delegation of intifada leadership that would fly to PLO headquarters in Tunis to negotiate with Arafat for a strong indigenous presence from the occupied territories at the Madrid Peace Conference. Later that year and in early 1992, she would travel to Madrid and Washington, D.C., as a member of the Advisory Panel to the Palestinian delegation to the U.S.-Russian-sponsored peace talks.

.10.

Suha Sabbagh

An Interview with Dr. Eyad el-Sarraj: Gender Relations during the Three Psychodevelopmental Phases under Occupation

Dr. Eyad el-Sarraj is founder and Director of the Community Mental Health Center and Research Program in Gaza. The objective of this program is to offer assistance to a population suffering stress as a result of the intifada, poverty, and lack of economic security. The center offers rehabilitation programs to women who have been imprisoned during the intifada and to women who are subjected to violence in the home. In this interview, which took place in 1992, Dr. Sarraj outlines a more or less psychosocial history of the issue of gender throughout the period of occupation.[1]

How do you approach the issue of mental health under occupation? Can one apply the same measure of mental health to the individual as in times of peace?

The intifada is in a constant state of flux, and the mental state of the population is constantly changing in response to new developments in the political arena. In order to understand the psychology of the individual, including women, mental health must be understood in terms of a dialectical relationship between occupiers and occupied. At different times this relationship demands different forms of response from the local population.

For many, the image of the intifada child or youth[2] carrying a stone has become the symbol of the Palestinian national liberation struggle. Images of youths throwing stones are the subject of many posters, postcards, and an endless number of book jackets. For the youths and teen-age girls the act of throwing a stone constitutes the restoration of their dignity and their humanness. From a psychological perspective, the act of throwing the stone constitutes a form of personal therapy for the Palestinian child of the intifada. The child who has taken an active role in the intifada is better adjusted than the child who has observed the violence but not participated. The latter has a much lower level of self-esteem and a much higher sense of anxiety.

Occupation is a form of language. The child is well aware of the difference between the living conditions in his or her dirty camp and the living conditions in the newly built Israeli settlement. The child learns at an early age that the father and protector is incapable of protecting the child. The child is bound to feel at that point a sense of anxiety and fear.

In my own childhood memories of the Gaza beach in the early 1950s, the beach was clean, and white flowers dotted the land around it. Green plants adorned some streets. As time went by the youths who saw no future for themselves in Gaza harbored a sense of resentment against all that was beautiful and clean. Green plants that had escaped destruction by the devastations inflicted on the environment under occupation were destroyed by the angry youths. Now, garbage and open sewers flow freely onto the Gaza beaches. The camps suffer from over population and people live on top of each other in homes made of blocks covered with asbestos or tin. Tall towers surround the camps, where soldiers can peer into the privacy of any home and into the corner of every street at any time. Youths cannot enjoy a moment of solitude, the child can never play alone. The lack of space, the dirt, heat, and constant surveillance by soldiers cause tempers to flare. In times of curfew the situation is exacerbated because the streets that provide added space are reclaimed by the soldiers.

Prior to the intifada a feeling of helplessness, of loss of control and disillusionment prevailed. Many patients complained of a feeling of *khanga*, meaning suffocation. The symptoms included shortness of breath. There was a general atmosphere of fear: fear of informants who might be in one's own family; fear of soldiers; fear of losing one's job. Many youths at that time came to the conclusion that life could not get worse and death would be welcome. At that very moment they overcame their fear of death and of the Israeli soldier. They opened their shirts, taunting the soldiers to shoot as they threw stones at them. At that moment the youths lost all fear of the soldier since the only thing the soldier could take away was their life. A new person who was not afraid of the occupiers was born at that moment.

How did occupation and the resistance to it affect the mental health of women?

Not only children's but also women's sense of identity was transformed in the intifada. Interviews conducted with women whose children were active participants in the intifada showed that initially women went out into the streets to prevent youths from throwing stones. They were fulfilling their traditional role as protectors and nurturers when they stepped between armed soldiers and their children, pulling the children away. But slowly mothers came to realize that the youths were right and occupation must be fought. They abandoned their traditional role and joined their children in the act of resistance. A new Palestinian women emerged to the same degree that women broke boulders and cinder blocks into smaller stones and chased soldiers away from their children. This new woman emerged with greater defiance, increased self-esteem, and a newly acquired political consciousness. For traditional women this moment constituted an unprecedented break with their traditional domain in the home, and it pushed them into the political sphere of the street. The extent to which this will have a long term effect on women's liberation from patriarchal constraints is still being hotly debated in women's circles on the West Bank.[3] However, the mother's participation has instilled a new sense of pride in the child who is active in the intifada, although the child's role model remains older active youths.

For women here there was both a sense of liberation from occupation and from traditional norms that were questioned further in the months to come. Palestinian women's identity was not transformed overnight. Just like the intifada itself, it was a process that took place over two decades, when women were active in all aspects of the intifada.

Not only women, but the entire society, including children and men, were transformed, in a psychological sense, through the experience of resisting occupation. Writing about the Algerian revolution, Frantz Fanon, the black psychiatrist from the Antilles, describes this transformation in his notion of the "New Man," which would better have been termed the "New Being." For his notion accurately describes the transformation that takes place in both men and women when society decides to reject the sense of identity imposed from above under occupation. Four years into the intifada the experience has brought about not only a new sense of identity but also new institutions. The intifada has become a way of life for Palestinians; and many facets of the intifada, such as the notion of self-reliance, have become institutionalized. It is highly unlikely that the population will return to the way things were before the intifada.

You said that the intifada is in a constant state of flux. Can you describe the developmental phases that can be discerned in the mental state of the population under occupation since 1967?

Three distinct mental and emotional phases can be discerned during the years since 1967 in the occupied territories. Women's situation has changed in response to the changing conditions. My experience is conditioned by living in the Gaza Strip, which has some special characteristics. Yet these phases also describe the conditions of life on the West Bank. Historically, Gaza has always been more conservative and less urban than the West Bank. It is also more isolated from the international arena. Living in Gaza is like living in a poor ghetto—it is geographically cut off and economically deprived. The situation in Gaza is far worse than on the West Bank because in Gaza the socioeconomic status of the population is lower. Many people are unemployed and suffering from severe poverty. This is reflected in mounting stress within the family, and it impacts on the situation of women.

I define the first phase as the period immediately following the occupation in 1967. As a result of losing the war, the population suffered from a deep sense of frustration and helplessness. Men in particular felt that they had lost control over all aspects of life. Many had to be bused to Israel to work on construction sights or to other jobs that strengthened the Israeli economy. And all of them felt humiliated in the work place. The standard of living was mounting and they could not always afford to put bread on the table. Outside the territories the situation was grim for the Palestinians. Black September, which resulted in the destruction of all PLO bases in Jordan, led to great disillusionment. Soon afterwards, the Camp David Accords were signed and this added to the general feeling that Palestinians had no control over their own destiny. All this time Israel had followed a policy of the carrot and the stick. While the doors were open to laborers who had no alternative but to work in Israel, any expression of political resistance was severely punished.

A feeling of helplessness and loss of control leads to clinical depression. Many patients complained of headaches and a feeling of khanga. For the first time in history, drugs were introduced into the territories and drug abuse became rampant. In some cases I treated whole families for drug addiction. Pent-up feelings of frustration, fear, and anger were directed against the self, as in drug addiction, or against weaker members of the family, especially women. Israeli soldiers were often called to break up family violence. In our culture the family is the repository of self-esteem and security. It is the source of identity. I am first recognized as a Sarraj before being recognized as an individual. By requesting that soldiers intrude on the family, society was violating a fundamental taboo in the culture, which dictates that problems must remain contained within the family. The fact that the intruder was also the occupier was a further humiliation.

For women the problem is twofold. Women suffer directly from the impact of occupation, like the rest of the society. But they also suffer as a result of tradition. In other words, they suffer in a direct and an indirect way under occupation. In our patriarchal culture, women and children have always been in a weaker position than the patriarch, the male head of the family. When a husband can no longer contain his anger, his humiliation, his frustration due to the conditions of occupation, he is likely to find an outlet for his anger within the home. Women are often the victims of this anger. To vent his anger at the source of oppression would mean that a husband would lose his job or go to jail. While the occupation is the source of frustration, the culture provides the channel for venting this anger within the home, and during certain political phases women become the victims of this anger.

In Gaza, a few women responded to the needs of the community and formed social welfare organizations to help other women. On the West Bank the situation was different, and many more women were able to participate through their work in women's organizations. These women found a positive outlet for their feelings of frustration. Still, the majority were not able to relieve their feelings of frustration and many developed psychosomatic symptoms. When women complained of a state of *khanga,* my strategy consisted of treating the entire family in their own home. In this way I was able to observe the interaction between all the family's members. We saw more women than men in clinics, and their symptoms fell under the general heading of depression: stomach problems, severe headaches, loss of appetite, loss of weight, loss of sleep, fatigue and exhaustion, and in more severe cases the cessation of the monthly period and the drying up of breast milk.

Fear and lack of security were two emotions that also dominated the lives of the population in the first phase. There was a strong fear of soldiers and settlers. Fear also infiltrated the private sphere. Nearly every *hamula* (extended family) contained one or two collaborators. Speaking out against the occupation was taboo at this point because the people suspected one another of being informants. In the *dawawin* (men's formal gatherings) a great deal of despair was expressed.

In this general atmosphere of discouragement, many women found themselves facing a new and serious challenge, that of being the single head of a household. Many men were either in prison or employed in the Gulf states. For the first time women became single heads of households and had to cope with the raising of many children. A study of the West Bank has shown that women heads of households developed symptoms of illness two or three times more often than men. From my own experience, I can say that the culture was supportive of these women and that this support has meant a lot to their mental health. The culture did not readily accept the idea that married women should be employed in Israel because people cannot accept the idea that a woman should be separated from her children on a daily basis. Experience has shown that most of these women were wonderfully resilient in their new role, while a few exhibited psychological symptoms and needed treatment. In general women managed to continue to provide security and care for the family, and they received the recognition of the society around them.

During the first phase of occupation, Palestinians had a fragmented sense of identity. Because most institutions in the occupied territories belong to the occupation authorities, female and male workers could not identify with their place of work. In hospitals this meant very poor care for patients. For laborers who worked on construction sites in Israel or for those who waited tables there, the situation was much more traumatic because the work place was often the source of humiliation. The victims of family violence, women and children, found it harder to feel the same sense of pride and security in the extended family system. And the population as a whole found it somewhat difficult to derive strength from their identity as Palestinians because of the occupied status of the territories.

The intifada, the second phase of occupation, brought with it a sense of euphoria. For the first time since the beginning of the occupation people felt that they could shape the course of history and that they had control over their own destiny. People felt that they took the initiative in their own hands, and they scored a very important moral victory over the occupation. The support of the Arab states and the international community brought a great sense of achievement. Helplessness was replaced with active certainty and with a feeling of being in control of destiny. The entire emotional outburst was there in the streets for the world to observe. The intifada quickly organized itself, forming a leadership and local committees to meet the needs of the community.

An Interview with Dr. Eyad el-Sarraj

What, in your opinion, led to the "second phase" of occupation, the emergence of the intifada?

Several factors led to the emergence of the intifada. The ouster of the PLO from Lebanon in 1982 made people feel that they had to take the initiative to liberate themselves. In Gaza women were among the first to respond to this call. The General Union of Palestinian Women was formed in Gaza in 1982 to organize women and to promote self-help programs. The mood that dominated the area just before the intifada had a lot to do with the beginning of the intifada. The situation was very volatile because people felt that life was no longer a better alternative than death. They were in a state of dismal despair, and that sparked unprecedented defiance. The gun no longer instilled any fear in the *shabab* (youths). They lost their fear of the soldiers, of occupation, and of all the symbols of power. Men of the older generation who worked in Israel did not have the luxury of resisting because that meant that they could not put bread on the table. So from the beginning it was clear that the youth and women would have a very important role to play.

It is not surprising, therefore, to find that at this point the culture came to appreciate the contributions of women. I think that initially women went out into the streets to protect their children, particularly in the camps. Their participation was a result of their nurturing role and not the result of their sudden politicization. It must be stated here that the intifada first started in the camps, where the entire population—including women—was more radicalized; only then did it spread to the villages and towns. The Gaza Strip has about eight villages and towns and about eight camps. Because of the poverty in the camps, the refugees became more radicalized than the conservative inhabitants of Gaza. Economically and socially they were on the lower end of the scale, and so it was natural that the intifada would start there. In addition to the social and economic dimensions, the division between villages and camps also reflects a division between traditional and radicalized Palestinians.

In terms of the overall picture of mental health, the intifada brought with it a healing process in many areas. Drug consumption disappeared, in part because the leadership of the intifada punished drug dealers. Violence in the home disappeared and divorce rates went down. Women received greater appreciation for their contributions. Gender relations improved and even evolved in a more positive direction. Many traditions that reflect the weak status of women began to disappear, for example, the dowry. Collaborators and informants were given a chance to return to the mainstream of society, and people no longer feared reprisals from them. The shabab, the youth who engaged the soldiers, gained a feeling of self-esteem. The society as a whole felt that it could affect the course of events and regain a sense of control over the future. These feelings of assertiveness contributed to a better sense of well-being. Briefly described, people used all their resources to meet the onslaught of outside violence.

A lot has been written about the contributions of women during this phase. Women demonstrated in the streets in defiance of the occupation and traditional norms. They saved their children time and again from the clutches of the soldiers, and they found the means to feed their families in times of curfew. They have become the cornerstone of the family. The children of the intifada now look up to their mothers, and women have demonstrated their innate ability to negotiate between soldiers and the youth, between the youth and their fathers.

What are some of the negative effects of the intifada on mental health?

Like all historical upheavals, the intifada also has a negative side. This negative side has also had an impact on the lives of women. First, there was a heightened state of insecurity and we began to see many more people, mostly women, suffering from extreme anxiety. Second, the father figure who was totally diminished under occupation now began to lose control within the home, and a form of backlash was widespread.

Before the intifada the clinics treated many cases of depression with some anxiety. During the intifada the clinics received many more cases of severe anxiety. This anxiety arose from the fact that anything can and does happen to the youth during demonstrations. People were anticipating Israeli raids into their homes at any time of day or night. Anxiety also resulted from not knowing what to do next. People wanted to know where to go from here or what would happen tomorrow. My colleagues conducted a study on the UNRWA clinics in Gaza, and we found that 90 percent of the attendants were women. Nearly 60 percent of these women suffered from psychological problems. The physicians diagnosed these women as suffering from physical symptoms. Only 1 percent was diagnosed correctly. The rest of the women were treated with sedatives and antacids, antibiotics, and analgesics. Because the doctors were not familiar with interhealth problems, they could not identify the problems. They also lacked the time to spend with patients. Each doctor had to see nearly three hundred patients per day.

It is interesting to note that the youths who participated in stone throwing were relatively well-adjusted members of society. One of my colleagues conducted a study during the first six months of the intifada, and he found that 28 percent of children under the age of fourteen suffered from symptoms of anxiety. The same study was duplicated six months later and the percentage had dropped to thirteen. These children learned how to cope with their anxiety, to endure and become more resilient. It is an important finding because it shows that while we cannot eliminate anxiety under occupation, it is possible to manage it. In my opinion the ability to manage stress is one of the positive developments in the early part of the intifada.

We are only now beginning to see the impact of the diminishing status of the male figure. In this case the intifada has only exacerbated a problem that has its roots in the policy of occupation. Much of the occupation policy is directed at humiliating the male figure in Palestinian society. Otherwise, how can one explain the workers' daily ordeal of lining up for work in what was dubbed the "slave markets"? Or the rules that prohibit the same workers from sleeping nearer to their place of work within Israel. Attitudes of Israeli society to Arab workers are reflected in an expression in the Hebrew language in which poor workmanship and work done by Arabs are synonymous. With the emergence of the intifada, the youths no longer looked up to their fathers as role models because fathers were not participants in the resistance. Youths regarded slightly older youths and to a lesser degree their mothers as role models. The father had now lost control of his destiny both outside and inside the home and it was only a matter of time before men would seek to reinstate some form of authority within the home.

What are the characteristics of the "third phase" and when did it begin?

It is not clear when, exactly, the third phase began. But it is evident that the early euphoria has been replaced by yet another period of depression. There are many reasons for it, the most obvious being that after four years, people are tired and disappointed in the political results achieved so far. Their financial and human resources have been spent. And in spite of the political and moral victory, no end is in sight. The intifada is fueled by an intensity that cannot be sustained for an indefinite length of time. And the deterioration in the psychological state of the Palestinians is evident in at least three recent developments: 1) the emergence of a fundamentalist Islamic movement and ideology bent on reasserting male authority over women; 2) the radicalization of the movement expressed through the stabbing of collaborators and Israeli civilians; and 3) the support that Saddam received during the Gulf war. Had there been progress toward a political solution, the Palestinians might not have looked to Saddam to champion their cause. All three involve a form of violence directed against the self. It is possible to predict that frustration will lead to a heightening of the cycle of violence between Israelis and Palestinians; more power perhaps for the fundamentalists; more violence against women and a return to drug addiction.

Women are the first victims of the failure to find a political solution. The emergence of Islamic fundamentalism has many political causes. On a psychological level, however, it has to be seen as the male desire to reinstate his power within the home. Occupation has robbed men of any form of control over their destiny. I have said that in the intifada the shabab have taken the power away from the patriarchal figure. This has led to a reaction by men who felt uncomfortable because they were prevented from exercising any control or deciding for themselves the direction to take. They were pushed into a corner, unable to formulate their position. Men of the older generation have tried to regain this authority by different means. One of these is to call on the tradition of discipline, control over children, and women's remaining at home. The perfect answer to their needs has taken the form of reverting to fundamentalist views.

It is clear why men desired to reinstate male authority within the home. But why did the women who stood up to Israeli soldiers relinquish their newfound rights to participation in the political sphere during the period you have termed the "third phase"?

Women in Gaza accepted the reinstitution of male authority because they were not yet solid in their assertiveness. They were not totally comfortable with their new role and were intimidated. Men, generally speaking, are capable of fits of anger when their demands are not met within the home; and women often react in the same way they react to their children—by pacifying them. Men can also be violent when their needs are not met, and women become terrorized. Some women comply with these Islamic regulations because they are intimidated. My sisters have gone back to the *hijab* (head and sometimes body covering) not out of conviction, although they are believers, but because they have been intimidated. There were instances when fundamentalists attacked women verbally and physically because they were not veiled. All women in Gaza now wear the hijab and many do so because they are terrorized. There are some women who wear the veil from conviction, either because of their upbringing or because of the way they see things now. In Gaza women quickly reverted to the older role of the oppressed, and that may explain why there are currently more cases of depression. Currently, many women come to the clinic complaining of what they described to me as khanga, a sense of suffocation and a

An Interview with Dr. Eyad el-Sarraj

desperate need for fresh air. This is not a medical term. The language used by these women denotes both an emotional and a physical state. Doctors must be very sensitive to the language used by patients, because they often describe the root of what is bothering them.

It is also important to note that women did not want to see their husbands humiliated in the workplace and totally diminished in society. Such a situation could have some very negative consequences for the family and for the mental well-being of the husband, and the women understand these repercussions very well. Consequently, many have chosen to give up their newly earned rights to participate in the political arena.

During the third phase we are seeing more cases of depression among men and more cases of anxiety among women. A study has shown that 37 percent of women suffer from anxiety, while there are 22 percent of men who suffer from higher degrees of anxiety than normal. I think that women feel more insecure than men. Women have gone through a lot of traumatizing experiences. They saw their children taken away from them or beaten before their eyes. Women with their protective nature fear for their children and for the future of their family. In many cases, they are now subjected to physical and verbal violence by their own men.

Most of the women we see suffer under the pressures on their personal lives. A forty-five-year-old mother of five complained of chest pains, a dry cough, and severe headaches during the preceding year. Delving into her background, we found that after her son was hit a year before, her monthly period had stopped. Since then, her husband had been sentenced to twenty years in prison. A forty-seven-year-old mother of twelve complained that her head had been hurting for twenty years and that at night she behaved like a zombie. This woman's husband worked as a street vegetable vendor and she had lost a lot of money trying to get treatment. A woman whose son had served five years of a fifteen-year sentence complained of pains and dysfunctions throughout her body. Another complained that she couldn't talk with anybody and that she was dazed and lost in thought all day. Her son, after being released from prison, insisted on living in the streets and has now been moved to a mental hospital.

Any effect on the general situation of adults will be reflected in the situation of children. Usually the family is the transmitter of happiness or misery, security or insecurity. The mother is the most important figure in the family. If she is affected in a negative way, then she will transmit her feelings to her children. In turn, this will affect the mother. Many children now suffer from debilitating phobias. They are afraid to go out of the house; afraid of the soldiers, which is natural; afraid of night because they're afraid of soldiers; they can't sleep alone and have to be cuddled and display clinging behavior. Bed-wetting is very common among children seven to ten years old. One of the most serious consequences is that these children are growing up without a childhood. Furthermore, because children come to think that violence is a natural means in daily life, this feeds on the natural cycle of violence. Victimized children will eventually seek a victim. The result will be a very violent society.

In my opinion the most important transformation in women is that they now consciously realize how much they are oppressed, individually or collectively. Individually, women have tried to overcome this problem by being active at the community level and sometimes politically; but these are still marginal cases in Gaza. Women are more active on the West Bank because the atmosphere is different, less traditional, and more exposed to international experience. Many women on the West Bank have been educated abroad. In Gaza the women's movement is still marginal. I am hopeful that this conscious realization of their situation will mean that women will not be oppressed for long.

In your opinion, what are some of the long-term consequences for society of the youths' loss of respect for their fathers and by extension for authority in general?

It is no coincidence that most stone throwers are male youths in their teens. Defiance of parental authority and the need to establish independence at that age are a normal part of growing up. During the intifada the challenge to the authority of the father was transferred to the occupying power, since paternal authority was severely damaged under occupation. The child lost all respect for his father because the father did not stand up to the occupying power and was humiliated by the soldiers. The father lost esteem in the eyes of his male offspring because he failed to join the troops of stone throwers. Most fathers are construction workers in Israel and by participating in resistance activities they would stand to lose their jobs from one day to the next. Yet the mother was and continues to be respected for her cooperation with the youths. We have found that the child who threw stones worked from his defiance of his father in the process of defying occupation, while at the same time he punished the occupiers for humiliating his father.

Currently, the child in the occupied territories looks up to older youths in the streets as his role model.[4] The long-term impact of this loss of parental authority on the child is not clear at the moment; experience elsewhere (e.g., among black families in the United States) has shown that this may lead to a weakening of the family structure in the future. And if the problem is left untreated, it may affect the way in which the youths will relate to the new Palestinian authority and possibly the way in which the current generation will manage and run the country in the future.

NOTES

1. Dr. Sarraj worked as a psychiatrist in the Gaza Strip for many years. The Gaza Community Mental Health Program has a network of activity in different clinics, where it provides therapy based on a community concept involving the whole family. The center provides a public educational program and an out-service training program for doctors, general practitioners, nurses, and social workers; and an in-service training program for the mental health workers themselves. The center has a research program that attempts to study and document different aspects of mental health and sociopolitical aspects of life in Gaza. Dr. Sarraj received his degree in medicine from the University of Alexandria in Egypt and his training in general psychiatry from the Institute of Psychiatry at London University.

2. The term "child" is used to describe children up to age twelve, while the term "youths" describes twelve to twenty-two-year-olds.

3. Discussions took place at the women's conference held at the National Palace Hotel in East Jerusalem on December 14, 1990; it was organized by the Palestinian development and research group Bisan. See *Al-Fajr*, December 24, 1990.

4. Interviews conducted with Palestinian women in Jordan; see United Nations Report of the Commission on the Status of Women, *The Situation of Palestinian Women in the Occupied Territories*, February 26–March 9, 1990.

11

Dima Zalatimo

An Interview with
Hanan Mikhail Ashrawi:
The History of the Women's Movement

Dr. Hanan Mikhail Ashrawi became known to the world through her numerous appearances on television as the spokeswoman of the Palestinian delegation to the peace process, which culminated in September 1993 in the signing of a peace agreement between Israel and the Palestine Liberation Organization. Before that, she was the head of the English Department and Dean of the Faculty of Arts at Birzeit University on the West Bank. In the following interview, which took place during the peace negotiations in 1992, she discusses her views regarding the Palestinian women's movement on the West Bank.

Is there a Palestinian women's movement? If so, when did it start and where is it today?

There certainly is a Palestinian women's movement, and it is one of the oldest women's movements in the Arab world. It was established in the twenties. The women's agenda was to form charitable organizations in which middle-class women would help rural women. Palestinian women always had access to education, to travel, and to what we call a liberal tradition set within a traditional society that was definitely male domi-

An Interview with Hanan Mikhail Ashrawi

nated. However, in Palestine, the oppression of women did not take on the very overt forms of oppression from which other Arab women suffered. Palestine had a tradition of education and openness because it was a center of multicultural interaction and it did not allow a closed society to evolve. A closed society that is self-evolved and convoluted tends to oppress its own people, particularly its own women.

In the period between the 1920s and 1967, women's work developed along traditional lines. Women formed philanthropic organizations, sewing centers, etc. These organizations were gradually incorporated into the infrastructure, becoming part of the Palestinian social fabric itself. In 1967 the shock of the occupation, like the shock of the dispossession, led to the emergence of a more politically aware women's movement. It was closely linked to the nationalist movement, and it saw its primary task to be national assertion and national liberation. Women worked together to implement the same political program as men, and they became extensions of their respective political organizations. They were doing nationalist work, the only difference being that it was women who were doing it. For some time women suffered from misplaced priorities because women's issues were defined as a conflict that could be postponed, or as a primary struggle for national liberation and a secondary struggle for women's liberation. The primary conflict was always defined as the national conflict, while the gender issue was relegated to the back burner and defined as an obstruction of, or distraction from, the national issue.

In the seventies the women's movement saw the creation of the women's committees, whose rise marked the beginning of the real grassroots movement among women. The committees reached out to women in remote and isolated areas, to women who were excluded from the work of the philanthropic organizations except for being on the receiving end as charity cases. Here was the beginning of the women's movement that reached out to women in villages and refugee camps, attempted to understand their needs and to evolve a gender agenda on the basis of women's issues. We, the women who took part in the debate around the direction to be followed, started meeting in the early seventies. It was very popular at the time to talk about consciousness-raising groups. Women's groups were trying then to read feminist literature and, at the same time, we were trying to see the ways in which we could develop an authentic Palestinian agenda based on the concrete situation of Palestinian women and the specific types of discrimination or oppression that we suffered. At the same time, we were reaching out to became part of the international sisterhood of women and the international theoretical women's feminist movement. With the formation of the committees, we saw the intensification and the mobilization of women who had hitherto been excluded from political or economic decision making. The committees focused on women's rights at work, as part of the labor force, or at home, in terms of social institutions. They addressed the question of divorce, dowry (*mahr*), the right of a woman to choose her husband, and the availability of economic alternatives. The occupation meant that women had to work, and they did not have a choice in the matter because the economic situation had deteriorated. But women did not use this as an opportunity and as a means of gaining power in the family or at the decision-making level in social institutions. Some women earned a salary outside the home but chose to hand over that income to the men in their household. In time, we developed a women's support system and women's consciousness groups that dealt with these issues. The literature of the committees reflects this stage.

When you say we, who are you referring to?

I mean many types of women, including academics and intellectuals who, instead of working at a distance with imported ideas, tried to work from a point within Palestinian society. We had all been exposed to the women's movement outside Palestine. There were also women who belonged to women's political organizations that later evolved into feminist organizations. With the intifada it became very clear that these women's organizations had to accelerate their work. The progression and development that takes place in the development of a feminist movement over a long period of time was a luxury that we could not afford because the intifada and Israeli reprisals made it imperative that we create economic alternatives immediately. Since we had to deal with women's issues immediately, this meant that we could no longer postpone the conflict; for a conflict postponed is a conflict lost. There was no such thing as a primary or secondary conflict, all social issues had to be dealt with simultaneously with national issues. This is the beginning of the evolution of the gender agenda on which we worked.

The receptivity of women all over was just incredible, especially because women created facts as they worked. In the popular committees and other popular structures, women initiated projects, they sustained efforts, they made decisions, took on responsibilities, and they produced results. In addition, many men, because they were oppressed or even jailed, felt that they could not take a very forthright position at the forefront of the struggle. Women did, not only in terms of economic alternatives, popular committees, neighborhood committees, and so on, but we also stormed the last fortress of male domination, which is the political arena. We did it by right and by merit, by proving ourselves and not by sitting back and accepting recognition as a gift from men. We won the begrudging respect and admi-

An Interview with Hanan Mikhail Ashrawi

ration of men but not their unqualified respect. Of course, there was and still remains some resistance on the part of men.

How would you describe male resistance to the progress made by women?

The traditional accusation levied against the women's agenda and women's organizations is that women's issues are distracting society from the primary conflict, the national issue. We have been accused of creating another front, which will have adverse effects on the struggle against occupation. In addition, there is the resistance from men at the economic level, where they feel that economic leverage gives them the right to decision making. When men lost that leverage because they lost their jobs in Israel or because they were imprisoned, women became the major wage earners in the family. That meant that gradually the decision-making authority began shifting to women. Men felt threatened by that. At times male resistance emerges from political circles—men who are working in the political arena but find it difficult to accept a woman decision maker. These men have a hard time accepting a woman on an equal basis. But I am amazed and gratified that men who think along these lines are a minority. There are many men who recognize the fact that women have achieved this role based on merit and hard work, and they work with women on an equal basis.

Discrimination can also take place on a subconscious level. There are many social and cultural habits that have to be brought up to the level of consciousness and addressed at that level. We are constantly checking out men's language, men's diction, men's expectations, and so on, in order to keep them aware of the fact that there is a subconscious level of discrimination even when there is a conscious level of acceptance.

You have described the conditions among urban and professional men, but what about the men in the refugee camps and villages? Do they feel the same way?

Women in camps made advances too. But there was a backlash during the last part of the intifada. For example, families started to marry their daughters at a very early age because schools are closed and the girls are likely to take part in demonstrations and other political activities. At the same time, major progress was made in the shifting definition of the concept of shame or female honor, which is now based on the degree of participation in nationalist activities and not on pride in a girl's virginity. In the past, women who went to jail were no longer marriageable commodities. Now there is a women's support system and a community support system for women who go to jail, and such women are seen as having gained tremendous honor, not shame. In our recent experience of the last few years, all the women who have been in jail were married. So the whole definition of shame has shifted, because again the major source of shame is no longer related to women's social and sexual behavior but is related to participation in the national struggle. It is a tremendous source of shame, it is the worst kind of disgrace and dishonor, to be a collaborator or not to work for the nationalist cause. So this has shifted the emphasis from women's behavior to nationalist behavior throughout Palestinian society. Because women became so active and so involved in resistance and in alternative structures, in many families parental authority was instituted again to protect these women, who were defying the family and traditions by demonstrating, by keeping night vigils, and by joining all sorts of political organizations.

The politicization of women has had other consequences. It has erased or eliminated many distinctions. A brother can no longer oppress his sister if she is of a higher level politically in the same organization. They say, "How can I tell her: 'You can't go out. You have to stay home and I am going to exercise my traditional male authority to ensure that you do so,' when, politically, she has more authority than I do." So this has again jarred and shifted the sources of authority. The same has happened with the children. They have gained more respect because of their involvement in the nationalist struggle. One backlash to all this was the drop in the marriage age for women. Parents sought to bind women to a family unit to keep them safe within the traditional structures. Unfortunately, many of these marriages are not very successful. Before the intifada women were trying very hard to deal with the question of early marriages, coerced marriages, and arranged family marriages. The intifada delayed all this, providing another example of the way in which forward strides by women could also contain some negative elements.

Along with consciousness-raising efforts and provision of a theoretical framework, we are trying to teach women some practical methods of resistance. We are teaching women that they are not the property of their families and that they have the right to direct their own lives. We need to change the laws that govern women's lives. But many of those laws are based on the *shariah* (religious law) and are therefore difficult to change. So we have tried to provide a feminist support system, women supporting each other, finding refuge for women who need it, finding a protective context, finding alternative sources of income—that again is important.

In terms of the economic aspects, women proved tremendously successful and creative at finding economic alternatives. They started different projects, taking on full responsibility for each project, including collective decision making and decisions about income and financial aspects. I am not saying that we have eliminated all sources of discrimination, but there is an increased awareness of women's rights and of women's options, because on the ground there are serious and concrete changes that are translating themselves into a new and irreversible reality. We are not merely reacting to immediate threats but are preparing for the long-term—by consolidating our gains and by ingraining new habits and attitudes while providing a new theoretical framework in the field of women's studies.

What measures are you taking to avoid following the path of Algerian women, who helped win independence from the French only to have their rights denied in the new Algerian state? Can you avoid the pitfalls faced by Western women who lost their jobs after World War II because they were disfranchised by the men returning home from the war?

Ours is a long-term struggle, and whatever is gained becomes integrated into the social pattern. It is most important that there is now an awareness of women's issues, that there is knowledge of the experience of women in other countries, and, at the same time, that there is a theoretical context which pulls these things together. Women are aware not just of the benefits but also of the potential loss of the gains made so far by women. Of course, this is all part of the assessment of our achievements. If you do not achieve much, if you are blocked, then people turn against each other and against themselves and can reverse and regress. But if there are achievements that are visible and tangible and can be assessed, this becomes an inducement for more work.

I am confident that we will not follow the Algerian model. When I hear women say we won't go back to the kitchen, that is music to my ears. I know that I can deal with any man on the basis of equality, as an individual, and not as an exception. If you look at the whole political picture, you will see that many women are in very responsible positions, making decisions, and are right at the forefront of the struggle. You will see that it is going to be very difficult to send these women back to the kitchen or to relegate them to the status of second class citizens.

There is always the possibility of a resurgence of traditional thought associated with religion. Hamas has always been viewed as the main threat to women's rights. We have seen attempts to imposing the dress code, for instance, on women especially in Gaza. A few months back there was a conference in Jerusalem arranged by women, with participation by women from across the political spectrum, including Hamas and all the com-mittees and organizations. The vast majority stressed the fact that it is a woman's right to choose her own dress code and that there should be no coercion whatsoever. Again, that statement was taken as symptomatic of all sorts of other activities. But the fact that there are now intellectual, cultural, and social events in which women's issues are being discussed openly and in a very candid and forthright manner is extremely encouraging.

The term "liberated" is a relative term; what is your definition of a liberated woman in the occupied territories?

There are various aspects and many components. There has to be economic liberation for women. But, at the same time, we must ask ourselves what is the availability of economic or career options for women at the present time under occupation? The opportunity must be present for women to take part on an equal basis in different types of social and political careers. Jobs and pay scale or work within the home must not be based on gender either in the home or outside it. The earning capability of women should not be defined according to gender. We must not consider certain jobs the exclusive right of men or the exclusive right of women, with women getting the menial and low-paying jobs. Women should not have the double burden of working both outside and inside the home; there has to be an equal sharing of work and equal sharing of responsibility and authority. There are so many aspects of equality that we need to deal with. We need to promote a better understanding of women's rights and of the essential equality of all human beings.

Do you believe that sisterhood is global?

Certainly I believe that there is a global sisterhood and that it transcends political, national, and cultural dimensions. But in order to reach out to a global sisterhood, you have to work in your own context, in your own setting, you have to put your own house in order. You have to create a sense of sisterhood among your own women, you have to deal with your own authentic agenda and not import other people's agendas or perceptions. If you fail to understand your own context, your own reality, and to move with it, to reach out to a global sisterhood, then you have failed where it counts and you will have no credibility and no rootedness. What use is it if you are part of a global sisterhood but you have lost your base. You have to move from your own base, you have to have the assurance of your constituency, of your own sisterhood, in your own society.

Would you say that Western feminists are trying to impose their own criteria and agenda on women in the Third World?

I think the Western feminist movement has made many mistakes. But of course all movements for national, social, or political liberation make mistakes, because there are no blueprints and no sure formulas for success. To me the major drawback was the political lack of responsibility and foresight in understanding women's position among all the oppressed of the world. This is an accusation that we level against the Israeli women's movement. We asked them, "How can you work for women's rights and against women's oppression in Israeli society when you see that there is a whole national oppression being practiced by your society against the Palestinians?" You cannot fragment these issues; the social oppression is the same. It is the same militaristic and macho mentality that oppresses women in Israel and oppresses the whole nation of the Palestinian people. So there is a lack of a politically comprehensive approach that fights against discrimination everywhere. We, as women, should be the first to understand the denial of the other's right to self-determination because we, as women, are globally denied the right to self-determination. You have to transcend your own narrow interest and be able to make the political and theoretical leap to understand that if you are fighting against the oppression of women or discrimination against women, you must fight against all sorts and oppression or discrimination. You cannot think in fragmented terms because the oppressor is not going to decide on oppressing one group and granting equality to the other. This is something that the women's movement did not accomplish in the early stages, although I remember that when I was a student in the United States, I worked for some time in the women's movement there, and they were much more receptive to the Palestinian issue than the men because they could understand the nature of our own oppression. But, at the political level, it was very hard to get the women's movement to reach out beyond itself. Western feminists will have to put their own house in order and see that there is not just sisterhood but also an affinity among all the oppressed, regardless of the nature of the oppression, before they address other forms of oppression. I was gratified that the National Organization for Women (NOW) did not choose to endorse the Gulf war. Yet one might have hoped that their position would be based on the fact that this war would inflict undue hardship on women and children in the Middle East. Instead, the position of NOW was based on the premise that the U.S. government should not support a country where women are treated like "chattels." Although NOW is showing signs of becoming more and more globally aware, there has to be a better understanding of ethnic issues and of NOW's responsibility regarding Third World struggles. We have yet to hear of the support of NOW for the struggle of Palestinian women and the Palestinian people in the occupied territories.

12

SAHAR KHALIFEH

TRANSLATION BY NAGLA EL-BASSIOUNI

Comments by Five Women Activists: Siham Abdullah, Amal Kharisha Barghouthi, Rita Giacaman, May Mistakmel Nassar, Amal Wahdan

Siham Abdullah

Siham Abdullah is from the Toutah quarter in the Old City of Nablus and is a graduate of al-Najah University. She is in her twenties and is currently employed. I met her in a gathering of about ten women, most of whom were in their twenties. While the rest of the women spoke of their experiences, emphasizing their heroic contributions to the intifada, Siham remained silent. She followed the conversation with her eyes by looking from one speaker to the next. Siham's mother, also present, was one of those generous and courageous women who was constantly laughing. The contrast between the two rendered Siham's silence even more mysterious. I asked her why she was not participating in the conversation. Had she undergone any experiences similar to those of the others that she could talk about? She said that in comparison with the performance of the older generation of women, what she had done merited no mention. When I expressed surprise that the picture had been reversed—the older generation of women far more active than the younger generation, which was shy about action—she answered in a self-defensive manner:

I want to work, and I want to contribute but the situation does not allow for it.

Are you afraid?

Of course I am, but not of the occupying power. With a mother like mine, how could I possibly be afraid of occupation? However, my mother and the rest of the women her age do not have to be concerned about the responses of society and are therefore in a stronger position than the young women.

Men are afraid of the bullets and prison because they are frequently exposed to both, but you are in the same position as the rest of the women, so what do you have to fear?

I disagree. The older generation of women is stronger because they have less to lose. They do not fear celibacy since they are already married, they do not fear not having children since they have had several each. Their reputation as honest, decent women has already been established. Nothing they do or say can tarnish this reputation. The same does not apply to the younger generation of women. In the early days of the intifada I took to the streets during a large demonstration along with many young women, and we all heard one of the boys from our neighborhood saying, "Look at the sluts. They are joining the demonstration in order to show themselves off and to meet men." If our young men were as politically mature as our young women, the intifada would have been much stronger. One should not dismiss this issue as irrelevant, because it affects the rest of a girl's life. Frankly, I am afraid of injury and of prison, because if I am maimed, there is very little chance of finding a man who will ask for my hand in marriage. The community will discourage even a widower or a divorcee from marrying me by telling him, "This girl must be an instigator of trouble since she joined demonstrations with other men." Take what happened to Rana Shaban as an example.

Rana who is twenty-three years old, was engaged to a young man from Tulkarem. One day when she was buying her trousseau from the market, she saw some soldiers violently beating up a young boy, and she quickly ran to his assistance. She tried to pull the boy away from the soldiers but failed. Then she noticed a knife sticking out of the boy's back pocket. She quickly pulled the knife out and stabbed a soldier with it. The soldiers immediately jumped on her and began to beat her. Eventually, she was sentenced to five years in

prison. When her fiance learned about the situation, he broke off their engagement.

I think that the young men should be more aware of the conditions that surround Palestinian women under occupation and should treat women the same way that women treat men. Women wait for their fiances when their fiances are imprisoned. Women are proud of men who resist and treat them as heroes. However, if I am imprisoned I might be treated as a "fallen" woman. Young women swear, "We will marry none other than a boy who resists in the intifada." The boys marry only superficial girls. Compare the reaction of my friend Nabila, engaged to a young man called Mustafa, to that of Rana's fiance. On the day they were to be married, Mustafa was injured by a bullet that left him paralyzed in one leg. Nabila has refused to break the engagement, and she took a solemn oath not to marry anyone else, even if it meant remaining celibate.

At this point two young women, friends of Siham, joined the conversation. All seemed to agree that when it comes to marriage, men still prefer girls who are concerned with appearance over girls who are politically active. Azza, a student at Hebron University, added that the intifada alone could not change the position of women and that there must first be a change in values "in the minds of people." She added that young men know that a girl like herself, in blue jeans and tennis shoes, is more likely to endure the current hardships and will contribute financially to the marriage. But they are programmed to seek a girl who cares about her looks. Since they all stressed the need for change, I asked who was to initiate such change?

Women will have to initiate change. Men don't have any interest in change because they have many privileges in our society.

But the national interest dictates that men should seek such change.

This is the case in theory. In practice the situation is different. Most men admit that women's participation is a necessary and important national act. Some go as far as to say that the liberation of the country will not be achieved without the liberation of women. But when the issue becomes personal, when it is their fiance or his sister that must take to the street, men refuse, preferring to assume this role in their place. In a political gathering in the university I was listening to a young man expound on the historical importance of women's participation in the intifada. I asked him to explain why it was, if women's role is so important, that young men prefer to marry women who are not politicized. He said that marriage is a matter of personal choice and that he did not feel compelled to marry a woman because she is politically active.

The third woman, Khawla, a teacher in the village of Tamoun, proposed that Palestinian society does not take women's political participation very seriously. I protested: all Palestinians in the occupied territories and outside have been singing the praises of women's heroic deeds in the intifada; how do you explain that?

This is true. Women have indeed contributed, but at a high price to themselves. In the media, on television, women's praises are sung, but in the street and in the neighborhood the situation is different. Here women's political activities and their participation in the intifada are not respected. In my estimation, roughly 30 to 40 percent of the general population is politically mature. The remainder, including the young generation of men currently in universities, have not changed their values.

I understand from what all three of you have said that you are against the participation of women in the intifada. They all shouted together:

Of course not!

What then?

[Siham Abdullah answered:] The problem is perplexing. Sometimes when I hear all the negative things said about politically active women, I say I will never again participate in a demonstration or any political activity. On the other hand, sometimes you find yourself in situations where you have no choice but to participate. Two weeks ago I was in the process of taking a bath when, suddenly, my mother opened the door and said, "Quickly wrap yourself in a towel. I want to bring in some men to hide here. I wrapped myself up quickly as five young men entered the bathroom. I forced myself to continue singing at the top of my voice in spite of my visible embarrassment while my mother could be heard explaining to the soldiers that they could not search the bathroom since her daughter was inside taking a bath. It never occurred to the soldiers that an Arab mother would allow young men to hide in the same bathroom where her daughter was bathing. The soldiers went away.

I was stunned and said, "This episode is far more daring than if you had joined the demonstrations."

No this is a more acceptable form of political activity because it took place in the house and not the public sphere where women are not easily accepted. It is also true that these young men will not admit in public that they had to hide in a bathroom protected by a woman pretending to be bathing. No one will ever know about it. However, if I am seen at night in the street returning from a political meeting, people might question my reputation.

These personal stories explain why, in the middle stage of the intifada, most of the female activists in the streets were older women, married women, mothers, and those who were past the first stage of youth.

Amal Kharisha Barghouthi

Amal Kharisha Barghouthi is director of a women's organization, Ligan Almaraa Al-a'mila *(committee of working women), in Ramallah*

In my opinion, national and class consciousness leads to an awareness of feminist issues. My active involvement with the national cause and with class discrimination was preceded by many years of discussing and reading and writing about these subjects in junior high and high school. During my high school days the Israeli secret police interrogated me for editing a school paper which, according to them, had a liberating and therefore a subversive tone.

When I graduated from high school, my parents wanted me to attend teacher training school. When they tried to force me to go, I packed my bags and prepared to leave home, declaring that I was on strike against their decision. My father could not understand my resistance and was very angry, but I continued to reject his decision, so he gave in and let me attend the University of Jordan in Amman.

My political consciousness began to develop at the university, where I became active in student organizations and the Writers' Union, which introduced me to the writings of Arab revolutionary authors: Altahir Watar, Hana Mina, Ismail Fahd Ismail, Mahmoud Darwish, and others. I also became involved in women's groups through the Jordanian Women's Union. Our camp activities were in two camps, Al-Baka and Shanar; through our visits there I started to feel the pain of Palestinian women's suffering. When I became involved in the Committee to Fight Illiteracy and the Committee on Women's Issues in the Al-Salt area, I learned about the shared problems of Palestinian and Jordanian women of the same economic background. These were important experiences for privileged university women; the scenes of misery and poverty that we saw made it seem as if these women belonged to a different world, yet this was the world in which most of our people lived.

In 1978, during a student uprising on the occasion of Land Day, I led a demonstration with some other women students. Until that time, any form of leadership at the university was traditionally male. I was elected with another woman, who led the demonstration to a student committee to negotiate with the board of directors of the university. All the student committee members, myself included, were expelled from the university.

Demonstrations continued and there were incidents with the military secret police and week-long arrests. In response to these arrests, we held a meeting attended by three thousand students and I spoke in front of this gathering. The women students were asked to select a committee to present to the board of directors the student body's demand that the recently expelled students be reinstated. All five women who met with the directors were automatically expelled from the university. But the student body continued to pressure the administration until all those expelled were reinstated after one year. This was my first experience of real victory, and I learned much from it.

In 1979 I returned to my hometown of Tulkarem and worked in the sewing industry as a laborer. There I became acquainted with the suffering of working women, women less fortunate than myself; sweatshops are located underground or under staircases; the working hours are long; insults, verbal abuse, and hunger are common—all in return for a meager twenty-five dinars a month. I concluded that the situation of these women is like that of workers in Europe during the Industrial Revolution, as described by Marx. Through my participation in unions, humanitarian groups, the fight against illiteracy, and organizing women's groups within unions, I learned that women will never be able to achieve real progress without education. I also witnessed a situation that has remained imprinted in my mind: I saw a husband beating his wife because she did not have dinner ready; the wife worked as a hospital cleaning woman, and on that particular day she was late returning home because of transportation problems and had arrived at the same time as her husband. When he found his dinner was not ready, he felt he had the right to hit her. This woman works outside the home, bears and raises the children, cooks, cleans after her husband, cleans her home, and yet she gets beaten. I will never forget the incident because at that moment I became aware of the oppression of women. My work in unions has played a large role in developing my feminist consciousness.

In 1981 I met my husband through my work with the union. He came four times to ask for my hand, defying his house arrest each time, and each time my parents refused him because he had no university education, was not a professional, and was poor. Although the traditional constraints governing marriages in the northern part of the West Bank are more stringent than elsewhere, I broke all these traditions and insisted on marrying him until my family had to give in. Since my husband is not traditional, our relationship does not fit traditional norms. In fact, during the period of his house arrest, he raised our first baby; he used to claim that he had a job as a baby-sitter.

What Changes Has the Intifada Brought?

There have been some changes due to the intifada, but we should not exaggerate their impact. Changes in gender relations are at the moment sustained by the high level of political energy among men and women.

Women are delighted by male recognition for what is generally perceived as their heroic participation, but recognition is not enough: there will be a serious regression in gains made so far unless women organize by joining existing structures and unless we unite our joint efforts. One example of such regression that can be pointed out occurred in 1982 when local municipal workers were asked by the occupying powers to resign. Women distinguished themselves then through their excellent performance, but this performance did not result in any gains for women because their work was not grounded in women's organizations. When the intifada of 1982 died down, women withdrew from the scene; women from the Ramallah and Bireh area had participated at the beginning in fairly large numbers, but because the women's committees were not yet activated, all of the women's efforts were lost.

During the intifada, the still-developing women's movement made important strides, which can be summed up as follows:

1. At the popular level, the women's movement reached the rural area, whereas prior to the intifada it was mainly in urban centers.

2. Regarding democratic practices, in the Women's Committee Movement, the decisions are made by the general cadre and the local committees, not by the executive committee or the leaders. The leadership only formulates the language of the decisions.

3. The Women's Committee Movement succeeded in establishing

links between the [local] women's movement and the [global] women's movement by participating in conferences, hosting delegations, exchanging information, and by providing mutual support for political and humanitarian causes.

4. There was a recognition that since the entire society and culture are under occupation, there is no possibility of separating social and political issues; goals of national liberation and women's liberation are interrelated and must be dealt with equally and simultaneously.

5. The organized sector has begun to realize the importance of publishing and recording the experience of women.

Areas of Weakness in the Women's Movement

To a great extent, the women's committees are considered an extension of the political factions and at times even act as an information center to the various factions. Thus, 1) those women who join the women's committees are so immersed in political struggle and thought that they are unable to give sufficient attention to women's problems and issues. This means that they do not achieve, in their views, the social depth that would allow them to touch the lives of many women; and 2) the national liberation movement, directed by the PLO, still perceives the role of women to be strictly within the Palestinian Women's Union—to the exclusion of other unions, such as the Writer's Union, the Student Union, the Lawyer's Union, and others. Unions and institutions have male leaders, which clearly reveals discrimination based on gender and means that the male National Leadership leaves no room for women to reach leadership positions in Palestinian organizations—political, professional, or cultural. It also means that the women's movement itself is still unable to impose its presence and change this political reality.

Did the Intifada Change Gender Relations?

Neither the intifada nor any other political organization can re-create the world: some aspects of gender relations changed for some people, but the change did not take place across the board. In spite of women's participation on a large scale, women are still totally responsible for all the household duties and all the requirements of the husband and children, in addition to their biological role of childbearing and breast-feeding. Whereas the husband comes home from a political meeting or demonstration and becomes absorbed in reading or preparing for his political involvement, the wife with equal political responsibility comes back home to her duties of cooking, cleaning, caring for children, and washing dishes. Believe me, when I want to enjoy reading I have to get up at four or five in the morning, before the rest of the family is up and making demands on my time.

The Women's Movement and the Palestinian State

I am optimistic and believe that our current intifada and our future government will be of a democratic nature. But I would like to make sure women understand that responsibility for the inclusion of women in the democratic process falls on the shoulders of the Palestinian women themselves. If the women's movement is capable of proposing programs and regulations that protect its own interests, women will surely gain their rights; if they fail to do so, we cannot expect that the male leadership will grant us our rights on its own.

It is our fear that what happened to Algerian women after Algerian independence is going to happen to us; we all talk about it. Certainly we want to avoid their fate; I believe that what occurs will depend on the programs and the activities that the women's movement is capable of developing and applying.

Dr. Rita Giacaman

Dr. Giacaman teaches public health at Birzeit University.

My sisters and I grew up in Bethlehem with a confused sense of patriotism and identity and the closed-mindedness of a Christian minority. When we were young, we didn't know very much about our society, partly because we studied in foreign schools. I personally studied with nuns in a private French school.

My mother was a strong woman. She influenced my life the most; I loved her as much as I feared her strength and domination. I had an exceptional aunt. She was one of the pioneers of the women's movement in Bethlehem and was a member of one of the women's organizations. She gave a lot to her community, despite the fact that she was raised in a traditional and repressed atmosphere. At fourteen she married a cousin and left with him for Nicaragua, but the marriage didn't work out and she returned with a son. Society made her lose confidence in herself and stay home to serve her mother. After my mother got married, strong ties developed between her and this sister. My mother encouraged her to apply to a college in London and to study social services by correspondence, then to live on her own. My mother took care of my grandmother so that my aunt could move away to have a career. My aunt did brilliantly. Thus my background contained two strong, influential women.

Political affiliation and political thought were not a part of the environment in which I grew up. At eighteen, I enrolled at Birzeit University and became immersed in the process of changing myself. Like all the rest of the so-called Kit Kat girls (this name was given to girls with enough money to afford the candy bars with that name but little social or political consciousness), I isolated myself at first and was afraid of becoming part of this politically changing environment. At that time Birzeit University was beginning to change from an elite private school to a popular institution imbued with political fire. Slowly we began to become part of what was going on around us and to take part in it. My sister was more active than I was. She fell in love with a young Muslim student from Nablus who led the protests at the university. When she confided in me about her love and the nature of her boyfriend's interests, I became very concerned. But she succeeded in convincing me to accompany them to the mosque for a sit-in, so I followed and was surprised to find the place far less tranquil than I had anticipated. The local population of Birzeit treated the politically involved students like heroes and brought us food at the mosque. I heard discussions and participated in the chanting of slogans, and I began to feel nationalistic sentiments I had never known existed within me.

From Birzeit I traveled to Beirut to finish my studies. The distance from my parents made me self-reliant. I began to accept what I was, who I was, and what I wanted. I am an Arab woman, I like my people, and I want to give back to the people. What I know and what I am capable of achieving is for their sake. But I am a woman and in their consciousness an incomplete person. From Beirut I traveled to America. Because of my father's sudden financial problems, I learned how to be self-sufficient. I was liberated and learned the meaning of progressive thinking about social justice based on my reality as a woman and as a Palestinian.

When I returned to Birzeit I found the popular movement growing and people resisting, rising up, and trying to change their reality. The air was charged and individuals were encouraged to give and work together for their common goal. Real attempts were made to resist occupation on every level. In the area of health, I found three strategies operating at once:

1. A strategy that gives Israel control over health care, which is in turn exploited by Israel for the purpose of carrying out its political policies.

2. A nationalist bourgeois strategy that hopes to control health care without offering any revolutionary ideas that challenge the present sociopolitical situation. The opinion behind this strategy can

be summarized as follows: "Anything that can be taken from the government should be considered profit." Basically, it works through legal means within the system and doesn't go beyond it. As a result, this strategy could not challenge the policies of the military government and it therefore didn't succeed in meeting peoples' health needs.

3. A revolutionary strategy that doesn't focus on medical treatment but on preventive medicine. This strategy aspires to establish health programs through cooperative committees that involve people in their health care programs. Work on the mass level is emphasized and individual focus is rejected. As a result, this method leads to some form of confrontation with the military occupation.

In the beginning, I didn't know which path I would take. My experience and training in the United States prepared me for laboratory analysis in the American system. Frustrated, I considered returning to the United States. Then, as a result of my increasing involvement in the women's committees and the medical aid committees, things started to crystallize, and I made two decisions: first, to remain in the country no matter what it took; second, to change my specialization from laboratory to pharmacological work, something our country really needs and that is related to the sociopolitical health situation we live in. Through the committees, I began to visit villages and see the reality of the health conditions facing women and children there. Female child mortality rates in some villages reached twice those for male child mortality because of the distinction made between males and females in traditional Palestinian society, where male children receive more attention. Also, women's health in general is worse than men's health for this same reason. This situation is compounded by the problems resulting from women's repeated pregnancies and childbirth. In the committees, we developed a feminist theory that views the health situation as directly related to our social and sexual reality; on one level, we wanted to deal with the health situation by developing women-oriented programs to make women aware of health problems specifically related to them and how they can treat them in the cheapest and easiest way. We also achieved our goals of completely undermining the military law and superseding its limitations and of filling people's health needs in their villages instead of waiting for villagers to come to the clinics in the city.

When we observed, studied, and traveled, we saw that the people in the villages needed cleanliness and general health care more than labs. Our health care system is based on the development of health services related to cleanliness and to the prevention of illness, and it is based on building an apparatus that doesn't rely on the resources of institutions or require the land of huge hospitals. The daily cost for a single bed in a conventional hospital equals the expenditures of an entire primary health care center in any village, and 70 percent of the inhabitants of the occupied territories live in such villages.

Some Issues Pertaining to Feminist Consciousness on the West Bank

In my opinion, the national liberation struggle contained the seeds of a growing consciousness among women about women's issues. This relationship between the national liberation struggle and the development of women's consciousness proved to be a mixed blessing: on the one hand, the national struggle forced women out of the domestic sphere and offered them a new political role outside the home, raising their consciousness to their own oppression as women. On the other hand, the struggle presented women's issues as a secondary front, the primary front being the liberation of the land. Yet the intifada could not have continued as it did if it had not been for the emergence of a feminist consciousness. This feminist consciousness is an integral part of the general national consciousness, existing with it simultaneously in a constant dialectical exchange.

The social change resulting from the intifada has created new roles for women. The women's organizations and the committees taught women the skills needed to be politicians and strategists, and the intifada taught them how to be political leaders. The important movement of women into leadership roles in the male arena was necessitated by the mass imprisonment of male political leaders. This movement was coupled with women's emergence into the political as opposed to the domestic sphere in demonstrations, where they broke up fights between the army and the youths. Very often the women who reached leadership positions were girls in their teens. Women also proved their capabilities in the popular committees, where they worked side by side with men. These changes widened the circle of women's concerns and contributed to their sense of belonging to the struggle. Whereas previously their sense of belonging was limited to the family, it was now extended to the neighborhood, the block, and even to the city as a whole. Their expanded horizons found them the focal point in the street and at the forefront of the struggle.

One fears that there will be regressions concerning women's roles and that women will go back into the home once the struggle is diminished or in the period after the national struggle is won, as is often the case. What makes me worry is the fact that this positive change did not have time to take root. The demonstrations and confrontations in which women participated en masse are not enough to produce permanent change on the structural and cultural level of society. After the eruption of the intifada, small changes took place in the distribution of labor within the home, but women are still responsible for most of the work. They are single-handedly responsible for cooking, cleaning, washing the dishes, and bringing up the children. Women leaders still suffer from a split allegiance to their traditional role, on the one hand, and to their new revolutionary role, on the other. For example, these women leaders, even during the most critical moments of the struggle, would suspend their political and organizational role in order to attend to such duties at home as cooking dinner or caring for a sick child. The husband, by contrast, does not suspend his political duties to do housework. We must conclude from this that women's participation is not considered by society to be equal in importance to men's participation. As long as women do not challenge the traditional division of labor, no serious transformations will take place in the structure of society.

Despite all the turbulence and potential for change, the expected role of women has not changed. For example, women are encouraged to become secretaries but not to become carpenters or to study commerce, and women who are studying medicine are always encouraged to become nurses rather than doctors.

In my opinion, the most important weakness of the women's movement is that the four factions to which women's groups belong are not independent of male leadership since they are part of the political ideologies of these factions. Because they are not independent, women's committees are not unified. The issue that illustrates this weakness is that of democratic representation in the women's movement; the Higher Council for Women, a body that is supposed to make decisions that affect the lives of all women, consists only of members of the four political factions and therefore represents only 5 percent of women. Is this democracy? I personally do not and never will belong to a political faction; this means that even though I am politically active, I belong to the 95 percent of women who are not politically organized or represented by the Higher Council for Women. Why is this council incapable of full representation when it is one of the arms of our official leadership (the PLO), whose structure includes independents and ensures their representation?

The third point of weakness is competition, which is a waste of time and effort. Before the intifada, the various factions used to compete with each other over who would establish child care, workshops, etc., in a village, the same neighborhood, or even the same street. The intifada reduced the amount of competition but didn't stop it completely.

Despite these weaknesses, the strengths of the women's movement are clear and numerous. The most important of these, as I previously mentioned, is that the committees taught women roles outside the realm of the home as well as the art of politics and planning. Further, the intifada produced superb women leaders who have proven themselves through their abilities and effectiveness. Yet the Unified Leadership perceives women only as mothers and wives of martyrs. What about our female martyrs? What about our struggle in the streets and the camps and the schools and the hospitals? What about all the things we women gave? Why is it that the Unified Leadership sees only the contributions that women make through men, as mothers and wives? Why did they address all of the sectors by name (in the flyers or *bayanat*) except women? Why do they insist on treating us as if we are mouths without tongues, as if our opinions are only peripheral? This situation will not change unless women are part of the political leadership in decision-making positions.

Specific Requests from the Women's Movement

The most important request I am making of the women's movement is that it unify women by representing independents in the Higher Council for Women and that it choose representatives on the basis of their efforts, not their contacts or the contributions of their families.

Second, feminist thinking and a strategy for women's liberation that are in accordance with the national ideology must be developed. National ideology is an important base, but it must not rule out progressive social thinking; the internal social conflicts in our society will not be resolved through the liberation of the land. It has never happened before that a national solution brought about solutions to social problems. I am also asking that the women's movement create a balance between national rights, social rights, and economic rights.

Third, I ask that the women's movement conduct more studies about the backward situation of women in our country and that the findings of these studies be used for the establishment of practical projects and programs to improve the condition of women. The projects should have political significance and not focus exclusively on nurseries, sewing centers, and illiteracy workshops.

Fourth, I am asking for a change in all laws, from the *shariah* to the civil law code. I am Rita Giacaman, the doctor, the professor, the mother. I don't accept having a protector or a legal guardian to grant me permission to travel or to prohibit me from it. I don't accept being married by a priest and then forbidden to get a divorce if need be, or having the priest prevent me from marrying a Muslim (my husband is a Muslim). Nor would I accept being married by a sheikh who lets my husband marry again or divorce me when he wants.

SAHAR KHALIFEH

May Mistakmel Nassar

May Mistakmel Nassar is an active member of the Committee of Palestinian Women, Ramallah

I began writing and expressing myself when I was in the fourth grade. The teachers were very receptive to my writings because they addressed national social issues. My father probably deserves the credit for that; he treated all of us equally (I have two sisters and four brothers). That we were male or female didn't change the way he listened to our ideas and arguments. We had freedom and equality in arguments and in forming our ideas. Males, however, had priority where higher education was concerned, and they had more pocket money than we did, despite the fact that my sister and I excelled at school. The result was that my brothers were the ones who obtained advanced academic degrees, even though we girls were better students and more self-reliant.

My intermediate and high school education was in public schools; my presence among girls in public schools played an important role in forming my personality because it gave me the opportunity to experience true poverty and hardship. During my junior year in high school I was transferred to a private girls' school, where the students came from a higher income bracket. It was there that I began to think of the issues of class. I discovered the large gap that separates me from them; there was a difference in the ideas and the way of dealing with people. I felt that my new schoolmates were not capable of commitment to any cause. I returned to public school, which I felt was my natural environment, where the give and take is not motivated by self-benefit and interests.

I had to get financial support from my mother to finish college. Despite financial difficulties, my mother convinced my father of the need for me to finish my education. She would say, "It was our joint mission. Who knows what the future will hold? An education is a weapon in the hands of a young girl." In college, I was very actively involved in volunteer work and was elected to my first work committee. Later I was elected president of the student council.

While I was working in student affairs, my views of sexual equality and the issue of women were idealistic: I rejected the distinction between women's issues and men's issues and I wanted women to take part in everything men did. I wanted to overlook the specificity of women's situation in our culture. It was after I graduated and started to work that I reached a new level of awareness: we began, as intellectuals, to meet in the libraries of Ramallah and Bireh, and we began to really think about the situation of women. I developed a commitment concerning women's status, and I understood the need not to overlook the specificity of women's situation. In the mid-70s, we began to look upon the women's question as a pressing issue: as young women we started to get together to openly discuss our problems and put them in a general social framework. We began to work exhaustively on issues facing women as well as the other issues arising from our present situation.

During my studies I was imprisoned twice. I heard my mother say more than once, "If she was a man I wouldn't have worried, but a girl. . . . It's too much." From other women I would hear, "Women shouldn't have to go through this much." It is understood that imprisonment for political reasons is honorable. But parents and others see it only as oppressive for women. These reactions proved to me just how complicated and sensitive women's issues are; they penetrate even the smallest details of upbringing, customs, and reactions.

During my imprisonment, I learned things about women that I couldn't learn on the outside, especially about the situation of women accused of prostitution. Once, two or three days after a severe interrogation, I needed to talk to somebody. I started to discuss things with an Israeli prostitute who had approached me earlier; I realized that Israeli society doesn't have any more compassion for women than ours does, especially as far as the Sephardim [North African or Middle Eastern Jews] are concerned. Prostitution among Ashkenazi women [the term Ashkenazi refers to European Jews] can be overlooked by their culture, whereas prostitution among Sephardi women would never be forgiven by their culture. As a result, they are left with no alternative for making a living. Even as a prostitute, the Western (Ashkenazi) woman has an advantage.

The result of my encounter with these Israeli prisoners accused of immorality was that I was left with a sense of compassion for them. Being imprisoned with them was supposed to be a punishment, but I gained from it. I began to see that these women are the biggest victims in society, economically and socially. Their acts—measured according to traditional social standards—are seen as immoral, yet it is their position in society that drives them to prostitution.

The third time I was imprisoned was during the intifada. The soldiers came in the evening and entered the bathroom as I was bathing my children, then started to rummage through our closets. I pointed to the soldiers and explained to my son, "These are the people who took your father." The soldier said, "You've started to teach your kids enmity now." It was 1 A.M. by then and I asked them to postpone my arrest until morning, but they refused. When I left, the women in the neighborhood came to my support and cared for my children. I credit this to the intifada, which has increased women's awareness and sense of giving. Before the intifada, when someone was arrested or searched, not one of the neighbors would raise a finger. During the intifada, things changed, and cooperation became the norm.

Comments on the Palestinian Women's Movement in the Occupied Territories and the Intifada

Women's activities can be divided into two groups: quantitative, or work that is an accumulation of women's projects that are not directed toward specific political ends; and qualitative, or work that is based on the interconnectedness of the political, social, and economic aspects of women's reality and that is goal directed. The two should not be separated.

Palestinian women began to be active in 1929, but their activities were fragmented and unconnected; the social struggle, political struggle, and economic struggle were all carried out separately. Their activities were positive, but they were missing something. Also, there was no leadership role for women; many became martyrs, sacrificing their lives for the national cause; but there was never an occasion for them to take much responsibility for decision making. Women's role was also wanting at the social level because they were always focusing on providing charitable services: in other words, the woman's role was humanitarian and no more. Further, from an economic viewpoint, women joined unions but did not reach positions of leadership in these unions.

This was women's situation until the early 80s, when a framework for women's organizations based on their political affiliations began to take shape. Since then, women have started to look at women's issues with more commitment; instead of viewing everything separately, as the charity organizations had done before, women began to see the interconnectedness of the three aspects—social, economic, and political—of their situation. For instance, women began to be aware that social oppression hindered their economic participation, and that economic repression subsequently led to a lack of political involvement.

During the 80s, most of the organizations with a political affiliation were composed of educated, single women of the middle class. But all political parties tried to reach out to housewives as well. While some polarization did exist among the various women's committees with different political affiliations, the intifada brought women closer together and emphasized the importance of cooperation between women's committees. There has been a fifty to one hundred percent increase in women's participation in organized committee work. In our committee, the increase in officially participating members has been about fifty percent. When you include sympathizers and those who are "affiliated" with us (e.g., through participation in demonstrations) it has risen by one hundred percent.

Comments by Five Women Activists

The general goals of our union are promotion of women's issues on the social, economic, and political levels so that women can participate in the liberation of the land from occupation and of women in society from oppression. We are striving toward these goals by working to place women in the political, economic, and social scene so that women can change society. We hope to achieve this through activities involving educational, political, informational, and organizational programs.

When the intifada started, we stopped all of our activities and took our work to the street—demonstrations, clashes, first aid, providing assistance to the needy and families of martyrs, visiting prisoners, etc. The nature of our work later provided the model for forming the popular committees. The importance attributed by society to our participation proved to us that it was the duty of the women's committees to keep the intifada going by moving our activities to the streets and neighborhoods. The intifada changed our way of thinking about and executing things and brought about the creation of new committees within our framework to deal with the economy of the home, the political factions, stocking of supplies, rationing of food provisions, and caring for prisoners during times of crisis.

What do we have to offer to women as a social entity with no rights? Right now we're cooperating with other women's groups to formulate new personal status laws that will make gains for women concerning paid holidays, inheritance, divorce, and alimony. (Laws are currently based on the *shariah,* the Islamic religious code). We in the Palestinian Women's Committee believe that the issue of sexual discrimination must be part of the program for liberation from occupation. The women's issue is part of the whole social structure. If women are not liberated, then society will not be liberated, and until women are liberated they will not rest. Rather, women will work for liberation from occupation because this will make their participation in society easier. We will not bring up the issue of women's liberation except within the context of national liberation. Our women's movement works with men to free the country, unlike in the West, where because of women's economic exploitation women's groups and organizations were established separately from men's groups. We are not separate; women and men, hand in hand, work together to liberate the country. We see that it is to men's advantage that women be liberated. The liberation of women will help them participate in the job of liberating society, which will benefit us all.

The Difference between Reality and Theory

For most men there is a conflict between theory and practice when it comes to women's issues. This is a result of our social conditioning. Not every politically conscious male has a clear vision of social interaction and gender relations. Most believe in national and economic liberation but are not aware of the need for social liberation and gender equality. This shows that their vision is not complete. In my opinion, only those who understand the necessity of both forms of liberation (national and gender based) can actually practice what they preach.

Palestinian Political Organizations Are Able to Initiate a New Consciousness

Palestinian organizations proved during the intifada that they are able to deliver on the popular level; they can be effective in bringing about social change. Therefore they must also have an agenda for examining gender relationships. Organizations should also give women a larger role in leadership so that they will take on decision-making roles. Needless to say, it is women's duty to exert serious efforts in order to become leaders. Women must achieve their liberation through their own efforts. But it is the duty of the leaders to understand the value of women's contribution to the struggle. Each sex gave in a different way. Although not as many women as men were killed, our contribution equals that of men. Because our society is a male-dominated society, one can't expect women to go down into the streets in the same numbers as men. When this society becomes less patriarchal, we will see more women in the streets. Women cannot be expected to jump into all political activities all of a sudden.

In Touch with Jewish Women

There is a need to form channels to Jewish/Israeli society in order to reach more women and to increase the number of women who believe and act upon a two-state solution. But we have not yet taken any steps in this direction.

Amal Wahdan

Amal Wahdan is a member of the Women's Work Committees for National Work (Lijan Al Mara' lilamal al nisai), *Ramallah*

I am of Bedouin origin and I am from al-Bireh, a conservative town where people's lives are ruled by tradition. Since early childhood I perceived discrimination against me when comparing the respective treatment my brother and I received: he gets what he wants and I am denied what I want. This disparity in treatment created a desire in me to challenge and to question. In time, as the discrimination against me as a woman became more apparent, I became more resentful of the degradation inflicted upon women. I expressed my resentment by refusing to dress or to behave in a feminine way. For example, I would refuse to wear a dress because dresses are for girls, and I would ride a bike because bikes are for boys. I would refuse to participate in social visits and weddings because such behavior was labeled female. I would play "male" games such as ball or jumping games. My behavior did not please my mother and my family, but I felt a sense of happiness when doing these things.

I refused to entertain thoughts about the relationship between women and men after marriage. The image of the bride was for me a repulsive one and reminded me of a doll. Why did I feel repelled by both images and dislike marriage? I am still not sure of the answer. Even my first emotional involvement as a young girl was affected by these feelings: I suddenly broke off this relationship, preventing it from developing further.

As I grew up, the constraints placed on me as a female increased. I was separated from the boy I used to enjoy playing with: he was to play with the boys and I was to play with the girls. I hated playing with girls.

Since then, I have started to think about the nature of social relations. So as not to become isolated, I joined the YMCA, which gave me an opportunity to continue to be with males and to join in some athletic games. The absence of my father, who had emigrated to the United States, made it easier to do this, and I was able to get around my mother. When my extended family brought up the issue, I would complain of being lonely and depressed and they would grudgingly leave me alone.

In 1983 I began volunteering with committees working for the national cause and also joined in discussions that took place in the public library. My family did not know of my participation, but my eldest brother began to inform my mother of my activities and set her against my behavior. Yet in the absence of my father it was easy for me to manipulate the situation by pleasing my mother.

In those days, it was common to marry girls off early, at about the age of fifteen, and there was a request for my hand in marriage. In spite of the fact that my father had emigrated to the United States, he remained a very traditional man when it came to women's issues and felt that the only avenue open to me was marriage. I used to avoid the subject; I dreamt of going to the United States in order to pursue my education and in fact was able to do this. After two months in the United States, however, a relative there asked for my hand. In the beginning I tried to resist the offer, but I finally had to succumb because of family pressure, because I was only eighteen, and because I was in a foreign country with no support system. I agreed, on the condition that I would continue my education; given my strong personality, I still found it difficult to give in and continued to seek a way out of this difficulty. I consulted with a Spanish professor who showed some sympathy for me. I consulted a lawyer. I thought of fleeing to Mexico, dreaming of every possible way to escape this fate. On the occasion of the 15th of May, the PLO representative was invited to preside over Palestinian events in Denver, Colorado. I took this opportunity to explain my situation to the representative and to ask him to help me flee to Lebanon. He gave me his telephone number and promised to arrange for the trip. After a few days, as I was speaking to him on the telephone, my brother overheard me. When he asked, I explained that I was getting ready to escape to Lebanon. My secret was discovered, and it soon became evident to my family that I was in a desperate state and there was no hope of reforming me. The situation was very embarrassing for them, since the prospective bridegroom had made all the necessary arrangements, including purchasing furniture, purchasing my trousseau, and printing invitations. As for me, I was making plans in a different direction. The situation of my family was a difficult and embarrassing one. How could they go back on a promise made between them and the family of the bridegroom?

They tried to threaten and to pressure me again. My father threatened that I would end up a maid in my brother's household, but to no avail. My relations and friendships at the university were my support system, as was my eldest sister, whom I was able to draw to my side. My father pretended to get sick, also to no avail. When my father and mother traveled back to Palestine and left me in the United States, I started to get homesick and think of returning. By then I had become convinced that the United States was not for me; I did not see myself staying there. Secretly, I planned my trip back, and I returned two weeks after my parents left.

When I got back home my father tried to place additional pressure on me. He ordered me not to leave the house or participate in any activity or even think of any projects. In the beginning I agreed, but soon I registered at Birzeit University. I worked and obtained education loans to become financially independent. I moved to Birzeit, away from my family. My relations with my family were interrupted for a period of five years.

Upon graduating, my professional life began and I started looking for a partner to share my life. I married out of conviction; we had been friends for many years and shared the same beliefs and convictions. He is a unionist, and he applies his principles in his daily life: he encourages me in my work with women's groups, he cooks, washes dishes, changes the baby's diapers. I can be away from the house all day without worrying about anything. He enabled me to see the problems in the lives of other women. Sometimes when I am visiting a friend, I notice how her husband orders her to perform her duties as a hostess while he sits like one of the guests. It disturbs me when I hear a husband tell his wife "make the coffee," or "change the baby's diapers," while he sits. My husband makes the coffee and changes the baby without trying to make it seem like he is doing me a favor. He even cooks, without problems. He is truly progressive and does not have all the traditional complexes, and he treats his sisters in the same way he treats me. I am one of the few women who are very lucky; I do not believe that my marriage is a typical one.

General Comments

In our committee (*Aoutor*) we address women's issues in the context of the national struggle. In the first two years, we focused on the integration of women into work outside the home. We also gave special attention to housewives since they belong to the category in society that is most oppressed but whose oppression is the least visible. We also focused on working women and were able to form work committees in institutions that hire women. When the intifada started our work committees were already operating; we used these committees as channels to transfer the intifada from cities to the rural sector.

I have a certain perception regarding traditions that prevent the mobilization of women: we will not be able to achieve any progress on the national front in the course of the intifada if we do not examine social and traditional problems. In the past, our culture condoned mediation between a husband and a wife, and many used to intercede on a woman's behalf with her husband. The time is now ripe for similar intervention on women's behalf, in this case by the national struggle; outside oppression makes it easier to raise issues involving the internal oppression of women, and women's contributions to the intifada have made it possible to support their liberation. People have shown greater ability to accept the changing situation of women; it is now acceptable for women to throw stones, wrestle with the soldiers, separate the young men from the grips of soldiers, distribute flyers, and perform all kinds of acts of resistance. The true capabilities of women are being discovered.

The following is an example of how women discovered their true capabilities through their experience under occupation: one of our most active members in Gaza was undergoing serious marital stress due to the strains placed on her marriage by involvement in political work outside the home. She was also pressured by her family, who opposed her involvement. Thus she was suffering from lack of support on both sides when she was imprisoned for a short time and then placed under military confinement. After she left prison, her husband and family began to interfere in her life again. At that point she found the inner strength to say to them, "If I have to choose between you and the work I am doing, I will choose the work." She had found this inner strength through her experience in prison: when she compared the two forms of oppression, she found that the oppression exercised by the family and husband was not unchallengeable after all. I understood her experience as follows: the intifada was able to bring out the issues facing women in the traditional realm, making it possible for women to resist this form of internal oppression at the same time that they were resisting occupation.

The experience of occupation during the last ten years has produced women's groups that have proven themselves by fully shouldering responsibility. The intifada in particular produced qualified women capable of assuming the highest leadership positions. But their ability to reach these positions depends entirely on the ideological make-up of the political faction of the PLO to which they belong: the more progressive factions, those that advocate a democratic approach by promoting political, social, and gender equality, also allow greater participation for women at the decision-making level.

Another by-product of the intifada is that negative competition between women's groups has diminished because the confrontation with occupation rendered all regional and factional rivalry secondary. I am worried, though, about women who joined only for the purpose of self-promotion, because they have not yet challenged traditional perceptions of the woman's role. I do not believe that we will be able to abandon the quest for women's rights once we gain our independence: the struggle in this direction will stretch way beyond the moment of independence. So that women do not lose the gains they made during the struggle, as was the case with Algerian women, I think it is very important that women's groups attached to the various political factions unite. I am afraid that once the political threat that unites us now is removed, women will give up the struggle to gain equality and their rights.

The responsibility for liberating women rests on the shoulders of women: there are all too many men, some of whom are in political organizations, who support women's rights in principle but do not apply these principles in their daily lives. For these men, theory remains suspended in the air, never reaching the ground. I personally despise men who grant themselves the right to be politically active and fulfilled while simultaneously denying these same rights to their wives. We must ask ourselves who is responsible for reversing this double standard, and I think that the various political organizations must give this issue serious consideration. It is a well-known fact that women's issues and discrimination based on gender are not taken seriously. These organizations give priority to political objectives over needs for social change. In any case, the responsibility for changing social perceptions regarding women rests squarely on the shoulders of women.

.13.

RITA GIACAMAN AND PENNY JOHNSON

Intifada Year Four:
Notes on the Women's Movement

In the wake of the Gulf War and in the midst of continued curfews and restrictions on the Palestinian population, Women's Day 1991 passed almost without notice in the occupied territories. A few young women were arrested in Jerusalem, some simply because the police were detaining all young women dressed in the ubiquitous color of black. The contrast to Women's Day 1988, during the first year of the uprising, was stark. On that day middle-class women in high heels, teenagers in jeans, and village women in traditional dress marched through the streets of Ramallah and other towns and villages throughout the West Bank and Gaza. Many women had tears in their eyes—not from the inevitable tear gas but from the exhilaration of a new spirit of women's solidarity and defiance.

The remarkable story of the first year of the Palestinian uprising has already produced a small body of celebratory literature. The Palestinian experience of a transforming mass mobilization in that year, like those in the history of other peoples and struggles, was marked by a release of popular energy, a new liberating consciousness, intense communal solidarity, and new forms of grassroots organization, particularly in the popular and neighborhood committees. The emerging role of Palestinian women was noted by political commentators and journalists and attracted the interest of feminist writers, including the authors of this piece. The images of women in street confrontations captured the imagination; the important role of the women's committees and their cadres—sometimes called the "new women's movement" in the occupied territories—in encouraging women's mobilization was combined with a declared interest in forging a women's agenda. The potential for a women's movement that seriously addressed both national and social issues and could make a significant contribution to improving women's lives and futures, was exciting.

However, just as the intifada in its initial stage offered remarkable opportunities for the development of the women's movement, the obverse is also true; the women's movement in the occupied territories, inextricably tied to the national movement, reflects each twist and turn of the national fortune.

Writing in a very different time, during the fourth year of the uprising and after the trauma of the Gulf War, in the midst of an American-dominated peace process that has so far engendered only deep cynicism, our aim is to use the lens of the present to examine some aspects of women's participation in and experience of the intifada and to identify some "missing questions" that need to be addressed.

In the spring of 1990, Salim Tamari offered an astute assessment of the predicament of the intifada in its third year: "The crux of the predicament lies in the routinization of the daily aspects of revolt (centered around the commercial strike and street confrontations with the army) which can neither be escalated in a campaign of total civil disobedience—and complete disengagement from Israeli rule—nor transformed into a political initiative which can engage the enemy on terms favorable to the Palestinians."

Tamari, among others, has argued that the political reality after the Gulf War blunts the second horn of the Palestinian dilemma. The first, however, has only worsened. The Gulf War has brought in its wake a reexamination of the tenets and methods of the intifada. This reexamination is taking place both at the level of the political cadre and in the street, and is marked by a sense of uneasiness and frustration, complaints and questions. The trend continues to be away from mass popular mobilization and toward actions by the "strike forces" and, increasingly, individual acts of violence, both primarily, although in the latter case not exclusively, male activities.

It is in this contradictory environment that the women's movement works today. The terrain of popular struggle has been replaced by a narrow arena with few actors and many spectators. What were the truths of year one are the heroic myths of year four, sometimes sustaining and sometimes constricting. One prominent woman researcher noted: "I sometimes feel like the subject 'women and the intifada' is a prison." Another writer on Palestinian women, Rima Hammami, argues that the very "culture of the intifada," with its focus on modesty and spartan values, has had negative consequences for women.

The Gulf War added another dimension; all Palestinians under occupation became spectators. For women, the confinement to the home under a strict twenty-four-hour curfew for most of the war replicated, by army fiat, women's mythologized role, and was coupled with real, terrible anxieties about their inability to safeguard the family against the possible horrors of war—particularly chemical warfare—and, as the curfew ground on, to adequately provide the daily necessities of life. The grassroots network of support developed during the intifada was, not surprisingly, inadequate to the emergency of regional and total curfew, with the partial exception of health committees and human rights work done by a number of organizations and activists to highlight the lack of protection afforded the Palestinian population. The role of the women's committees, however, was minimal at best. In towns, villages, and camps, the sustaining network was the traditional one—family, kin, and neighborhood.

We conducted in-depth interviews with three women who were grassroots activists during the first year of the intifada, listening to their opinions, problems, and perceptions of the current reality, as well as their experiences during the war and their reflections on the future of the intifada and of the women's movement. Combined with our own experience, we hoped to capture the questions that women are asking and the questions that need to be answered.

Wahida

No one really knows the age of Wahida. Her birth certificate says she is thirty-three. She maintains that this is a mistake and that she is actually twenty-nine. She is tiny, slightly plump, and doll-like. And she loves life.

Wahida was active in the past in one of the women's committees. During the first two years of the uprising, she spent more time in the streets than in any other place. She was one of the women of the *mataris* (road blocks). She idolized the stone, as she does today, as the symbol and the form of Palestinian struggle against the occupier. Within the *shabibeh* (youth) section of her group, she led both young men and women. She was responsible for organizing the entire street activities with the youth within an area that went far beyond her neighborhood. Wahida was one of those rising stars, a leader of both men and women.

Yet she resigned from the committee two years after the beginning of the intifada and continues to be inactive in the area of politics today:

> It is useless; no one listened. They wanted us to move in wrong ways. They did not understand the makeup of young people. They treated them badly, just ordering them around. They did not take into account their needs, and the way things really were. In the end, they did not even take into consideration my recommendations because they stigmatized me as someone who takes the side of the youth too much. For what mattered most was which group scored more points in relation to others.

Wahida's life is a paradoxical tragedy in Palestinian culture. While the backbone of society continues to be the family, Wahida has had hardly any family life. Her father left her mother when most of the six children were young. For some reason that she still does not understand, Wahida and the two younger children ended up living alone in one West Bank town, the other children scattered all over. At that stage, when Wahida was fourteen, she left school and began to work as a child laborer to support the two children, who were hardly two years younger than she. She worked at one of the "national institutions" and faced what appear to have been unspeakable conditions, including gross violations of workers' rights. She was eventually thrown out of this institution when she joined one of the women's committees.

Wahida grew up way before her time. With the burden of child support weighing heavy on her shoulders, she embarked on a life full of responsibility with no backing. With no more than seven years of education, she could only engage in manual labor; she confused numbers and could not tell left from right easily. But she had the gift of being able to write short stories and even poems, and this creative outlet increased her self-esteem. Yet she found her strength within the context of the committees. And soon, the committee became her family—a refuge in time of need, something that would defend and protect her in society.

Over the years she learned much about politics. She learned the difference between strategy and tactics. Although uneducated, her political discourse is much like that of political savants and avid readers. She did read, for that was part of her education at the committee; Marx and Engels, Pablo Neruda, and all the others that cadres must go through for a political education. In this sense, the group widened her scope, exposed her to analysis, and indeed provided her with the will to move forward.

The exceptional conditions of the intifada allowed Wahida and others to move swiftly into the world of men and into positions of leadership. Soon, Wahida's efforts in reading, educating herself, and practice in the streets bore fruit; she began to assess, criticize, and attempt to participate in decision making. She also began to form relationships with the youth in the streets, relationships that went beyond the group and involved cooperation and even befriending those belonging to other groups. For what mattered to her was the intifada, its course and how to move it forward:

> The decision makers and the persons responsible for me did not understand me. They did not understand that if I visited someone from another group it did not mean that I was in danger of betraying mine. They could not see the value of listening to the bottom echelons, their views and arguments. They could not face criticism from below. They could not tolerate differences in opinion. . . . I was to execute orders and that was that. And when I tried to get to the high officials, I could not, because the persons directly above me would not let me. I felt lonely and not understood. Then the pressures of my personal situation, financial insecurity, loneliness, and the pressures of the political conditions all together did something to me. And I began to forget important details and things. It was becoming too dangerous and I was too alienated. So I withdrew from the group: what else could I have done?

The Gulf War dealt yet another blow to Wahida. On the day the war broke out, she looked around her and found no one. She tried to contact her brothers, but they were busy with their own families. The only brother that she had maintained a close relationship with, because they in fact lived together for much of their lives, was in prison serving a two-year sentence. She was worried sick about him because he was located in a prison inside Israel and she knew that they provided no protection to prisoners in the face of sophisticated war arsenals and chemical warfare. Yet, more than ever she needed protection, needed to be with a group. And she could not bear to think of facing the war and the chemicals—*kimawi* she called it—on her own. Besides, being a woman on her own at home also meant that she could be exposed to incidents of theft and other forms of attack. For in local culture women should never live alone, especially in times of danger.

She found a friend with whom to stay. During the first part of the war she was constantly depressed, and she spent the rest of the forty-five days crying. To Wahida, although she was appreciative of the opportunities the committee opened up for her, especially in terms of personal growth, in the end, the impact of the committee and also of the political groups themselves virtually disappeared during the war, precisely at a time when they needed to make their mark on Palestinian history. She recited what her educators used to maintain about the importance of public relations with the West and the backing of the socialist bloc countries and insisted:

> Haki fadi (nonsense), for what have we gained from either side during the war when we needed help most and when we became a lost and forgotten nation? What have we gained from this during our entire history.... Public relations? Presenting a good image? It builds people and makes them important, but what do those do to our nation?

Laila

Laila's relationship with the local political movement began when she was fourteen years old, when her interest in national politics was ignited by the events of the time. The early and middle 1970s were times when Palestinians under occupation were beginning to organize and move into the streets in new ways. So Laila first drifted with the crowds of young people who were beginning their mobilization experience. Her context—a mature and aware father and a politically active brother—helped to the extent of providing an opportunity for her to experience national politics. But she swears that her brother was not the major influence in eventually making her join the same political group he belonged to.

After much struggle in politics and in her personal life as well, Laila today finds herself alone and weakened, despite her tremendous inner strength and determination. To Laila, what happened to her during the Gulf War came as a bitter reminder of the weak position in which any woman, even the strongest woman, finds herself. Despite an illustrious political career, a divorce, single-parent childcare, and a hard struggle to make ends meet on her own, Laila could not face the war living alone with her daughter. She needed protection, the protection of men, and she felt lonely, so lonely. So she first moved to her sister's house for about two days just before the beginning of the war. But soon she moved back to her house, because she feared that it would be vandalized, as was beginning to happen to empty houses in her area. Yet she knew that she could not protect herself in such circumstances, even though she was physically and mentally strong enough:

> I had to find someone, a man, to live with me. It was not a matter of me not thinking I could take care of myself and my daughter. It was a matter of what society thought about my status and what this can bring about in terms of danger. I could not go on being alone facing the

threat of the army or settlers barging into the house at night. I could not face this knowing exactly what my neighbors think about me and what they would think about that situation. And I was afraid of loneliness too. So I asked my eighteen-year-old cousin to live with me. Can you imagine a young, immature eighteen-year-old being a good substitute? Do you think that I actually thought that he could protect me? Ha ha, I am physically much stronger than he is and am sure that it is I who is the protector, and in terms of maturity, I actually can easily run his life. But what mattered was what people thought, not reality. He is living with me even today, you know, even after the end of the war, for I have discovered that this is a good arrangement. For him, it is quiet and he can study and is excited about my lifestyle, meeting new people, and—as he puts it—"living in a civilized environment." For me, he makes people shut up and turn their eyes away, and that is the purpose of the whole operation.

Laila's life was marked by political engagement early on. It was university days that turned her into a leader of both men and women in her group:

University days were special. Most women belonging to my group and other groups as well could not become leaders, although many were hardworking and skilled. They could not become leaders because of social restrictions on freedom of movement, coming back late at night, and going to different parts of the country. Besides, young women did not have much free time, for they had to help around the house. In contrast, men could move freely and seemed to have a lot of time on their hands; so of course they had more of a chance to move up in the student organization's hierarchy.

But Laila was different. She came from a liberal family and struggled to achieve her rights, sometimes by publicly shaming her father into acceptance. She had guts. Between her courage and her determination, the men in the group soon began to deal with her as an equal and she eventually guided them in their daily political activities.

Although Laila's marriage did modify her role in politics for part of the time, especially because of childbearing, she continued her activities after university graduation and eventually reached the mid-level cadre positions. As with other women in politics, the intifada provided Laila with an additional impetus to work hard and achieve. Yet the problem always remained that women did not hold powerful and decision-making roles, despite the presence of exceptions like her.

Laila's views of the women's committees are realistic and astute:

The committees have been an important factor in assisting women in realizing themselves in politics. It was through the committees that

Intifada Year Four

women managed to activate other women, help them in their daily lives at times, and push the women's movement forward. But let's face it—the committees continue to be subservient to the institutions of men. Women are part of the political decisions of men rather than making these decisions. Women reach a certain point in decision making and then defer to men. Part of the problem is the women themselves: they bend instead of fighting them through. The other part of the problem is of course the men themselves, for even when we began to practice democracy in a fuller way—through elections and the representation of the views of the bottom in policy decisions—many of the men continued to behave toward women as before—not listening to them, underestimating their comments, and sometimes even stifling them. We see a lot of that among those who are married and working within the same group. You often find that the husbands try to undermine their wives' political activities in order to keep them down. And the best way to do that is to coerce them into having more babies so that they will stay down.

Amira

If the women's movement possessed a checklist for its grassroots cadre, Amira would score high. Rooted in the life of her Ramallah-area village, Amira, a single working woman with a high school education, is politically active, hardworking, intelligent, and equipped with a rare broad vision, perhaps because she grew up in Colombia and has the breadth of experience offered by exposure to dual cultures. Her nationalist and feminist principles are sincere and deeply felt, but she is also flexible and practical in her approach to people and politics.

Yet Amira, after the Gulf War, seems less active and connected to the organized women's movement than in the past, when she enthusiastically led a committee in her village and tried largely on her own to invent and implement the program of education on political and social issues. Today she believes the women's committees are "lazy" and not focused on her top priority—"real education for women."

Amira's observations on her village during the Gulf War are valuable, because her remote village was not regularly patrolled by the army, so villagers did not endure the isolation and confinement to the house that was the experience of city and camp residents. In the village, political activists had the opportunity both to offer assistance to people in need and to have a voice in interpreting wartime reality. But even in this context, it was the *shabab* (the young male activists) who exclusively manned (an appropriate word in this case) public terrain.

Amira lives with her mother and twenty-three-year-old brother,

Hatem. Two other brothers are currently in Ansar III prison camp in the Negev desert. In the tense days before the war, Amira notes, "We talked a little bit about how we could help each other, but only informally, maybe because for everybody, this war equaled chemical gasses, and we did not know what to do." A few days before the war, Amira found, in Ramallah, the leaflet on chemical warfare that had been prepared by the Union of Medical Relief Committees. She made a number of photo-copies and "gave them to the small shabab to distribute. They were very eager to do something." Amira also made some large-size copies for the shops and got a few read to the elderly in the village. This personal activism—and the comfortable exercise of some personal authority— seem typical of her relations with her neighbors.

The news that the war had begun came to the village in the early morning hours of January 17. All over the village, lights went on and radio and televisions began to blare. The next night was the first Iraqi missile attack on Israel, and Amira recounts one incident that illumi-nates how the young men, the shabab, tried to use the organizing methods developed during the intifada to face the new realities of regional war—of missiles and bombs, rather than stones and bullets:

> I stayed awake listening to the radio. The news came and I woke everyone up. My mother brought clean water and first aid materials. It was both funny and painful. They told everyone to put on their gas masks. My mother and aunt, who had moved in with us that day, were particularly scared.
>
> My brother said he had to leave the house; it was the duty of the shabab to be on the streets in case people needed anything. My mother tried to protest—what can the shabab do against the chemicals—but he said he must go. So I left the room and went to the veranda. There was nobody in the streets but shabab. Soon a loudspeaker sounded; "This is the voice of the Unified National Leadership in Kobar. We ask the people of Kobar not to enter the sealed rooms until we tell them."
>
> I recognized the voice of a young man I know and I thought; How will he know? Maybe after he is vaporized by the gas, we will know it's time to enter the rooms.

The inefficacy of teenagers with a bullhorn in a remote West Bank village trying to guide an unprotected population to face sophisticated warfare is obvious; the fact that they nonetheless tried, however, affirms that the intifada continued to be alive in people's actions and responses. During the course of the war, the shabab received two leaflets from the newly formed Palestinian Civil Defense Committees and tried to follow its instructions. The attempt to incorporate the war into the familiar truths of the intifada could express an underlying skepticism, as is evidenced when Amira tried to comfort her mother, who was very worried about her sons in Ansar III: "I kept telling her," Amira said, "that Saddam would never hit our shabab in prison. Don't worry. But I was really thinking that Saddam didn't care at all about Ansar."

Today, reviewing the women's movement, Amira feels its inactivity during the war had deeper roots: "Before and after the war something was lacking in the women's movement. I think it is pure and real education for women. The committees use politics and ideas but they don't really educate."

Amira's main example was her own experience during a year as the leader of the village branch of a women's committee. She created, literally from scratch, writing summaries of the more difficult readings, a program of political education that ranged from the 1936 revolt to the Shamir Plan. The readings were unsystematic; one popular book was a local history of a famous Jenin collaborator who lured young women into collaboration. "Everyone read this," Amira says, "their brothers in prison had told them about collaborators and how to behave."

Her attempts to hold similar sessions on social issues ran into problems. The other women viewed Amira as exceptional; her relations with her brothers, for example, were on a different basis. They both questioned the usefulness of discussions on these issues and were nervous that anything they talked about might be repeated in the village. A woman who had separated from her husband was the only one who really wanted to begin discussions.

Ironically the committee's greatest public success was when women symbolically took on a male activity. For a march on Palestinian independence day, their committee practiced marching "like the army" and made their appearance dressed in *tobes* (traditional embroidered dresses) and *keffiyehs* and carrying a flag (usually reserved for young men). "Everybody gasped," said Amira, "and then the shabab said, "*momtaz*" (fantastic)."

In evaluating her experience, Amira says ruefully, "I thought in three years we'd have leaders to compete with men—not nationally but at least in Kobar. Perhaps if the main office had helped me, if someone with some experience had come and given us advice, we would have succeeded in our program." Amira is critical of the "main office," which, she says orders "fifty girls for a demonstration" but was unable to provide guidance or resources for their village committee. She wrote a proposal for a village pickling cooperative and the women awaited the decision of the main office; it was negative: "They were very disappointed but I told them the main office is not God."

"Sometimes the women's movement seems to be about competition and conferences," Amira says reflectively. All that presently remains of the committee she worked with is a kindergarten. Amira reserves her unqualified enthusiasm for a project of the first year of the uprising— popular education, an attempt to provide alternative education to children after the army closed West Bank schools in February 1988. It is a moving story and shows what can happen on the grassroots level given the proper environment:

> For about one month after the schools closed, the political factions discussed a plan but got nowhere. Then Amjad, my brother, and I decided to start. I told everyone: "There is a school in our old house." One day, six or seven kids came with us and we walked through the village. We told the kids to call other kids who were in their class and say, "We are going to school. Finally, we had about twenty-five kids walking through the village with us to school. We divided them up and started to teach. That night, several shabab came and said they wanted to teach. And then the girls joined in. Then the popular education committee was formed; it was representatives of all the factions and me—people said I was "hizb Amira (the political party of Amira)." I felt good.

Amira's story shows both the positive and negative elements of the experience of the past three and one half years, the opportunities as well as the constraints. Under the present circumstances, opportunities such as those existing in the first wave of popular mobilization in 1988 cannot be expected. The capacity of the women's movement to actively intervene is a critical question.

Laila, Wahida, and Amira do not "represent" Palestinian women, but their reflections and experiences as activists and women point to a need to examine the achievements and the limitations of the women's movement in new ways. The uprising created the conditions that allowed for the women's movement as well as for individual women to participate in political life as actors and sometimes as partners of men. Consequently, the Palestinian women's movement began to be recognized for the grassroots political mobilization that successfully pushed women from invisibility to a high profile; the image of women shifted from the household to the streets, from the confinement of domestic work to public political activity within neighborhood committees. While this image reflects a reality, give or take peaks and troughs, its sensationalism has also obscured the serious obstacles that the women's movement continues to face in assuming political and social power. If we listen to the voices of activist women and combine them with our own observations, three areas of inquiry suggest themselves: the question of power, political ideology, and culture.

The first striking theme is power and the role of women in national politics. Women continue to be subservient to men, not only at home but also in the domain of political activism. The secondary position that women hold in national political organizations has several causes. Women often do not have the skills, confidence, or recognition to assume public and organizational roles and thus lag far behind men. They are restricted by their inability to move freely by family and society, and they are hampered by the many tasks and duties imposed on them within the household, from childbearing to tasks at home. As Laila has repeatedly pointed out, unmarried and married women alike must face the double burden of housework and activities outside the home, whether in politics, at the university, or in the workplace. They often end up exhausting their personal resources in trying to avoid and deal with parental and social restrictions and in completing their obligatory household tasks before they can even contemplate a public role. Even when qualified and confident, they meet what Laila aptly calls "the problem of men themselves," patriarchal attitudes that block the way for women's development. Amira could exercise informal leadership in her village, but her political goal—of women exercising an equal role in the political leadership of the village—remained unreachable.

The second impediment is the political ideology that shaped and defined the way in which political organizations were formed and the manner in which the process of politicization took place, especially in the period before the uprising. Here we emphasize the absence of democratic process within the organizations of both men and women: only a few make decisions and hold power—for what seems like an eternity—and the rest, men and women, execute their decisions. A general lack of understanding prevails among the leadership concerning the problems, aspirations, and views of the different sectors of the population involved in politics, especially women and the youth; and these sectors are unable to express themselves and influence decision making. Amira's village committee was exclusively on the receiving end of orders from the main office; Wahida believed that young people were denied their opinions and were "pushed around."

This problem is a natural consequence of the lack of democratic experience in society at large, including within the basic unit of the family. In this sense, processes and interactions within political groupings are to a large extent a reflection of the way in which Palestinian society is structured and the way in which it operates; this is how the process of politicization took place and continues to take place until today. Political activists draw on family and kin to increase the number of their cadres. An easy path to success in politics is putting to work

Rita Giacaman and Penny Johnson

mothers, sisters, wives and daughters. People from one group often marry only members or family members of the same group. As Wahida tells it, if social relations extend beyond the group, then suspicions are raised as to possible defection. In a nutshell, with some exceptions, political groupings form by virtue of family and clan relations. Indeed, they substitute for the family and clan and are tightly woven to exclude others from political or social interaction. While variations do exist between the different groups, it would be safe to state that in the context of our discussion, such variations cannot be described as breathtaking.

But the period of the intifada came and gave the population new momentum and a new consciousness as well. Apart from the successes and failures of the intifada, this period allowed for the mass participation of all sorts of people in national street politics. Participation brought with it "a revolution of rising expectations" and the desire to actively participate not only in action but in decision making as well. Women and the youth were particularly affected, as they were the sectors that were most active in the streets, the neighborhood committees, and consequently in the intifada at its high point. By the third year of the uprising, when activities were on a clearly downward trend with the weakening of the neighborhood committees as well as other factors, these newly awakened and "empowered" sectors, both men and women, found themselves with this new consciousness yet with very few chances of real participation. The reaction to this among the different political groups was varied; in some the rift between leadership—the *mashayekh* (or clan leaders, as they are called) and the grassroots *shabab al-mataris* (or the youth of the road blocks) began to be manifested in the formation of different subgroups operating under one umbrella but experiencing serious differences that began to be expressed overtly to the public. At least partially because of this "democracy / participation" problem, another group underwent a clear split into two—and so unfortunately did its women's committee. Yet another attempted to address the problem by bringing about thoughtful and potentially far-reaching changes in its structure and decision-making processes. But it must now face up to resistance from without and within, for those who are within have also been shaped by a culture and political ideology that make it difficult for them to absorb these changes.

The third problem is that of cultural patterns of behavior and die-hard attitudes that are difficult, and sometimes impossible, to shake. Even with the process of democratic reform having begun within some political groups, the prevailing attitudes of men in politics toward their activist wives, sisters, daughters, and other women appear to stand in the way of implementing this reform. As Laila has indicated, having more babies is a tactic politically active men use to keep politically active wives in their places. And despite attempts at raising the consciousness and the education of both men and women, men continue to downgrade the views and achievements of women, and women continue to defer ultimately to men's judgment at all levels of decision making, from the grass roots all the way to the top. As Laila remarks, the problem is both "the men themselves" and "the women themselves . . . who bend when they should not."

In structured conversations we had in the spring of 1990 with teenage girls about to enter Birzeit University, the girls all confirmed their interest in political activism and the intifada. When we asked if any of them wanted to be on the Student Council, they answered with embarrassment, denial, and a few giggles. When it was pointed out that women had been on student councils before the intifada, they still demurred, although interest flashed in the eyes of one particularly lively young woman. As the discussion progressed, we realized that the intifada in some ways intensified traditional cultural patterns because girls desperately wanted to be accepted by the community, which now stands for the heroism of the intifada.

This social conservatism, expressed in its most manipulated form in the campaign by Islamic fundamentalists to impose the *hijab* on women is, of course, only one side of the coin. If we flip it over, we find the December 1990 women's conference in Jerusalem, sponsored by the Bisan Institute, which brought an unprecedented number of women activists and community leaders together to discuss a social agenda for women as well as such issues as the hijab and its forced imposition.

The questions raised by Laila, Amira, and Wahida are crucial not only for the further development of the women's movement but for the viability of the national political movement as well. These questions are not easy to resolve: How does one change cultural patterns of behavior when consciousness raising and education are necessary but not sufficient conditions to bring about change? How can democratic processes be instituted in a society that continues to regard them as alien and when society is structured in such a way as to negate the formation and development of these processes? How can women assume powerful positions to affect change when they themselves continue to feel an internal "weakness" fostered by institutions and relations that have long existed in society? Most importantly, perhaps, what direction should the women's movement take in its path of liberation given the decisive limitations existing in society at large?

REFERENCES

Hammami, Rima. "Women's Political Participation in the Intifada: A Critical Overview." *The Intifada and Some Social Issues: A Conference Held in Jerusalem on 14 December 1990.* Women's Studies Committee, Bisan Center, Ramallah, 1991.

Tamari, Salim. "The Uprising's Dilemma: Limited Rebellion and Civil Society." *Middle East Report,* no. 164–65 (May-August 1990).

PART FOUR

Anticipations
after Oslo

.14.

Amal Kawar

Palestinian Women's Activism after Oslo

The Oslo Agreement of 1993 signaled the transition from the Palestinian liberation struggle to autonomy on the West Bank and in the Gaza Strip and was to be followed by a final settlement of the question of Palestine. An important consequence of the Oslo Agreement and resulting Palestinian self-rule is that Palestinian women are presented with a new political environment that has its own opportunities and constraints. Indeed, women activists have begun to create a new agenda that is focused on women's rights and women's empowerment, and to devise strategies for the political arena emerging under the Palestinian National Authority (PNA). This chapter reviews the new developments in women's participation, focusing on women's new agendas, institutions, and leadership.[1]

The pre-Oslo activism of Palestinian women was focused on national mobilization and nation-building rather than on women's rights. Also, while women were represented in the entire framework of the revolution, including the militias, their primary organizational homes were the partisan women's organizations and the charitable societies. During the 1980s and the intifada, women's charitable societies and party-sponsored women's action committees participated significantly in the nongovernmental organizations (NGOs) movement on the West Bank and in Gaza. Indeed, the consensus is that the NGOs' health, educational, and charitable services constituted the infrastructure of the intifada.

In previous studies, I noted that the development of an agenda for gender equality during the national liberation struggle was constrained by the political imperatives of crises and war, especially the war in Lebanon and the intifada.[2] The slow development of gender equality was bolstered by the social conservatism of Palestinian society and its organizations. In fact, throughout the national liberation period, social conservative gender attitudes permeated cadre relationships and were only superficially addressed by the PLO's male leadership. This was evident from the fact that no programs to advance gender equality were initiated during the decades of the struggle, apart from permitting women to join the militias and party cadre ranks, and the 9 percent quota in the Palestine National Council. Furthermore, since the intifada, social conservatism has been bolstered by the success of the Islamist movement.[3]

Women's activism since Oslo has operated in the context of four important Palestinian developments. One is the decline of PLO political parties (other than Fateh), which have been marginalized by Yasser Arafat's tight control of the PLO, their own internal competition, and their opposition to the Oslo Agreement. So far, other than Fateh, PLO parties have been unable to regroup or amass any significant public support.[4] This has also been reflected in the decline of the women's committees movement, with the result that activists turned to a growing movement of less partisan and nonpartisan women's centers and societies.

A second development in Palestinian politics is the influx of donor support, especially European, to the Palestinian NGOs. This international involvement reached its height during the intifada, and it is likely to continue to influence Palestinian agendas and activities. Particularly for the women's movement, the availability of external funding helped activists gain a degree of autonomy from their parties; they were consequently better able to engage in addressing women's empowerment.

The rise of the Islamic Resistance Movement (Hamas) and other Islamist trends is the third development of significance for Palestinian women. The Islamist promotion of conservative gender roles has already impacted women's agendas by toning them down, and this is likely to slow down, for some years, the progress of women's rights.

A final Palestinian development is the establishment of the PNA ministries, which opened up to women new avenues of participation and influence. The Palestinian Legislative Council, however, with less than 6 percent women (five of eighty-eight members), remains very limited in its promise of institutional power for female members. Nevertheless, women activists find they must learn how to influence the council which, in the next few years, will pass legislation in all gender-important areas, especially education, lending, employment, and personal status law.

The rest of this narrative reviews developments since Oslo, in the General Union of Palestinian women, the women's committees, women's centers, and among the women of the legislative and administrative branches of the PNA.

The Status of the General Union of Palestinian Women and Women's Committees

In Palestinian women's organizing efforts, post-Oslo meant the demise of the historical frameworks of representation and agenda setting. The women's agenda from the mid-1960s to the late 1970s was defined by the General Union of Palestinian Women, which was created in 1965 along with the Palestine National Council. Its purpose was essentially nationalistic—to mobilize women for the liberation of Palestine. The women's union's counterpart on the West Bank and in the Gaza Strip were the PLO factional women's committees' associations, created during the late 1970s to mid-1980s. In contrast to the external women's framework, which was controlled by Fateh, dominance in the territories was in the hands of three main leftist parties: the Democratic Front (Women's Action Committees), the Popular Front (Palestinian Women's Committees), and the Communist Party (Working Women's Committees). Later on, especially during the intifada, Fateh's group (Social Work Committees), gained ascendance after the influx of Fateh funds—and this continues to be the case under the PNA regime.[5]

Much of the partisan women's activism occurred within these frameworks, and its primary goal was the mobilization of women to help preserve the nation and the culture. Occasionally, female party cadres raised issues of discrimination and gender-sensitivity inside their factional organizations *(tanzimat)*, but those voices were almost always silenced by the primacy of the national struggle. Women's rights were relegated to the background as secondary. The dominant model was the traditional female service role, taking care of children orphaned by the violence, establishing kindergartens, vocational classes, and small income-generating enterprises.[6]

Women's charitable societies represented an older, more traditional generation of middle-class women, who had no agenda for dealing with gender issues beyond the social welfare services they offered. Most charitable society leaders were not overtly political, and the question of how much to be involved has been a running theme in the history of the women's charitable societies movement. A current notable exception is Samiha Khalil of In'ash al-Usra (Society for the Rejuvenation of the Family), located in al-Bireh on the West Bank. She has been politically active for decades, as president of the West Bank branch of the Palestinian women's union and, more recently, as a candidate for the PNA presidency in the January 1996 elections.

With attention turning to self-rule, the PLO women's leadership, regardless of party, was hopeful that a Palestinian state would be bound by the PLO's promise of equality of rights for women and men. This principle was declared in the 1968 Palestinian National Charter and reaffirmed in the 1988 Palestinian Declaration of Independence. The women's organizations also felt that it was time they bring forward a women's rights agenda. In 1994, in an unusual coalition of women's charitable societies and women's committees, a common set of articles for women's rights was proclaimed. The three-page Women's Charter, which was submitted to the PNA, reminded the nation of women's contributions to the national struggle; and it called for the incorporation of equality for women in political, civil, economic, social, and cultural rights. The Women's Charter was a Palestinian women's union and women's committees initiative, and it signaled the return of the diasporan leadership to the Palestinian territories, something made possible by Oslo.

The Palestinian women's union, relocated from Tunis to Gaza City, found it had to search for a new role in the more pluralistic political arena of the West Bank and Gaza Strip. Now that the mobilizational model had passed, it had to deal with many questions. What role would it play vis-à-vis the PNA? Would it be a nongovernmental organization like any other? Or would it have a special relationship as a semigovernmental organization because of its historic tie to the PLO? These questions, however, have not received adequate consideration because of the fact that the union lacks a grassroots membership, and it is mainly a leadership group. This structural weakness is likely to remain until the union's sixth congress, which is scheduled for 1997, is held. Preparatory committees, however, are actively recruiting throughout the territories, and in particular in the Gaza Strip, where the union has not previously had any structures.

The Palestinian women's union goal of recreating a women's grassroots organization will encounter no competition from the women's committees. That movement came to an end in the early 1990s, reduced to a few local committees that rely primarily on European donors for funding. With the exception of Fateh's women's group, these local committees are more loosely organized and independent of their parties than they were during the intifada. Their agendas are focused on supporting women's development through support services for women and children, for example, through a children's day care service, a kindergarten, and a children's library. Within the women's committees movement, however, there are some who are attempting to revive its mobilizational structures. Given the weakness of the Palestinian political parties, there is little indication that they can succeed.

The 1990s also witnessed the rise of a nongrassroots, nonpartisan women's centers movement. And under the PNA, such centers have made themselves the primary voice for women's legal rights.

Rise of the Palestinian Women's Centers Movement

The women's centers movement is made up of well-educated, politically sophisticated, and feminist women. These are academic and professional women who gained visibility during the intifada, speakers and researchers on the conditions of Palestinian women under the Israeli occupation. The women in this leadership group are either independent in their party orientation, or are partisans with a strong interest in women's autonomous action and empowerment. All these women's centers rely on European and Palestinian funding for their maintenance. In their steering committees, especially those that are politically active, the centers painstakingly maintain a multiparty representation. This is to indicate the importance of political consensus rather than hostility in relations with the political parties.

The central strategic goal of the women's centers movement is women's empowerment, and the agenda focuses are women's political education and women's rights. Activities are primarily educational: conducting research, publishing a women's magazine, holding training workshops, and providing forums on such topics as democracy, women's rights, and women's leadership. There are also women's centers that specialize in legal counseling for women or in social and psychological counseling. And there is one center with West and East Jerusalem offices; its mission is to build a bridge between the Palestinian women's movement and the Israeli women's peace movement. That role, however, has not been particularly successful, to a large extent due to the closures that limit mobility between the territories and Jerusalem.

All these centers share the purpose of promoting women's political and legal rights, and they are particularly interested in creating data banks and supporting research on women. However, the most politically active among these centers is the Women's Affairs Technical Committee (*taqem shu'un al-mar'ah*). Since 1995, this group, headquartered in

Ramallah, has positioned itself to become the foremost Palestinian women's lobbying group.

The Women's Affairs Technical Committee was formed following the Madrid peace conference as one of several specialized, transitional committees set up to prepare for the PNA. The Women's Affairs Technical Committee was authorized by Arafat, but, unlike the other technical committees, it had to solicit its own funding. The effort to create a women's structure in the PNA was led by Zahira Kamal, a leader of the women's committees movement and the Arafat-allied Palestinian Democratic Union Party. Kamal headed the Women's Affairs Technical Committee until she moved to her new role as General Director for women's affairs in the Ministry of Planning and International Cooperation—and she remains very active in it. Earlier in its history, Kamal and her colleagues hoped that the Women's Affairs Technical Committee would be elevated to a ministry, as the other technical committees were supposed to be. That idea, however, was rejected by Arafat, and he also shelved the proposal for a presidential women's advisory council, which he had provisionally supported.

One of the earliest proposals the Women's Affairs Technical Committee promoted was a gender quota for seats in the Palestinian Legislative Council. However, this idea did not receive PNA support or, for that matter, the consensus of all the women in the committee itself. All but the People's Party (the former Communist Party), however, rejected the women's quota, and the parties generally did not seriously promote women for legislative seats. Interestingly, 60 percent of the public supported the idea of a legislative quota for women.[7] Polling data, however, indicate that the public tends to have a mixed bag of opinions about women's rights, and this should act as a caution against readily describing Palestinians as liberal or conservative.

This mixture of views can be illustrated by the fact that the public supported women's right to vote and that women's support for this view was higher than men's (86 percent versus 76 percent). Furthermore, about 75 percent of women and 60 percent of men said women should be present in the legislative council. Indeed, several female candidates received a larger number of votes than the men on their party slate. Interestingly, women viewed their support for women in the legislature somewhat differently from the men. Thus, while 61 percent of women found it necessary that women be in the legislature to demand their rights, only 34 percent of the men thought so. In the end, however, only 42 percent of the women went to the polls, compared to the men's 56 percent participation.[8]

On social issues, the Palestinian public tends to be fairly conservative. A survey taken in 1992 shows it to be generally conservative, supporting the existing personal status law and the veil. Women, however, were slightly more supportive of secularism in the law and were less likely to engage in religiously based political activism.[9]

The existence of a gender gap in the Palestine National Council was ultimately predictable since only twenty-eight women ran for office of a total of 628 candidates.[10] There is consensus among the political elites that the single-member district electoral system and tribalism are the two most important reasons for the small number of women who ran. Furthermore, families often align along partisan lines, and if there were both men and women potential nominees, then the chances are that the family selected the men. There were some exceptions, of course, but then women aspiring to be on their party's ticket found that their own parties were also not particularly enthusiastic. This was a problem in particular for Fateh's female cadre, who hoped to be nominated by virtue of their local party leadership posts. But they had to contend with Arafat's strategy of balancing Fateh's slates with representation from certain families, and independents, and of covering the quota set up for Christians.[11]

One of the most notable changes in women activists since Oslo has been their willingness to criticize their parties for resisting the promotion of women. For example, a leading female member of the secretive Popular Front noted her surprise at discovering how much tribalism dominated the leadership ranks, as evident by the fact that male leaders chose their female relatives for certain women's leadership roles. She pointed out, however, that her party organization instituted a gender-based quota, in August 1996, for the selection of delegates to the Popular Front's sixth congress, scheduled for 1997. That quota, however, will be slightly higher for the cities than for the villages in recognition of the social reality that it is difficult to recruit women in the more conservative rural areas.

In this environment of social conservatism and cautious parties, the Women's Affairs Technical Committee and the network of women activists it encompasses have found an important niche as lobbyists for women's rights to the PNA. In 1995–1996, they successfully lobbied against PNA regulations that discriminated against women. The two issues were the Palestinian passport and the driver's license test. In the case of the Palestinian passport, the Interior Ministry, following regulations in some of the Arab countries, had required that a male guardian sign for females who applied for a Palestinian passport. The Women's

Affairs Technical Committee led the fight with letters to the PNA head, Arafat, and the Interior Ministry, with street demonstrations, petitions, and letters to the newspapers.

In regards to the driver license test, the Ministry of Transportation, fearing sexual harassment of females taking the test, had sent a directive requiring the presence of a family member during the driving segment. This time, the Women's Affairs Technical Committee succeeded in having the policy overturned, without much effort, through direct communications with the minister. In both instances, the retreat of the PNA ministries helped empower the women's lobby and enhanced its visibility.

At the present time, the most important legal gender issue in the Palestinian autonomous areas concerns the drafting of the Palestinian Basic Law. During summer and early fall of 1996, the draft law was held up in a committee of the Palestinian Legislative Council awaiting Arafat's readiness to move it through the PLO and PNA decision-making processes. Two proposed articles directly affect women's rights. Article 7, which states the principles of equality and nondiscrimination before the law—including sex—is likely to pass without much controversy.

The second article addresses sources of the law, and here there are at least three competing drafts. One omits any mention of Islamic law; another states that "shariah is one of the sources of legislation"; and a third, sponsored by Dar al-Fatwa—a Jerusalem Islamic committee— says that "shariah is the primary source of legislation." At this time it is difficult to tell which version will win, but they are being debated in the circles of the women's and human rights communities. If the clause "shariah is the primary source of legislation" passes, it might not have much affect on employment and education legislation. It will most certainly, however, stop in its tracks the prospect of gender equality in the legislation on personal status, especially rights relating to inheritance, divorce, and child custody.[12]

For the near future, however, some in the women's leadership, such as the famous Palestinian lawyer, Asma Khader, are debating what a new Palestinian personal status law should be. Others are interested in educating rural and uneducated women on their rights under whatever personal status law exists. Interestingly, the women's community is resigned to an inevitable Islam-state legal relationship, which is likely to be formalized in the proposed Article 4 of the Palestinian Basic Law, which states that "Islam is the official religion of Palestine." Also, discussions with several members of the Palestinian council have convinced me that the chances of a purely secular basic law are nil. Perhaps this will be the most prominent success of the Palestinian Islamic movement. But I suspect there will be fierce resistance from nationalist forces and from women's and human rights organizations against a fundamentalist agenda of gender segregation in schools or the workplace.

Women Legislators and Bureaucrats

So far, the Palestinian Legislative Council, including its five female members, have had to take a backseat to the central authority embodied in PNA president Arafat. There are several obvious reasons for this, including the fact that most members are from his group, Fateh, and the independent minority is in no position to take the initiative. The council is in its first session and no one knows yet how the power of this body will evolve. Finally, the Palestinian Basic Law bill, or any other legislation, are highly bound, certainly in the way Arafat sees it, to the progress of the negotiations. Nevertheless, women activists, mainly the network comprising the three politically active groups—the Women's Affairs Technical Committee, the Women's Legal Counseling Center, and the Feminist Studies Center—have begun to lobby the legislature for more commitment to gender equality in the articles of the Basic Law.

Finally, interest in gender issues in the PNA ministries has come primarily from an ad hoc group of directors of women's affairs in five PNA ministries: Planning and International Cooperation, Agriculture, Health, Social Affairs, and Youth and Sports. These directors have a common mission to lead in the development of gender-sensitive policies in the ministries and in strategic planning for women's development. This group of women is part of a sizable group of high and middle-level (from minister to section head) female members of the PNA executive branch.[13] The United Nations Development Program (UNDP) supported this focus on women in the PNA with a three-year project that helped establish the women's affairs directorates, assisting them in strategic planning, action plans development, and with equipment and furnishings. The UNDP project also facilitated networking among these women by providing them with a framework of ongoing communications through the ad hoc committee.

Finally, there is a wider group of women, an eleven-ministry ad hoc group, which has also been meeting to devise goals and strategic plans for gender-sensitive policies. Their effort is funded by the United Nations Development Fund for Women (UNIFEM), part of an all-Arab project to implement the resolutions of the 1995 Beijing World Congress on Women. This international interest in women's development has had the effect of bestowing official legitimacy on Palestinian women's activism in the PNA ministries. To what extent these strategic plans become part of the general ministerial plans or of the PNA strategy for Palestine remains to be seen.

Conclusion

Oslo has contributed to the decline of an already disintegrating model of a centralized, partisan, and PLO-led women's leadership group. Under autonomy, the domestic political arena can be characterized as having weak political parties; limited grassroots organizing; European donor participation; and a new, more pluralistic model of women's leadership. Among the women in the Palestinian leadership, there is a consensus for equality of rights and for gender-sensitive legislation. There is also evident a greater urgency to be more vocal for women's concerns. Clearly, the old argument that women's liberation must wait for national liberation has been replaced by the imperative to promote women's interests during this critical stage of state formation.

Under the PNA, women activists engaged in a great deal of networking across party lines. Even those in the Popular Front, who are adamant in their rejection of the PNA, have participated in post-Oslo, agenda-setting activities. For example, they participated in drafting the Women's Charter of 1994 and recently became members of the Women's Affairs Technical Committee. The Palestinian women's leadership can be characterized as an interlocking group of women, spanning women's committees and centers, the legislative council, the PNA ministries, and the charitable societies. In fact, their activism cannot be completely divided into governmental or nongovernmental since leading women move with ease between the two spheres.[14]

How Palestinian women choose their specific agenda interests is, to a great extent, determined by events in the national arena. The issue they turned their attention to during the summer and fall of 1996 was the upcoming municipal elections. Thus, Arafat was urged to select women to the transitional city and village councils that he was in the process of appointing.

Women's groups remain active on the national issue, of course, responding to the frequent crises in the negotiations. For example, during the clashes surrounding the opening of Jerusalem's underground passage, in the fall of 1996, women's groups participated in demonstrations, first aid training, fund-raising, assistance to martyrs' families, and other relief work. Under the self-rule regime, however, they have a new role: to educate women in democratic politics and to train them for leadership. In this mission, they start not from a grassroots base but from their symbolic role as activists and leaders with a proven record of commitment to the national cause.

What are the prospects of success for the old and new women's institutions, and how will they impact policy in the PNA? I suggest that women activists already achieved some success in exerting influence during the initial stage of state formation. Women's institutions, however, operate under precarious economic and political conditions and in a somewhat inhospitable conservative social environment, especially in the Gaza Strip.

In particular, women's representation in the political arena is weakened by the absence of women's political or economic grassroots organizations, and this is likely to continue until women are able to enter the job market in greater numbers. In the short run, women's economic power is likely to remain weak due to high unemployment rates for men and the desperate economic conditions in the territories. The women's leadership is also fully aware of the constraints imposed by the conservatism of Palestinian society. This reality has forced them to make more modest demands for women's rights—especially concerning personal status legislation—than they would have otherwise.

Finally, the support of the international community has given women's agendas a boost with both funds and expertise. But funding will decrease in a few years, and then, hopefully, the new women's institutions will be in a better position to compete in the political and legislative arenas. Palestinian women activists have shown that they are able to adapt to the changing political environment. And they understand that their long-term plans are likely to go forward in small increments. They are, however, committed to waging the long battle for women's rights and for empowering a new generation to carry the banner in a Palestinian state.

NOTES

1. This chapter draws on the author's field work on the West Bank and in the Gaza Strip during summer 1996. Several sources were consulted, including members of the Palestinian Legislative Council, others who were candidates during the January 1996 elections, women in the PNA ministries, and leaders of women's NGOs. Personal observation was further facilitated by my role in the United Nations Development Program (UNDP) as advisor to PNA women's departments during that summer. Several Arabic-language research publications and newsletters of women's organizations were also consulted.

2. Amal Kawar, *Daughters of Palestine: Leading Women of the Palestinian National Movement* (Albany: State University of New York Press, 1996); and idem,

"National Mobilization, War, Conditions, and Gender Consciousness," *Arab Studies Journal* 15 (spring 1993): 53–67.

3. See Ziad Abu-Amr, *Islamic Fundamentalism in the West Bank and Gaza: Muslim Brotherhood and Islamic Jihad* (Bloomington: Indiana University Press, 1994).

4. For a recent treatment, see *Crisis of the Palestinian Political Party.* Proceedings of the Conference held at Muwatin Palestinian Institute for the Study of Democracy, Ramallah, November, 11, 1995 (Arabic).

5. See Kawar, *Daughters of Palestine,* chap. 5; Zachary Lockman and Joel Beinin, eds., *Intifada: The Palestinian Uprising Against Israeli Occupation* (Boston: South End Press, 1989); and Kitty Warnock, *Land Before Honor: Palestinian Women in the Occupied Territories* (New York: Monthly Review Press, 1990).

6. Ibid. And see Julie M. Peteet, *Gender in Crisis: Women and the Palestinian Resistance Movement* (New York: Columbia University Press, 1991).

7. Islah Jad, "The Palestinian Women's Movement and the Legislative Elections: Report Based on an Election-Day Poll," *al-Siyasa al-Filastiniyya* (Policy studies) 3, no. 10 (1996): 19–40 (Arabic).

8. Ibid.

9. Marianne Heiberg and Geir Ovensen, *Palestinian Society in Gaza, West Bank and Arab Jerusalem: A Survey of Living Conditions* (Oslo: Fagbevegelsens Senter for Forskning, 1993), pp. 249–82.

10. For a review article on the women legislative candidates, their characteristics and agendas, see also "We Lost the Quota Battle but It Is Not Over: Let Us Elect All the Women's Candidates," *Kul al-Nissa³.* A one-time publication of the Feminist Studies Center, Jerusalem (January 1996), pp. 1–16 (Arabic); and Jad, *al-Siyasa al-Filastiniyya.*

11. For additional discussion, see ʿItaf Abu Ghadhib, *The Role of Palestinian Women in the Legislative Elections* (Nablus: Women's Affairs Center, Nablus, 1996); Gada Sughayr, "Briefings," *al-Siyasa al-Filastiniyya* 3, no. 10 (1996): 143–49; and Jad, "Palestinian Women's Movement."

12. For discussion of the legal status of Palestinian women, see Adrien K. Wing, "Custom, Religion, and Rights: the Future Legal Status of Palestinian Women," *Harvard International Law Journal* 35, no. 1 (winter 1994).

13. Data collected by the Feminist Studies Center, Jerusalem, in 1996 indicates that in a sample of six PNA ministries, 26 percent of high and middle-level employees are female; the high level category contains 14 percent women.

14. Two prominent examples are Zahira Kamal of the Ministry of Planning and International Cooperation and Dalal Salama of the Palestinian Legislative Council. Both women are members of the Women's Affairs Technical Committee, and they participate actively in its lobbying and educational work.

.15.

SUHA SABBAGH

The Declaration of Principles on Palestinian Women's Rights: An Analysis

On September 13, 1993, Yasser Arafat, chairman of the Palestine Liberation Organization, and Mr. Yitzhak Rabin, prime minister of Israel (as-
sassinated on October 4, 1995), shook hands on the south lawn of the
White House as President Clinton looked on approvingly. What will
this handshake—touted as the most important and most televised handshake of the century—do for Palestinian women? Will this handshake
lead to change in the direction of equal rights? Or will it simply lead to
a perpetuation of the status quo in gender relations once a new Palestinian government is established? In Arab culture and tradition, Arab men
are considered to be the guardians and protectors of women, justified in
their role by the words of the *shariah*, "al-rijal quayyamun a la al nissa"
(men are the protectors and providers for women). In the present context, this statement could come to serve as a tool for excluding Palestinian women from competing for new job opportunities or from seeking
higher office, although they helped preserve the fiber of society for
many years under occupation.

To ensure that their rights will be safeguarded during the upcoming
period of political transition, women on the West Bank have been actively involved in drafting the Declaration of Principles on Palestinian

Women's Rights. If they succeed in having this document incorporated into the constitution of a new Palestinian state, it will mark the first time in the history of the West Bank that women have linked their struggle for equal rights with a document that serves, at the same time, as the cornerstone of Palestinian national rights.

It is interesting to trace the path of this document from a draft proposed by the General Union of Palestinian Women (with headquarters in Tunis and somewhat cut off from women's groups in the occupied territories), to the third draft supported and signed by most of the women's organizations, including some that oppose the Oslo Agreement but see this as empowering women. Not surprisingly, the draft (see appendix) displays some of the symptoms of a "tired text," that is, one that has been so thoroughly worked over that it has almost lost its directness in projecting women's demands. This "tiredness" is an indication of the amount of time spent in discussion, compromise, and outright haggling between the various women's groups that prepared the draft. The two previous drafts were written by groups that shared a greater degree of consensus, while the third draft was endorsed by most women's organizations, from the conservative In'ash al-Usra headed by Samiha Khalil, to the more progressive groups, for example, the Bisan Center in Ramallah headed by Eileen Kuttab. Each organization in this vast spectrum has its own agenda and political affiliation, and this is reflected in the demands made in this document.

The women who attended the meetings to ratify the document were impressed with the fact that it reached the semifinal draft stage and that such a broad segment of women's organizations signed on to it. After the dust has settled, women's organizations intend to rewrite the draft in a way that will reintroduce the directness exhibited by the second Tunis draft, yet without altering the delicate balance achieved by all groups and without disturbing the more democratic nature of the third draft.

In an interview, Eileen Kuttab, a member of the Women's Document Committee and a professor of sociology at Birzeit University, explains the purpose of this document and the controversy that has surrounded its ratification by women's organizations.[1]

Comments on the Second and Third Drafts

Both draft documents were signed in the name of the General Union of Palestinian Women, an umbrella organization that is part of the PLO and that was formed in 1965, one year after the inception of the PLO. It includes women from all four Palestinian political factions. In the past, women's groups in the occupied territories had little contact with the leadership structure of the General Union of Palestinian Women. Headquartered in Tunis, the latter group was coopted by the leadership, and female participation in PLO structures represented little more than tokenism. Cut off from the leadership structure, the women's movement in the occupied territories developed a more serious agenda, focusing on issues of equality and exceeding the "feminine" activities of women's groups outside the West Bank. Because their demands were based on women's essential role in preserving the very fiber of society both before and during the intifada, women on the West Bank felt more secure in making these demands. The third draft was written on the West Bank, on national soil, where women's contributions are well recognized. Consequently, this draft reflects a more self-assured posture, and women do not feel the need to first reiterate the means by which they have contributed to the national struggle since these facts are well recognized.

If we analyze the "we" of the speaker in the second draft and that in the third, it becomes evident that the third draft projects a generally less hierarchical and more democratic tone than does the second. In the second Tunis draft, the "we" of the speaker is announced univocally; it stands for the General Union of Palestinian Women, which speaks for all Palestinian women. Despite the fact that not all women belong to this organization, the text states: "We in the General Union of Palestinian Women (GUPW) declare in the name of all Palestinian women that we look forward to assuming—on equal footing—the responsibility in the independent stage. . . ." Implied here is a certain hierarchical relationship, according to which the GUPW presumes to speak for all women; yet even the different groups of women are not mentioned.

Who is the "we" of the speaker in the third draft? Although the document is also written in the name of the GUPW, in the section entitled "General Provisions," the "we" is defined as "the women of Palestine, from all social categories and from the various faiths, including workers, farmers, housewives, students, professionals, and politicians [who] promulgate our determination to proceed without struggle to abolish all forms of discrimination and inequality against women. . . ." Of course, the women who wrote the draft are not from all the groups listed; yet a more democratic spirit is noticeable since the different groups of women are at least listed as those standing behind this statement.

It is equally interesting to compare the areas in which each group of women supports women's demands. In the first paragraph of the second draft, the writers feel compelled to name, first and foremost, the issues that still concern Palestinian society as a whole, for example, "Zionist settlements . . . set up in large parts of (Palestine)." This is a reflection of the fact that the women's agenda in Tunis has always prioritized the national issue over equal rights for women. The writers also first state their concern for the national agenda: "The people and their political leadership have yet to achieve a number of their national goals, such as the right to return, the right to self-determination, and the establishment of an independent state." Later in the text, the writers buttress their demands for equal rights with a "Palestinian Declaration of Independence," followed by the "Universal Declaration of Human Rights" which, along with the "international charters pertinent to political, legal, civil, and religious rights, as well as the various conventions that aim at the elimination of all forms of discrimination," provides the basis for the "Palestinian Declaration of Independence."

In the third draft, the authors do not feel compelled to state their concern for the national issues and agenda first. This is a reflection of the fact that women's groups on the West Bank have a separate women's agenda; it is also a reflection of the fact that the third draft was written at a later period. Since the signing of the peace agreement, women on the West Bank have felt an urgency about pushing for a women's agenda because failure to do so at this moment could mean that Palestinian women will not reap the benefits of their long, hard struggle for both national and equal rights.

What is curious about the opening paragraph of the third draft is the emphasis immediately placed on the need for the government to respect the rights of minorities: "The rights of minorities shall be duly respected by the majority, as minorities shall abide by decisions of the majority." This right is stated even before the "civil rights of men and women." One must assume that the religious and political minorities present at this meeting felt a need to ensure their rights as minorities before ensuring their rights as women.

Another interesting feature of the third draft is that on more than one occasion the document seeks to ensure the rights of "women and men." This may be a tactic designed to avoid confrontation with men and with the more conservative groups within the women's movement. Although the stated objective of the document is to "enhance the principle of equality between women and men in all spheres of life," the binary opposition that governs this text is not always relations between men and women; rather, it is the relationship of men and women to society.

The body of the text stresses three main areas in which women seek equality: political rights; civil rights; and (taken together) economic, social, and cultural rights. Their order in the text clearly reflects the concerns of the authors. First and foremost under political rights is the right to vote and run for office. Women fear becoming disfranchised in the political arena now that their participation in the process of liberation is no longer necessary. Women seek guarantees that they can represent the state in "international and regional organizations as well as in the diplomatic corps."

Based on the interpretation of the shariah in some Islamic countries, women are not considered fit for certain judicial positions, specifically for that of judge, because their "emotional fluctuations" can cloud their judgment. While the declaration does not address the issue directly, there is an implied demand for reconsideration of these archaic notions so that women can compete for government positions on all levels.

The category of civil rights also reflects the concerns of women at this historical juncture. In all Arab countries (except Syria), citizenship is passed on from the father to the children or wife. Women do not have the right to pass on their citizenship to their husband or their children. In 1989, after the declaration of independence was passed by the Palestine National Council (PNC) and the leadership started issuing Palestinian passports (not valid as travel documents), women petitioned the PLO leadership for the right to pass their nationality on to their husbands and children. This was because in the diaspora many Palestinian women married non-Palestinians but wanted to share their identity with their offspring. The leadership agreed, but no steps were taken to guarantee this right.

Also in this section women demand their right to be protected from family violence and their right to "express themselves." The right to "express one's self" could, of course, imply the right to choose one's husband, although it might have been far more effective to state that right explicitly, as is the case in the second draft. Interestingly, the third draft calls for compensation for chores carried out by women within the household: "Motherhood should be looked upon as a social post. Household chores should be regarded as a task of social and economic value." This constitutes a very progressive position, although to date this demand has not been implemented by more progressive countries with greater resources.

The section on economic, social, and cultural rights stresses equality of work opportunities and wages, security and compensation, training and promotion, and women's right to maternity leave and other services that enable women to combine family duties and work. Palestinian society in general is not averse to women's seeking positions of power in the workplace. However, because of the extreme shortage of jobs under occupation, women anticipate that they will be elbowed out by men seeking employment once Palestine gains autonomy.

Childbearing could be used as an excuse to keep women out of the job market. Palestinian society is very family oriented, and bringing up children is an important consideration. Therefore, to enable women to work, there must be excellent day-care facilities and a maternity leave sufficiently long to prevent critics from claiming that working women cause undue hardships to their children and their families.

Equality of educational opportunity is only hinted at in the document. It is possible that women did not feel a sense of urgency in requesting this right because institutions of higher education generally do not bar women who seek to be admitted. Palestinians have a near obsession with education, perhaps because, with the loss of their land in 1948, an individual's only path to income was through education. Many Palestinians were able to work in Gulf countries, underdeveloped at the time, and some amassed great fortunes because they had the advantage of an education. However, as a result of financial hardships, parents now often have to choose between sending either their sons or their daughters to school.

While the third draft exhibits a more democratic and self-assured tone, the second Tunis draft is more direct in presenting the rights of women. It might have been preferable in the third draft to address separately the issues discussed in the third section on economic, social, and cultural rights, since treating them all together sometimes makes the text confusing. However, as one of the authors of this document has said, the real achievement is that a majority of women's groups agreed on a single draft.

More difficult than all obstacles encountered in ratifying and drafting this document will be the process of incorporating it into a future constitution. At present, the leadership's position is that the document will be incorporated as long as it does not contradict the shariah. This is a political statement that leaves the issue open to interpretation, and much will depend on the resistance expressed by political Islam in general and Hamas in particular.

NOTES

1. Part of the interview with Eileen Kuttab is included in *Arab Women: Between Defiance and Restraint*, ed. Suha Sabbagh (New York: Olive Branch Press, 1996), pp. 121–26.

Appendix

DECLARATION OF PRINCIPLES ON PALESTINIAN WOMEN'S RIGHTS

THIRD DRAFT

GENERAL UNION OF PALESTINIAN WOMEN JERUSALEM-PALESTINE

Preamble

Based on the Declaration of Independence, which was the outcome of the Nineteenth Session of the Palestine National Council in 1988 and which reads:

> The State of Palestine is the state for all Palestinians wherever they may be. It is the state in which they enjoy their collective national and cultural identity and in which they can pursue complete equality of rights. In it will be safeguarded their political and religious convictions and their human dignity by means of a parliamentary, democratic system of governance, itself based on freedom of expression and freedom to form parties. The rights of minorities shall be duly respected by the majority, as minorities shall abide by decisions of the majority. Governance shall be based on principles of social justice, equality, and nondiscrimination in the civil rights of men and women, whether on grounds of race, religion, color, or sex, under the aegis of a constitution that ensures the rule of law and an independent judiciary.

Based on the United Nations Conventions, Universal Declaration of Human Rights, and other international documents and conventions pertaining to political, civil, economic, social, and cultural rights, specifically the Convention on the Elimination of All forms of Discrimination against Women:

Appendix

For the purpose of building a democratic Palestinian society that believes in equality and social justice for all its individuals;

We the women of Palestine declare the Document of Principles of Women's Legal Status to be ratified and incorporated into the constitution and the legislation of the future Palestinian State.

General Provisions

We the women of Palestine, from all social categories and the various faiths, including workers, farmers, housewives, students, professionals, and politicians promulgate our determination to proceed without struggle to abolish all forms of discrimination and inequality against women that have been imposed by the different forms of colonialism on our land, ending with the Israeli Occupation, and which were reinforced by the conglomeration of customs and traditions prejudiced against women and embodied in a number of existing laws and in legislation. In order to build a democratic society that ensures equal opportunities for women in rights and obligations within the following principles:

The future Palestinian state and the National Authority must be committed, regardless of its jurisdiction, to the Declaration of Independence and to all international declarations and conventions pertaining to human rights, particularly the 1979 Convention on the Elimination of All Forms of Discrimination against Women; and must enhance the principle of equality between women and men in all spheres of life and declare this, clearly and unequivocally, in the constitution as well as in the legislation of the national authority. This is in addition to guaranteeing the practical implementation of this principle by adopting legislative and administrative procedures to prohibit all forms of discrimination against women and repealing the status of inequality against them by endorsing legal protection for women.

The commitment to women's right to hold public posts, whether through elections or appointment, whether judicial, legislative, or executive, should be on an equal footing with that of men, and this should be ensured in a law that is compelling, functional, and can be implemented.

In the vision of Palestinian women for a society of justice and equality, the general provisions stated above are basic guidelines from which we acquire support in order to:

Appendix

Preserve a cohesive Palestinian society. We the women of Palestine comprise half of Palestine. We are an integral part of this society. We also believe that the issue of women's liberation and equality with men is the task of the society as a whole. Thus, we believe in the necessity of working hand in hand with men to establish a Palestinian society permeated with social justice and equality for all.

Enhance Palestinian culture and uniqueness. We the women of Palestine join all democratic forces in our vision, which affirms that the level of human development is measured by the implementation of women's rights and the availability of equal opportunities for women in all spheres. Palestinian heritage embodies different visions of the role and positions of women in society. Therefore, we see that enhancing women's equality and respect for their rights requires from us the promoting of the positive side of our Palestinian and Arab heritage and culture.

Reinforce the national and social struggle of Palestinian women. The Palestinian women's struggle has been depicted over the decades of the Palestinian national struggle as an immeasurable contribution in all spheres; women were martyred and thousands were imprisoned. Palestinian women also played a vital role in the preservation of the unity of the Palestinian family as a social base to support individuals in the absence of a Palestinian national authority. Palestinian women were forced to delay many tasks associated with their social position and instead focus all their attention on the issue of the national and political struggle. It is now time to affirm that the issue of women's legal rights is in all respects a cornerstone for building a democratic Palestinian society.

Achieve equality. We, the women of Palestine, see equal rights for both men and women in all spheres as a basic principle of the emancipation of women and men. This requires a clear statement that unambiguously guarantees the equality of women and men in all Palestinian legislation. This also requires having legislative and administrative procedures to ensure its implementation. This demands that we unite our efforts to remove those social norms that prohibit women from achieving success in society, and in order to guarantee the respect of human rights and the principle of rule of law. At this historic juncture, we demand equality in the following:

–Political Rights: To guarantee the right of women in voting, running for office, involvement in public referendums, and the ability to hold political and public judicial posts on all levels. This is in addition to equal opportunity with men in political parties, nongovernmental organizations concerned with political and public life in Palestine, and the representation of the state in international and regional organizations as well as in the diplomatic corps.

–Civil Rights: To grant women the right to acquire, preserve, or change their nationality. Legislation must also guarantee that marriage to a non-Palestinian, or a change of a husband's nationality, while married, will not necessarily change the citizenship of a wife. This includes freedom from imposition of a husband's citizenship. Women should also be granted the right to give citizenship to husbands and children, be guaranteed full freedom to move, travel, and choose their place of residency, and have a guaranteed right to adequate housing. Motherhood should be looked upon as a social post. Household chores should be regarded as a task of social and economic value.

The law should stand by women to protect them from family violence and practices that infringe on any of their guaranteed rights—including their right to express themselves and their right to join any activity, assembly, or association—by guaranteeing their right to go to court as citizens with full rights.

–Economic, Social, and Cultural Rights: To guarantee, through the Constitution and Palestinian legislation, the equality of women at work, ensuring equal pay with men working at the same work, providing equal opportunities in promotion, training, compensation, rewards, health insurance, and maternity rights; equality in making contracts, administering property, obtaining banking contracts and property mortgages, and in all procedures practiced in courts and judicial bodies. We also affirm the importance of equality in social welfare, health benefits, education, and training services, and the guarantee of women's full equality regarding issues pertaining to personal status.

The efforts of women as well as all democratic forces in Palestinian society must unite to remove all obstacles hindering the equality of women with men. We must work hand in hand toward a democratic society based on comprehensive national independence, social justice, and equality.

This draft was signed by numerous West Bank women's groups that participated in rewriting the previous draft of the document.

Contributors

ILHAM ABU GHAZALEH is Assistant Professor of Linguistics and a member of the Women's Studies program at Birzeit University on the West Bank.

HANAN MIKHAIL ASHRAWI is currently Minister of Higher Education with the Palestinian National Authority on the West Bank. In the early 1990s, she served as Palestinian spokeswoman during the Middle East peace negotiations between the Palestine Liberation Organization (PLO) and Israel. She is author of *This Side of Peace*, in which she recounts her personal experiences during these negotiations. She was a founder and director of the Palestinian Independent Commission for Citizens Rights, and she is a former Associate Professor of English and Dean of the Faculty of Arts at Birzeit University on the West Bank.

RITA GIACAMAN is Assistant Professor of Public Health at Birzeit University and author of many articles on gender issues and community health.

JOOST R. HILTERMANN, sociologist and writer, is author of *Behind the Intifada* and is a frequent contributor to *Middle East Report.* He has lived on the West Bank and has taught sociology at Birzeit University. He is currently with Human Rights Watch, Washington, D.C.

ISLAH JAD is Assistant Professor of Political Science and a member of the Women's Studies program at Birzeit University on the West Bank; she has published on the development of the women's movement on the West Bank.

PENNY JOHNSON is Assistant Coordinator of the Women's Studies program at Birzeit University and a contributing editor of *Middle East Report.*

Contributors

ZAHIRA KAMAL, a leader of the Democratic Front, is founder of the women's committees movement and president of the Women's Action Committees. She currently holds the portfolio of Women's Affairs in the Palestinian National Authority.

SHARIF KANAANA is Associate Professor of Folklore at Birzeit University on the West Bank. He is coeditor, with Ibrahim Muhawi, of *Speak, Bird, Speak Again, Palestinian Arab Folktales*.

AMAL KAWAR is Associate Professor of Political Science at Utah State University and author of *Daughters of Palestine: Leading Women of the Palestinian National Movement*.

SAHAR KHALIFEH is a novelist. Six of her novels have been translated into nine languages. She is director of a women's research center in Nablus.

ROBIN MORGAN is former editor-in-chief of the magazine *Ms*. She is author of *The Demon Lover: On the Sexuality of Terrorism* and of *The Word of a Woman: Feminist Dispatches*.

SUHA SABBAGH currently teaches courses in women's studies at Birzeit University on the West Bank. She founded and directed the Institute for Arab Women's Studies in Washington, D.C., and was the recipient of a Fulbright Grant to the West Bank in 1994/95. She has published extensively on gender issues in the Arab world and in Arabic literature, and she is editor of *Arab Women: Between Defiance and Restraint*.

EYAD EL-SARRAJ is a psychiatrist and Director of the Gaza Community Mental Health Center. He is Director of the Independent Palestinian Commission on Human Rights and has written extensively on the issue of mental health and the Palestinian community.

PHILIPPA STRUM is Professor of Political Science at City University of New York and author of *The Women are Marching: The Second Sex and the Palestinian Revolution*.

DIMA ZALATIMO is a journalist and television producer; she is currently working with Dubai television from Washington, D.C.

A number of individuals assisted with the preparation of the manuscript or with translations: Nagla El-Bassiouni, Ramla Khalidi, Emma Naughton, Karen Healy, Laica Dajani, Magida Abu Hassabo, and Victoria F. Halstead.

Index

Index